The New Competitors

The New Competitors

A Report on American Managers
from D. Quinn Mills of the Harvard Business School

D. QUINN MILLS

JOHN WILEY & SONS
New York • Chichester • Brisbane • Toronto • Singapore

Library of Congress Cataloging in Publication Data

Mills, Daniel Quinn.
    The new competitors.

    (Wiley management series on problem solving, decision
making, and strategic thinking)
    Includes index.
    1. Executives—United States. 2. Industrial management
—United States.   I. Harvard University. Graduate School
of Business Administration.   II. Title.   III. Series.
HD38.25.U6M55 1985   658.4'00973   85-616
ISBN 0-471-81026-6

Printed in the United States of America

10 9 8 7 6 5 4 3 2 1

To Louise, Dan, and Deb

Preface

Today's *status quo* is change. Yet many companies face a changing reality with a certain amount of reluctance. Managers may think they are making necessary changes through actions like reorganizing their company's structure but in reality they continue with the old ways in a new environment. *The New Competitors* is about new ways of thinking about and approaching work that companies —and more importantly the managers of companies —must take if they are to survive. The changes necessary touch the organization from top to bottom and include senior managers, middle managers, white collar professionals, unionized workers, blue collar workers: everyone from the CEO to workers on the shop floor.

My goal in writing *The New Competitors* has been one of making an authoritative statement about the state of management and what managers can do to improve both their own performance and that of their companies. The sources of information underlying these chapters are several. One significant base is my experience as both a consultant and teacher of management. The thousands of managers I've met in these two roles have had a major influence on my thinking. I've learned as much from them as they have from me.

The second base is field research done by persons associated with the Harvard Business School and embodied in cases taught at the School. These cases are a rich source of material indigenous to actual companies. My approach has been to use the dramatic event of a case and to build on it with material from conversations and interviews I have had with executives over the years. In this way, I have attempted to recapture the excitement the casewriter must have experienced while conducting the research and that groups of managers experience in discussing a case. I have tried to convey a feeling of discovery to the reader. All individuals and companies are real. Some have disguised names, however. Readers can easily distinguish where the actual names of companies and people are used because names and companies listed in the index are real; those not listed in the index but appearing in the text are disguised.

A third significant source is a series of interviews conducted for this book with executives of many companies. More than four hundred executives at over three hundred firms were interviewed by LDG Associates, Inc. of Gardner, Massachusetts.

Among the companies at which managers were interviewed are all those on *Fortune*'s most admired companies list. Unfortunately not all the companies which deserve to be on the list are selected for recognition by *Fortune* or other business magazines.

In particular, the coverage of smaller companies has been inadequate in other books. Our research shows that often smaller companies are making the most effective and up-to-date efforts to be competitive. As we all know, effective smaller companies generally far outperform the giants in growth and on the stock market as well. Management literature has been seriously deficient in describing the innovative and successful techniques of smaller, but still substantial, firms.

When all is said and done, this book is not about companies, but about managers. A basic problem with much management literature is that it assumes organizations do things. Yet one of the most profound insights into business is expressed in the simple observation: organizations don't do things, people do. What matters most is the effort, imagination, and adaptability of the individuals who make up an organization. Individual managers take actions that make it look from the outside as if the organization as a whole did something. Because of this, the focus of the book is less on companies than on individual managers.

It follows logically that this book is dedicated to the belief that what individuals do makes a difference to the success of their business. This is especially true of managers, but is not limited to them. Many companies are now recognizing the contribution to competitiveness that each individual can make, whatever his or her level in the company; they are trying to give people an opportunity to make greater contributions.

Because individuals make a difference in the success or failure of a company, this book rejects the popular social science notion that circumstances and environmental factors determine the course a company takes. Each company is challenged by its changing environment, but that challenge does not dictate the right response to the company.

Conditions allow different responses. Managers and other people in each company choose which responses to make. Some are successful and prosper, but not all. To observers looking at events after the fact, the correct response looks inevitable. This is an illusion—the illusion of the Monday morning quarterback who thinks that yesterday's game could only have turned out as it did; that the coaches and players on both teams made no mistakes and missed no opportunities or made exactly offsetting errors. The fact is that success is created by choosing the proper plays and by the proper execution.

So it is in business. Managers cannot presume that conditions will drive their company in the direction of success. A changing environment creates opportunities; and competitors are as anxious to seize the opportunities as anyone else. The following chapters illustrate how successful people are molding companies which can seize the opportunities in today's fast-changing environment.

Behind the buzz words and current fads of management lie substantial, long-lasting methods. It is the latter that this book tries to convey to persons trying to develop their managerial skills. The material in the book is up to date, but attempts to exclude the ephemeral and superficial. Top performers succeed

by a judicious combination of old principles and new ways of
applying them. We will explore both.

D. QUINN MILLS

Boston, Massachusetts
February 1985

Acknowledgments

I owe a particular debt to Rae Ann O'Brien, Research Associate at the Harvard Business School, who helped write several of the chapters of this book, and to LDG Associates, Inc. of Gardner, Massachusetts, a survey research firm which provided data on which I relied in many of the chapters.

Some of the case situations referred to in this book have been drawn directly or derived from Harvard Business School cases prepared by my colleagues. To these present and former colleagues at the Harvard Business School who have done the field work and writing of the cases which have enriched these pages, I am humbly grateful. They are G. W. Baird, Mary Lou Balbaky, Michael Beer, A. Bhambri, Clinton Bourden, C. Roland Christensen, J. Stewart Dougherty, Robert G. Eccles, Fred K. Foulkes, Donna Hale, Ann Harlan, John P. Kotter, David Kuechle, Frank S. Leonard, E. A. Lipton, George C. Lodge, A. Morgan, Claudia Pharis, David O. Rikert, Robert Rodat, Leonard A. Schlesinger, J. A. Siegar, C. Wickham Skinner, Jeffrey Sonnenfeld, Bert Spector, E. Stein, Richard Vancil, Richard O. Von Werssowetz, C. Weigle, and J. Wilson.

Finally to the legion of students of management practice at Harvard and the excellent companies at which I've had the opportunity to consult and to teach, I owe a debt for the insight which I hope is evident on each page of this book.

All errors, omissions, and other shortcomings are my responsibility.

D. Q. M.

Contents

The New Competitors

1

The Best Organization You've Belonged To

What are the characteristics of the best organization to which you have belonged? Perhaps that organization is the business office where you now work. Possibly it was a church group, a volunteer fire department, a private club, or an investment group. As you think back, what aspects of its operation made it effective?

If you are like several hundred managers with whom I have raised this question in recent years, you will list some or all of the following:

The mission was clear; everyone knew what was to be done.
People were creative and cooperative.
Communication in the group was open.
Each member carried his or her part of the work load.

This list may seem innocuous, but in fact it has some very telling omissions. Did you mention strong leadership, clear lines of authority, exact directions? Most executives today do not.

A few years ago business leaders would have put these factors at the very top. Their experience in World War II had taught them to do so. During that war confused command, indecisiveness, and GI participation in decisions added up to mortal danger. The successful fighting organization had strong leadership, a clear chain of command, decisiveness when decisions were needed, and clear direction for the rank and file. The exigencies of war demanded top down, hierarchical organization. Directives were based on commands implementing top level strategy that had been developed in secret—the classic military paradigm. Ways of doing things based on military conceptions became deeply ingrained in a generation that applied this model to peacetime occupations in the nation's industries. Having seen their hierarchical military model work, former servicemen carried a belief in its efficacy forward into their new endeavors. In business after the war, the one organization that was everyone's common denominator was the military.

Not that managers necessarily thought of the military as an organizational paragon. They did not. It was too inefficient, too bureaucratic, too frustrating. But front line units had managed to win the war, and the most effective front line units were ones with clear direction and authority.

The war that created this military model is now forty years past. Most of today's work force had no personal involvement in it; the memories of those who did have sometimes lapsed. Subsequent wars in Korea and Vietnam have tarnished the military's image, rather than enhancing it.

When they think of successful organizations, young people today do not think first of the military. Instead they reach widely, to businesses, churches, political groups, clubs, and associations. They rarely associate clear lines of authority and unambiguous direction with the most successful of these. They do not identify with carrying through a task given them by others. The effective situations they recall are those in which they were participants or partners.

Not that today's manager is entirely comfortable with the implications of a list of the successful organization's characteristics. If asked why decisive leadership and clear direction are omitted, the manager is likely to claim that they were simply an oversight, and probably belong.

Members of the World War II generation, however, would not have overlooked them. The marketplace as a battlefield is a popular and in many ways apt metaphor. But it is more applicable to the external environment than its internal dynamics. The adaptation of the military model into corporate life has been too wholehearted. For some time it has worked against our ability to manage today's labor force and, therefore, to meet both domestic and foreign competition.

Every generation lives in a different world from its predecessors. Often this difference is expressed in terms of the technological developments made during a generation's lifetime; these developments serve as benchmarks of change. Technology frames and defines our world in an outward and tangible way. When changes occur, technology can fundamentally change the way we think about the world in which we live and redefine the parameters of our imaginations. Political events and social movements have an equally profound effect on us. This generation of managers is different because of these social and political influences, just as they are different as a result of technological changes in their lifetimes.

NEW GENERATION OF MANAGERS

Today a new generation of managers is advancing to leadership positions in American companies. After a decade or so of experience in the specialized aspects of business—in accounting, sales, production, or personnel—they are entering general management positions.

As a group they are well educated, ambitious, and capable. Knowledgeable about the new technology, many or most are conversant and comfortable with computers' ability to answer "what-if" questions. Today's manager almost has a second brain at his or her fingertips.

Experience, intelligence, and computer literacy are significant advantages to take into higher management positions. Yet today's new managers also experience a certain unease. Though they know a great deal, they wonder what they do not know. Though they have considerable capabilities, they wonder about those they may not have.

Current experiences and capabilities have served today's managers well in specialized applications. But as they rise in managerial ranks, their roles become increasingly less specialized. Management is a profession unlike any other. In discipline-based professions, including law, medicine, and architecture, for example, a person's career begins with fairly broad training in a professional school and progresses toward specialization. Management follows an opposite course. Beginning in specialization, managers progress to more and more general responsibilities.

As production supervisors, young executives are experts in the technology of that department and the skills of its work force. When they become plant managers, additional departments and persons of additional skills report to them. If they try to learn the new departments and skills as well as they mastered their original jobs, they will be unable to keep up with the detail. When they progress to division managers, marketing, sales, research and development, and personnel will join manufacturing in reporting to them. In top corporate jobs at the end of their careers, staff functions such as finance, accounting, and planning will be added to a list of responsibilities that still includes production, marketing, personnel, and research and development. At each step in their careers as general managers they have not specialized, but rather generalized.

Embarking on this career path, or midway into it, young executives are concerned with the applicability of what they have learned in their careers so far. What talents, methods, and values will assist rising executives to climb the business ladder? Which will be hindrances? Is it true that the new technology means that all traditional management verities are suspect? Or, are the old ways still valid in some instances? As a person progresses in management, what style fits today's conditions? What can be learned from the past, and what of the past is best cast aside in today's business world? What did previous generations of managers learn that remains useful? What skills does today's new manager need to invent?

HOW OLDER EXECUTIVES CAN STAY IN TOUCH

Today's new managers have been shaped by different experiences during their lifetimes than the people they are beginning to replace in top managerial jobs. Experiences shape the expectations, attitudes, and behavior of each of us. Where experiences have been different, values will be different; if not for every person in the new generation, then for many.

Older executives sometimes deny that the younger generation is much different. "They are just as ambitious; just as driven for money," older people will say. Some certainly are; but many, if not most, are not. The mistake of older executives is trying to compel younger managers to be like themselves. This is done by promoting people who behave as older executives think they should—often not realizing that such behavior can be, and often is, feigned. When older executives locate and promote those in the younger generation who are most like themselves, they take a large risk. The danger is that persons who are too much like the older generation may be ill-suited to be successful in tomorrow's business world—they may be too different from their own generation to understand its needs and objectives.

Reginald Jones, Chairman of General Electric Company (GE) from 1970 to 1981, is one of America's most admired managers. Yet when faced with the selection of a successor to guide GE though the 1980s, Jones intentionally chose someone with a very different personality than his own, and a much younger man. Asked about his choice, Jones described his two rules for selecting a successor: first, don't select someone like yourself, and, second, choose someone attuned to the future.

What did Jones see as the future? The three key elements in his vision were greater competition, an enhanced role for technology, and a new set of mores for the American people. The personality characteristics he sought in a successor were derived from his vision of the future: an intensely competitive person, a technologist, and a younger person who embodied the experiences and mores of the generation now coming to dominate American society.

Because few older executives are as thoughtful as Reg Jones, American top management is in danger of becoming isolated from those they manage. Their formative life experiences were different from those of the current generation of managers in their 30s and 40s.

All human communication is based on the ability to understand others; to know with whom one is speaking, trying to motivate, develop, encourage, and summon forth the best. Successful managers must understand both the individuals and the perspective of those managed. For today's managers environmental factors define what will be effective to motivate, reward, encourage, and develop employees. What does this environment look like?

Our country's work force is divided into four groups according to their life or work style:

1. The *traditional employee* is a male sole earner whose wife and children are not in the labor force.
2. The *single employee* often works, but is not part of a family unit, though singles sometimes live together.
3. The *nontraditional employee* is in a household with more than a single earner, whether spouse or child.
4. The *least traditional employee* is a woman who is the sole earner, and has others, possibly including her husband, to support.

The entire American labor force of more than 100 million people may be described in these four categories. What proportion of our labor force is in each? If you could ask American managers to express their own estimates of the relative importance of these groups in today's labor force, as I have done, you would find a very interesting pattern in the results.

The more senior the group of managers in position (and generally in age), the more likely those individuals are to fall in the traditional family group, and the more likely they are to *overestimate* the proportion of their fellow citizens who are also in that category.

Today 90 percent of chief executive officers, chief operating officers, and chief financial officers will ordinarily fall in the traditional family category (i.e., their spouses do not work, and any children living at home do not work). Asked to estimate the proportion of traditional employees in the labor force or in their companies, most CEOs will guess from 90 percent down to a low of 40 or 50 percent. The correct figure is 14 percent as shown in Table 1.1. Upon learning this, many executives were incredulous.

Middle managers are equally divided between the traditional group, and singles or multiearner families. Similarly they are likely to estimate the traditional family's numerical importance more accurately, at 25 to 50 percent. Some few even have made it their business to know the living styles of their fellow citizens and answered 13 to 14 percent.

These statistics are not of mere academic interest. They reflect a profound change in the nation's life-styles. In the 1940s almost

Table 1.1
The Traditional Employee Is Disappearing

	Percentage
Traditional employee where husband is the only earner	14
Husband and wife family where wife only earner	1
Wage earners in multiearner families	63
Single employees	22
	100

half the work force was in traditional, one earner family units; and the decline to today's one in eight has occurred steadily over the decades.

Persons in multiearner families think differently and behave differently about work. They must be concerned about the jobs of other family members, so they may require more flexibility at their own work places. They may be more concerned about certain benefits, and less about others. They may be less willing to travel or to relocate. They may tend to be less concerned about working for a particular company than remaining in a community where their spouses are also employed.

Considerations necessitated by employees' life-styles are often interpreted by top management as excessive self-indulgence; a self-centeredness at the expense of the corporation. Rather than seeking to accommodate the needs of people, managers complain about a supposed lack of loyalty and commitment.

Managers are sometimes dismayed at the apparent shortsightedness of younger employees who attach little importance to the future. The future is far more uncertain today than in the past, however, and not only because of the risk of nuclear war. The country's demographics and economics are evolving in ways that make the future more risky. Planning for the future is very difficult.

Consider the problems of providing for retirement. Inflation and our tax code have weakened the value of individual savings, while population dynamics are undermining the promise of publicly provided programs such as Social Security and Medicare. This is very difficult for the World War II generation to understand, because it has been an especially fortunate generation since the war.

Social Security, for example, has been kind to the war generation. In 1945, 50 workers contributed to the Social Security trust fund for every retiree. With a large cash flow, benefits from the fund could be and were increased. In 1960 a person retiring at age 65 would have paid $7,311 (adjusted for inflation) into the fund and, given average life expectancy, could expect to receive $49,554 (adjusted to remove the impact of inflation) over the term of his or her retirement.

Then more and more people began draining benefits. By 1980 only three persons—not 50—were working and paying Social Security taxes for each person draining benefits. As a result, a person who retired at 65 in 1980 would have paid $34,694 in Social Security taxes, with an expected benefit level of $78,804 over the retirement period. The 1980 ratio of inflation-adjusted benefits to costs was about 2:1 compared to the 1960 ratio of 7:1. Social Security was not as good an "investment" for the 1980 retiree as for the 1960 retiree.

But by 2025, when a person entering the labor force at 20 in 1980 would reach 65, there will be only two people working for each retiree. A person retiring at 65 in 2025 will have paid more into Social Security in taxes than he or she can expect to receive in benefits. Social Security was a good deal for the World War II generation but not for today's employee.[1]

To make this comparison more striking: by 2025, if retirees are to live at the same standard of living as the average worker, each working person would have to pay some 20 percent of his or her pay in Social Security taxes alone (presuming the employer paid the rest). Is it any surprise that many young persons today do not think workers will agree to this high level of taxation, and expect that there will be little or no Social Security system left for them?

Similarly corporate pension funds will be placed under great pressure as they attempt to provide benefits for a rapidly increasing group of retirees, while overall employment in the country grows less rapidly than in the past.

To younger people the promises made to them by politicians and corporate executives about a secure financial future must seem suspect. Given the underlying facts, it should not be sur-

[1] Board of Trustees of the Federal Old Age & Survivors Insurance and Disability Insurance Trust Funds, "1980 Annual Report" (Washington, D.C.: U.S. Government Printing Office, 1980), p. 85.

prising to managers if younger people are groping for different forms of security; or simply discount the likelihood of it entirely.

A top level manager sitting down with an employee for a performance evaluation, a planning session, or a discussion of career progression or compensation faces someone who may see the world and the future from a different vantage point. The younger person is facing a slow growth economy and is competing with a large number of baby boom peers who are also striving for top positions. The younger person is also a member of a more educated work force in an economy where traditional manufacturing jobs are declining and opportunities are emerging in new sectors. The top manager's family style is probably different. A top manager may make assumptions about shared goals and values and assume that the person he or she supervises shares a fundamentally similar world view. But such assumptions can serve as a basic source of miscommunication between people.

Managers in their 30s and 40s face stiff competition from a large number of other baby boom generation workers. This competition will continue, if not intensify, as life expectancies lengthen and birth rates decline. The postwar baby boom has created a work force profile in which the largest group of workers is in the prime age group of 25 to 54. As managers perceive this environment, their response may well be to pursue a high credential, low loyalty stance in regard to their standing in the work force, counting on wits, transferable skills, and credentials to create the security lacking in today's corporation. The problem for the top manager, then, is how to provide the opportunities that will enable the company to retain good employees and to enlist the loyalty of managers whose futures are actually more limited, or at least not as clear, as the top manager's.

Incorrect assumptions about life-style can be an important barrier to communication. The largest increase in the female labor force has been among women with husbands present in the home—a remarkable 108 percent since 1950 when today's top managers had already begun their corporate and married lives. Between 1980 and 1985 two-thirds of the growth in the labor force consisted of women workers. This means increased pressure on top level management for job redesign to address special needs, flexible hours, shared jobs, and shorter workweeks for employees with working spouses to enable them to raise a family (albeit a small one) at the same time. These pressures can provide opportunities to address the special needs of this generation of managers as well as the needs of the company. The challenge, of course, is how to recognize, understand, and reconcile these needs so that both the manager and managed benefit and the legitimate interests of both are served. Taking these demographics in the aggregate, top managers are not viewing younger, mirror images of themselves and their own earlier life-styles and sets of personal expectations.

Today, top managers are not very likely to be managing employees who followed the same routes to their present positions. The stories are legion of how CEOs began their careers in the mailrooms of various enterprises and devoted their lives to learning and achieving within one company. In the vast majority of cases today, the route to middle management has not followed that path. Serving as the basis of today's younger manager's business acumen is some combination of formal education as well as job experience with one or more companies. Today's employees have the highest level of educational attainment of any previous generation. The veritable explosion in law and MBA degrees is typically associated with fast-track corporate aspirations. Although this somewhat serves as a proxy for the "up from the mailroom" kind of experience the top manager may have, it cannot go the whole way. Education is not a perfect substitute for experience. The manager has the task of taking away with one hand the perquisites employees may feel due them because of their investments in education, while with the other hand offering the opportunity to cast in their lots with the organization and gain the long-term, in-depth, industry-specific experience required to manage today's complex organizations. This will be an increasingly difficult task as the professionalization of business continues.

As a result of these factors, combined with other variables, today's managers as well as professional, clerical, and hourly workers show a decline in job satisfaction over the past 20 years and an even greater decline in satisfaction with companies and their policies. This is a long-term trend. Central to this review of the performance of corporations by managers is their belief that top managers have lost touch with employees at all levels of the organization.

In response, managers express a desire to be included in the inner circle where decisions are made about how things are to be done. Denial of this request may bring out the worst in a work force. Managers may read this denial as a lack of good faith by top management to do what is within its power to improve their situation in an increasingly competitive labor market. Why not job hop if not given the opportunity to dig in and invest oneself? Middle managers or other employees may lessen their commitment to the performance of the business and express this directly through a lack of concern for the customer. Faced with the lack of op- portunities to earn the security of the 1950s generation, managers continue the present trend of looking to the law and to technical rules as the only apparent means to assert control over their situations. The spate of law suits attacking the employment at will doctrine is one indication of a heightened sensitivity to fair treatment and an attempt to define rights by law where they have not been offered voluntarily.

Related attitudes may emerge in the form of oversensitivity to real or imagined criticism based on an overall feeling of insecurity. An accompanying psychological stance of helplessness is in part based on a very realistic appraisal of whether hard work will lead to enhanced security and other rewards. These insecurities may strike the more senior management at a minimum as inap- propriate and at a maximum, as a sign of real maladjustment. But the manager lives in the world of the 1980s corporation which is more competitive and in many ways made less secure by de- mographic trends and foreign and domestic competition than the world to which the top manager is accustomed. These differences should be acknowledged as real and addressed in tangible ways by top management. One observer has described the broken link between the company and its employees in the following way: "Calvinism once united virtue, salvation, work, and motivation in a productive package, but that package has come undone. Perhaps people now look only to themselves for the motivation that used to be supplied externally and emerge prisoners of their own insularity. The fire to lead others may soon be rekindled under a reformulated ethos, but the legacy of these shifting values in our culture may be a firm warning from humans that corporations and organizations in general can no longer with impunity take their loyalty and involvement for granted."[2]

ADJUSTING TO THE NEW MANAGERS

Signs indicate that senior management is well aware of their changing environment and willing to make efforts toward winning the loyalty of managers and through them, the work force. Responding to a recently administered human resources planning survey, a senior vice president commented: "Our environment is changing. The whole approach to personnel planning is entirely different from what it was when I started 37 years ago. It requires having more compassion for the individual, and doing away with old concepts. It's difficult to digest. It requires flexibility and tolerance."

And it does matter very much how people are treated. Different generations have different experiences; this leads to differing conceptions about how people should be treated. For the most part, these concepts slowly get institutionalized as people treat others as they have been treated. It is hard for a generation to give up these old ways of doing things and begin to use other less ingrained and value-laden methods. A change in values is required and this is difficult territory for any of us to rearrange. The circumstances created by a changing work force cause ad-

[2] Ann Howard and James A. Wilson, "Leadership in a Declining Work Ethic," *California Management Review*, 24, no. 4 (1982): 46.

justment problems for some companies and opportunities for others. To fail to see these developments as opportunities is to fail to capitalize on them. This is a failure of management of the first order and leaves a company very vulnerable to more imaginative and effective domestic or foreign competitors.

How can these changes create opportunities rather than road blocks? How can the link be reestablished? Corporations are not alone in their need to revitalize trust. People distrust institutions of all kinds, but there are signs that people want to change this. In the 1980s government, unions, and managers will all be competing with each other to regain the loyalty of the various constituencies and the public at large. A vice president of manufacturing summarizes the need for change: "We have been profitable but have not met the expectations we set for ourselves. The reason was that we are not effective in how we treated and developed people. We have high expectations. We haven't accomplished as much as we should."

Generally in the past, management has not treated people with as much respect as they deserved. Management did not fully accept the reasons given when an employee raised questions. The employee felt demeaned, like a kid. Management in the future cannot get away with this position. The attitudes of the leaders have to change.

How can this be accomplished? Managers tend to view themselves as the center of the business around whom other persons revolve. This view is enhanced and given visual legitimacy by hierarchical organizational charts showing lines of authority shooting downward and reporting responsibilities reaching upward. This "art of the corporation" in graphic presentations heavily influences how people grasp the basic dynamic of the organization as well as their place and role in it. Often such a chart is part of an employee's first introduction to the company. Because of this, it makes a particularly lasting impression.

As we have seen, people think of effective organizations not as those in which they play a standardized, specialized part, but as one in which they are part of a group and yet given an opportunity to contribute individually to the effort. A wise manager seeks a way to get out of the center of the universe, permitting others to help define how they might contribute and how they could foster cooperative and committed relationships. Top managers can find a way to join the group without giving up their basic responsibilities to lead and manage.

In order to motivate subordinates, managers must understand where employees are coming from, and which values determine their decisions. Simple responses to life-style concerns, such as protecting against employee burnout by pacing work where possible, is an easy step toward gaining the loyalty of employees and their families. In exchange, employees and their families will probably willingly, and even enthusiastically, support a situation requiring extra hours and effort if the company has not cried wolf too many times before. Better yet, let managers design and control their work as much as possible so that the inevitable crunches are of their own doing. People are usually more committed and willing to take responsibility for their own logjams; in this way they learn from them.

Managers in their 30s and 40s are sometimes less willing to make accommodations for the good of the corporation; this may be misread by some top managers as a lessening of ambition or willingness to climb the corporate ladder. The younger manager, however, may be defining a different type of ambition—to advance in the company and to balance other responsibilities at the same time. If these life-style concerns are treated as legitimate, they can serve as a powerful means of winning loyalty to the company in exchange for the loyalty to the employee as a person. Top managers, if they are "working smart," will turn this new-style ambition to motivation by not thwarting it.

One way of tapping into this ambition may be to turn the self-improvement craze into a means of encouraging employees to develop skills and capacities related to their current and potential job responsibilities. This will require direct one-on-one communication with employees to determine what their interests might be and how they might coincide with those of the company.

We will turn more fully to this central question of communication in Chapter 3.

COMPOSING A MANAGEMENT STYLE

The danger for older executives in today's changing environment is that they may look for management potential only among people as much like themselves as possible. They search for persons adept at meeting the kinds of business problems they encountered in their careers.

The principal danger for today's new generation of managers is discarding thoughtlessly all that their predecessors have learned about management. For today's new managers some old approaches are ineffective, but others continue to work well. Tomorrow's successful manager must identify which approaches work. Managers who use new processes when old are more appropriate, or who rely on the traditional in novel circumstances, are both unlikely to be successful.

A manager's choice should achieve the proper fit between today's environment and the managerial approach selected. For example, the old fundamentals of delegation of responsibility and measurement of performance are of renewed importance when issues are technologically complex and need to be decided by those who best understand the technical issues involved. On the other hand, traditional approaches to labor relations are performing poorly in today's environment for both management and labor.

In the chapters which follow, old and new techniques of management are measured against today's environment to determine those which fit successfully and those which do not. This approach differs from those who argue that everything is different today, and that nothing can be learned from traditional approaches to management. It also differs from those who say that nothing in the environment is really new, that all the old practices continue to have value, and that things will be done in the future just as they have been done in the past. Works of the proponents of the first view are easily found in today's bookstores; advocates of the second view abound in corporate offices throughout the land.

SUMMARY

A new generation of managers is advancing after garnering experience for years in specialized functions. They are now assuming general management positions or are creating their own companies. They are bringing special values and interests to both endeavors. These include independence, a wider range of personal life-styles, and a concern for the humanistic aspects of the corporation. Today's organizations are adjusting to accommodate these new managers. But what managerial styles will the new managers adopt? How should things be done? Can the good aspects of old management styles be kept while incorporating new and better approaches? How can new managers distinguish between the good and bad in each style? What will work in today's world and what won't? This question cannot be answered in isolation and it depends in crucial ways on the circumstances in which the manager is to operate.

A key characteristic of today's business environment is renewed and vigorous competition. In many ways hot competition fits the new generation of managers well because they want to have the opportunity to respond to challenges in the business environment. Today's vigorous competition also defines which managerial approaches will and which will not work.

2

New Competition

The most important characteristic of today's business environment—and therefore the yardstick against which managerial techniques must be measured—is the new competition. Today's successful techniques are those that contribute to the competitiveness of an enterprise. Those that do not will be found wanting.

This is the age of the new competition, of the toppling of many old and established companies and the building of great new ones; an age in which adaptation is the greatest virtue. Today's large companies will survive by completing a metamorphosis into something very different than they were in the beginning. This new age is reflected in the following examples:

On the highway leading into Chicago from O'Hare Airport Toshiba has erected a large billboard: "Competition Brings Out the Best" it exclaims as a challenge to rivals of all nationalities.

"This is not our business," a chief executive officer explains to his assembled staff. "It's no one's business. No one owns this industry. It belongs only to the best—to those who can keep it growing, producing, alive. We're in it today, but tomorrow it belongs to whoever does it better."

CHALLENGE FROM ABROAD

Since World War II, America's business sector has been preeminent. Today ambitious managers in other industrialized countries target key American industries and attempt to take their markets. Governments and entrepreneurs in the Third World look to their burgeoning populations and low labor costs as a competitive weapon to wrest production from American plants and bring it into their own manufacturing centers.

We know of 100,000 years of human existence. Of all the people who have been on this earth in that time span, almost 1 in 10 is alive today. More than 4 billion people struggle for food, shelter, and clothing—for necessities and luxuries.[1] The world's population grows rapidly. Between now and the end of this century some 750 million people (all of whom are already born) will have entered the world's labor force—nine-tenths of them outside the industrialized countries.

What a labor cost advantage the nonindustrialized countries have! In 1984 compensation in manufacturing (expressed in U.S. dollars at current exchange rates) averaged a bit less than $2.00 per hour in Mexico, Korea, Malaysia, and Taiwan. This is about one-sixth of the average U.S. manufacturing hourly wage and benefit package. These countries are areas in which electronics assembly, auto parts manufacturing, and textile production have been increasing rapidly. In India, where American companies are now establishing assembly plants, total compensation is 30 cents per hour. In China, which is now a major exporter of apparel and footwear to the United States, total compensation is estimated to be 25 to 30 cents per hour. The Indian and Chinese compensation rates are roughly one-twentieth, or 5 percent, of comparable U.S. rates in apparel manufacturing and only 3 percent of all the U.S. manufacturing rate.[2]

[1] John Noble, "Nine Percent," *New York Times*, 6 October 1981, p. C1.
[2] Sources include individual companies and unpublished data from the Bureau of Labor Statistics, U.S. Department of Labor.

Have these wage differentials always existed? Were they of little importance in the past? These are questions commonly raised, and appropriately so. In other words, is this situation any different than before? Unfortunately, it is different in degree. The pay differentials are larger due to the strength of the dollar and to the rapid rise in living standards in the United States following World War II, a rise unmatched in much of the Third World.

Furthermore, the competitive significance of wage differentials is far greater than in the past. Advances in communication and transportation technology make it far easier today to use low-cost Third World labor as a competitive weapon in the contest for market share in industrialized countries, especially in the large domestic marketplace of the United States. American companies are rushing production abroad to compete with foreign producers who are also turning to Third World labor.

These labor cost differentials are not likely to change in America's favor in the next several years. Behind them lies a fundamental cause—the very different demographics of the industrialized and Third World countries. In America, Western Europe, Japan, South Africa, and Argentina population growth is slow. Populations are slowly aging as the World War II baby boom generation grows older and has few children. A graph of the population by age group resembles a somewhat flattened sphere—with its bulge just below the middle. Only some 30 percent of the population is under age 20. Because of the relative scarcity of young people, labor shortages are widely feared for the United States in the years to come.

But the population dynamics of the Third World, where the majority of the earth's population lives, are very different. Population growth is rapid. The average age of the population is declining. A graph of the population by age group resembles a very flat triangle. More than 50 percent of the population is below age 20. Unemployment is massive as governments search desperately for useful work for people to do. In much of the world, particularly in Latin America, average living standards have been declining rapidly for a decade—adding to political turmoil and revolutionary insurgencies. The demographic dynamic lies underneath both political instability and increasing international business competition, as companies headquartered in the industrialized countries rush to gain an advantage from the low-cost labor of the Third World.

Because the majority of the globe is awash in people, no early end to low-wage competition for the industrialized countries is in sight. Even if population growth should decline precipitously abroad, the children now living are sufficient to refresh the spring of low-cost labor until the end of this century.

Labor cost is not the only advantage new competitors are bringing. A capable managerial class has been developing. The Japanese have been so successful and so publicized in recent years that many American managers do not want to hear about them any more. Other nationalities are mimicking the Japanese, attempting to imitate their successes.

Foreign managers have become effective competitors, turning apparent weaknesses to market plan strengths. For example, only 10 years ago American companies held virtually all of the office copier business in this country. Not only was the technology sophisticated, but also a large network of service personnel was in place to keep the equipment operating properly. A large sales force existed to market new products and replacements. High technology and an established distribution and service network nationwide—these were formidable barriers to foreign competitors.

Yet today American firms hold less than half the nation's market in copiers. How did this occur? A combination of low-price products—founded on low labor costs—and inventive marketing by foreign competitors is the answer. The Japanese first entered the copier market at its low-price, few-features end. Unable to send service people on calls, they were forced to rely on the customer either to repair the machine or to ship it to a regional service center. To make the machine repairable by a customer, its technical complexity was reduced and parts which could not be simplified for customer repair were bundled into a cassette which the customer could remove and replace.

Customers liked the convenience of repairing the machine or replacing a cassette themselves. Rather than returning cassettes for repair, customers simply bought replacements; cassette sales became a profitable item for the foreign competitors. Finally, since they were unable to provide service at the customer's site, foreign firms built greater reliability into their machines, winning from customers a reputation for high quality.

American firms relinquished control of the bottom end of the market with surprisingly little resistance. After all, it was not very profitable and was costly to service. For several years American firms were financially successful, while foreign competitors took a firm lodging in the lower end of the American copier market. Finally, from this base Japanese firms introduced upgraded equipment borrowing popular features from their lower-cost models. Customers welcomed the combination of larger machines, popular features, and prices well below the American companies' levels. Thus the American firms began to lose the profitable end of the market as well—and today they scramble to regain competitiveness in what was only a few years ago virtually their own private preserve.

Low labor costs alone are not enough to support a successful competitive challenge. Combining low labor costs with aggressive marketing and a sound business strategy, however, creates a combination very difficult to beat.

The challenge to management in this country has never been greater. Speaking about foreign competition in March 1984, John Young, Chairman of Hewlett-Packard Company and Chairman of the President's Commission on Industrial Competitiveness commented: "Some competitive disadvantages we'll probably have to accept as 'givens.' With our high standard of living, the human resource cost is one of those. That means we'll have to find ways to make our labor worth what it's paid."[3]

---

[3] John A. Young, "Industrial Competitiveness" (Remarks at Stanford Graduate School of Business, The International Management Development Institute, and the National Association of Manufacturers, March 1984, mimeographed.).

One thing American companies ought to have learned from recent experience is that it is very difficult to let the unprofitable part of the market go to an aggressive competitor and yet keep the rest. Over time the competitor not only grows up in the business but also expands to take from the established companies whatever sales they have left.

That American companies are learning this lesson is evidenced by General Motors Corporation's Chairman Roger B. Smith who commented about his company's new effort to build a small car for the American market: "Without the Saturn project, we don't stand a chance against the Japanese."[4]

Many American companies hope that they can insulate themselves from foreign competition by having trade barriers, such as tariffs or domestic content legislation, erected against imports from abroad. Although initially effective in protecting American labor from the competition of cheaper foreign labor, trade barriers are less effective for American employees. This is because foreign companies can vault over trade barriers by buying plants and hiring labor in the United States. Fearing that the American government will start to close our domestic markets against imports, foreign companies are now dramatically increasing their acquisition of properties and facilities in the United States.

CHALLENGE FROM WITHIN

Foreign competition, however, is not the only source of new competition. For some companies foreign competition is not significant at all. Yet many of these seemingly fortunate companies are facing new competitive challenges every bit as serious as those from foreign companies. In fact, though less publicized, new domestic competition may be more important in today's hotter business climate. Americans are good businesspeople, so it is not surprising that much of today's new competition for established firms is from other Americans.

[4] Amal Nag, "Gearing Down," *Wall Street Journal*, 14 May 1984, p. 1.

Government deregulation is a major source of new competition in many industries. Beginning in 1968 when the Supreme Court permitted AT&T's competitors' equipment to be connected to the AT&T system, a series of major industries have been exposed to the harsh winds of new competition. The deregulation of financial institutions began in earnest in 1975, of airlines in 1978, of trucking and railroads in 1980, of bus service in 1982, of public construction (via changes in federal regulations under the Davis–Bacon Act) in 1983.

Although the impact of deregulation has been substantial everywhere, it has taken different forms in different industries. In trucking the number of firms offering transportation services to the public rose 40 percent in the four years following deregulation.[5] The industry has been flooded with new entrants and many old established firms are toppling.

Construction in the United States has always been a competitive business with a multitude of firms. Because the industry is localized, many medium-sized companies had established comfortable niches for themselves by the 1960s. Furthermore, the industry was then largely unionized, so that a new company could not gain an initial entrance based on lower labor costs. In the 1970s the unions' hold on the industry began to weaken. A few large nonunion companies developed in the South, then extended their operations to other regions of the country. Also, because housing construction was less profitable than building commercial, industrial, and public office buildings, union contractors and the unions allowed this work to go to new nonunion companies.

Soon new firms copied the tactics of using low-cost nonunion labor as a competitive advantage in breaking into commercial, industrial, and public building construction. By the early 1980s the unionized sector had lost so much market share that the federal government ceased to require de facto union pay scales on federal and federally assisted construction. Thus, the

---

[5] Agis Salpukas, "Trucking's Great Shakeout," *New York Times*, 13 December 1983, p. D1.

public construction market was wide open to nonunion contractors.

For years large American engineering and construction companies had the lucrative Middle-Eastern construction market largely to themselves. Then they lost out to Japanese and Korean construction companies which initially offered far lower labor costs to their Saudi and Persian Gulf customers.

In the early 1980s, having lost most of the overseas market, large American companies reentered the U.S. domestic construction industry seeking work. At the same time Japanese companies, having lost work in the Middle East to the Koreans, began to bid for work in California. Thus, as American firms were driven out of markets abroad, they returned to intensify competition in the United States.

For medium-sized union contractors the market was squeezed from all directions: from small nonunion companies with a foothold in housing who were upgrading into more profitable nonhousing markets; from large nonunion southern firms branching out into other regions of the country; from giant previously worldwide design and build companies driven out of their foreign markets back into competition in the United States; and finally from a large number of new nonunion firms entering the business continually.

Airlines present a particularly instructive case of the emergence of new competition due to government deregulation. When the government deregulated airlines in 1980, a number of entrepreneurs prepared to enter the industry. The established carriers were not particularly concerned. They thought their position was protected by the following substantial obstacles to any new entrants becoming major factors in the business:

First, airlines are a capital intensive business. The existing carriers presumed that the financial markets would not provide capital except at prohibitive cost to unproven companies.

Second, airlines were highly unionized. As a result they had similar high compensation costs. Officers of established companies reasoned that even if a new nonunion carrier could begin operations, it would soon be organized, raising its cost levels to equal their own.

Third, the established carriers thought they had customer loyalty. Under government regulations airlines had not competed on fare levels but on service. They believed customers would reject new carriers whose low cost might be based on a no frills approach to customer service.

Fourth, the growth of a carrier is governed by its ability to get airport space. Hence, in competition with established carriers a new carrier could not determine its own rate of growth. The new company would have to move fast to get airport slots prior to established companies seizing them defensively to shut the upstart out of additional localities. Hence, a new company must grow very fast or not at all. If it tried to grow very fast, its management, financing, and operation systems would each crack under the strain.

Fifth, if despite the other arguments, new carriers should threaten to bankrupt existing firms, the established companies reasoned, the government would reregulate the industry, just as it had stepped in to stop ruinous fare wars between the carriers in the past.

To date not one of these barriers to entry has turned out to be effective; and several new entrants—in particular People Express— have apparently surmounted them all.

Wall Street made capital available to People Express on cheaper terms than to the established carriers. Unions have been unable to organize the new company's rapidly growing labor force. Customers have flocked to People Express's combination of no frills service and low fares. Although it has had to grow very rapidly (from 200 employees in 1980 to more than 5,000 in 1984), the new entrant has somehow managed its growth. Finally, several established carriers continue to wobble at the brink of bankruptcy, imposing cost-saving concessions on their employees, while Congress gives no indication of a willingness to reregulate the industry.

Trucking, construction, and airlines are instructive examples of what deregulation has done to foster the new competition, but the most significant impact of all has been in the financial services business. Commercial banks, savings banks, brokerage houses, mutual funds, and insurance companies are among the most important institutions of the American economy. For most of this century federal and state regulations have kept them each in separate compartments—able to offer only a certain list of products or services to certain customers in certain geographic areas.

Deregulation is changing all this. Brokerage houses via money market mutual funds lured billions in deposits from the banks. In return, banks now offer brokerage services. To cast wider nets for depositors, large banks now solicit by mail in all states and are seeking to open branches in states other than those in which they are chartered.

Seeing an opening, nonfinancial companies have been moving into financial services in a big way. Some industrial companies have done it on their own—like General Electric Corporation through GE Credit Corporation (GECC). For example, GECC now offers a package of short-term construction loans and long-term facility financing to other industrial companies building new plants. Previously unable to provide long-term financing, commercial banks are thereby put at a disadvantage. Looking at a *Wall Street Journal* advertisement placed by GECC, offering the full new facility financing package to industrial companies, a top executive of a major New York bank was heard to comment, "My God, are they that far into our business now?"

In contrast, other nonfinancial companies have entered the burgeoning financial services market by acquisition. In 1981 Sears, Roebuck & Company bought Caldwell Banker and then Dean Witter. In the same year American Express acquired Shearson. Talk began about the possibility of a full-line financial services organization for the future, and insurance companies rushed to keep up by acquiring brokerage houses.

Everyone, it appears, is trying to get into the financial services business. The new entrants are not necessarily going to be short-termers. The retail houses and industrial companies have a possible competitive edge in the financial services marketplace: Sears by its direct access to the investing public through its stores; General Electric by the possible product pull to industrial companies of its proposed factory of the future.

If this turmoil were not enough, security markets are becoming increasingly internationalized. Joint ventures are beginning between American banks and Japanese security brokerage houses. A more open Euro-Yen market is being created, and the competition for place and survival in the financial markets is more intense than ever before. In the course of the competitive struggle, falling profits, increased risk of financial failure, cost cutting, and a wave of mergers and acquisitions are foreseen for financial services companies. From a conservative, complacent backwater, financial services has become chaotic, exciting, and opportunity driven. This change is increasingly stressful for the executives charged with gaining success for their companies.

Technology is also driving the new competition. The semiconductor has made clear what government regulation of the telephone industry had disguised, that computers and communication equipment are to a very large degree the same industry. The result is direct competition between the giants of both industries, not only in the United States but on a worldwide scale.

Finally, diversification also drives the new competition. Oil companies seeking to invest billions in cash flow have moved into retailing, paper products, electrical equipment, and other businesses. Large industrial manufacturers seeking a window into the new electronic technology have purchased semiconductor companies. "One never knows from which laboratory in the Silicon Valley or the Research Triangle one's new competitor will spring," GE's chairman observed. To respond to all this change, he continued, GE had in 1982–83 entered into 118 new ventures and disposed of 71 others.[6]

[6] Jack Welch, "Managing Change" (Dedication Convocation Keynote Address, Fuqua School of Business, Duke University, Durham, North Carolina, April 21, 1983), General Electric Executive Speech Reprint, p. 2.

MEETING THE CHALLENGE

How have American companies reacted to intensified competition? Have they aggressively responded, trying to regain lost markets by outcompeting the challengers? Some have; but far too many have not.

In the late summer of 1983 line executives of 224 companies were interviewed about increasing competition. Far more than half of the companies had been affected by either increased foreign competition or deregulation and its associated heating up of competition. But compared to companies not facing increased competition, those which did were much more likely to have adopted a strategy of simply trying to hold market share. To a degree this defensiveness can be validated by citing a lack of resources to use in aggressively responding to competitive challenges. Perhaps more imagination would be an important factor in causing a company facing competition to be more aggressive.

IBM has been very successful in holding its own against foreign competition in the 1980s; a key reason for that was its efforts in the 1970s to cut production costs by upgrading facilities, technologies, and practices. When foreign competitors began to challenge it in the 1980s, IBM was already well on its way to its goal of being the low-cost producer in key product lines.

Company officials were asked if this strategy put a lot of pressure on IBM executives. And, if it was difficult to get managers and employees to respond in advance to potential competitive challenges. IBM's answer: "Our research shows that companies trying to preserve outdated products burn out their sales and production people fastest. Rapid technological and product changes create some stress, but not as much as trying to play catch-up in every inning."

Aggressiveness and success have problems associated with them. So do decline and failure. For most people the problems of growth and success are preferable to those of decline and failure.

For both successful and unsuccessful American firms, the impact of the new competition is substantial and growing. Even firms which have no new direct competition themselves are also being drawn into the vortex.

Because of deregulation and the intensified competition in air transportation, aircraft manufacturers are being forced to invest a more substantial stake in their airline customers. McDonnell–Douglas Corporation and Boeing Company, Inc. are now extending credits to the established carriers to help them finance equipment purchases. Competition identifies the strong firms in an industry, whether they are upstream or downstream from the companies initially affected, and forces them into the marketplace struggle.

In air transportation the strong companies are upstream; aircraft manufacturers are forced to intervene to support their customers. In the computer business the situation is the opposite. The stronger companies, such as IBM, Digital Equipment Corporation, and Hewlett-Packard Company deal directly with the final customer, but intense competition brings pressure to cut costs while advancing technology more rapidly. Suppliers to strong companies are often smaller companies lacking the resources to meet the competitive pressures being transmitted from the consumer marketplace. The strength is downstream, with the large companies. To drive costs down and yet keep suppliers viable, large companies are abandoning long-established patterns of supplier relations.

Sole sourcing, always considered too risky because of the chance that a strike or other eventuality could disrupt supplies to the downstream company, is staging a comeback. Large companies now accept equity positions in suppliers, furnish technology, advance capital, and sign long-term purchase contracts. Because of the high costs of these involvements, they are limited to few suppliers of any given product, often becoming virtually a sole sourcing relationship.

If the relationship between suppliers and industrial customers becomes so close, should the larger companies simply acquire the supplier, or produce its product themselves? This answer is also found in competitive pressures. Often the larger company believes it cannot obtain the lower costs of the smaller company, particularly labor and overhead costs.

Another symptom of increased competition is the spin-off of casualties—those large company divisions which are likely to be permanently unprofitable. The desire of parent companies to forego operations in declining businesses has promoted a small boom in employee buyouts and other rescue efforts. Often the spin-offs remain suppliers for the previous parent company, but labor concessions and overhead reductions cut the spin-off's costs and allow the parent to obtain supplies at a lower cost than it could achieve if production were kept in-house.

The lean organization is a further manifestation of competition. Staffing and overhead cost cuts made during the recession of the early 1980s are persisting in response to competitive challenges. In the recession thousands of middle managers in various staff positions in large corporations lost their jobs. A survey by LDG Associates reported in *Fortune* magazine found that most large companies in a wide range of industries have felt it necessary to reduce the number of middle managers.[7] In a subsequent survey managers were asked if the loss of these positions damaged the company in the economic rebound. Not at all was the common answer. Have the people been replaced or the positions been reestablished? Generally not. "Who is performing the functions these middle managers used to perform?" respondents were asked. "A combination of subordinates and other middle managers," was the common answer.

Increased competitive pressure requires a company to minimize costs. Reducing inventory expense has been a key target in many companies because companies that have cut inventory have experienced unexpected savings in other areas as a result. In fact the long delay in the recovery of industrial construction activity is partly due to the attempt of manufacturers to maintain leaner organizations. Facing competitive pressures, American companies worried about the cost of planned new facilities. Modernization

[7] Jeremy Main, "The Recovery Skips Middle Managers," *Fortune*, 6 February, 1984, pp. 112–120.

was required, but its costs seem suicidal. Inventory controls had been tightened and inventory reduced as a cost cutting measure during the recession. Managers asked, how much plant space was allocated to inventory? In some companies the answer was staggering. Final product and materials inventories sometimes consumed as much as 40 percent of the floor space of an American plant. Separate storage was provided for final product inventory and for materials inventory; and often each production worker had an additional cache of parts or materials at the work station. The American system, aptly labeled "just-in-case" inventory management, was ballooning not just inventory cost but plant space needs as well. A severe restriction on inventory allowed reductions in the facility space needs of many companies, and extended the weakness in the industrial construction market.

At the strategic level, many industrial firms have reemphasized their core businesses in response to more vigorous competition. Some companies shed divisions and subsidiaries poorly related to their principal venture. Others acquired closely related firms in an attempt to create economically logical companies that could be managed more effectively. Businesses were both narrowed and strengthened.[8]

Yet other firms took precisely the opposite tack: Sears diversified into financial services. Citicorp began selling merchandise to its customers through catalogues accompanying Mastercard and Visa credit card bills. Far from narrowing and focusing their business, these important companies and others as well appeared to be diversifying into largely unrelated fields.

One commonality reconciles these apparently completely divergent strategies. It is not simply a case of companies flailing wildly under the impact of new competition, some doing one thing and others another. Instead, each company is trying to gain greater leverage on whatever it identified as its key asset in the marketplace.

[8] "How the New Merger Boom Will Benefit the Economy," *Business Week*, 6 February 1984, pp. 42 and 50.

Sears's most significant asset is its contact with millions of consumers through its retail outlets. Citicorp's is its contact with millions through its credit card operations. Leveraging these assets by expanding the range of products and services offered to customers is the logical next step of a competitive strategy.

For many manufacturers, the key competitive asset is proprietary technology or managerial know-how. That asset is most effectively leveraged by a refocusing on undertakings directly related to the technology and know-how. Hence the movement toward diversification in retailing and financial services and toward refocusing in industry.

In responding to foreign competition American firms have substantial strengths upon which to build. Our firms have greater freedom and discretion in the marketplace than firms in other countries where marketplaces are more constrained by government regulations. Our firms also have relatively low debt to equity ratios, signaling substantial financial strength.

These strengths have been too little leveraged by the efforts of people throughout our business organizations. The competitive strength of American firms has tended to be at the top—in the capabilities and hard work of top executives. In many foreign companies, particularly the Japanese, competitive strength is in the rank and file—in commitment and performance that yield a consistently high quality product or service. In order to remain competitive, American firms are now challenged to strengthen the organization downward.

MANAGEMENT CREATES VALUE

The new competition is contributing to a renaissance in the fundamentals of management. A professor of business strategy used to teach a course to MBA students concerning mergers and acquisitions.[9] The course stressed finding a proper fit between com-

---

[9] Norman Berg, *General Management: An Analytic Approach* (Homewood, Illinois: Richard D. Irwin, 1984).

panies that would enhance the prospect of creating value in the companies' ongoing activities. This is the fundamental task of a manager.

But times change, and students polarized into two extremist groups. One drew its inspiration from modern financial theory and opposed all diversification, holding that no merger or acquisition had any value and that stock portfolios alone should be diversified. According to that theory, there could be no value added in the operations of diversified firms.

The other group was interested only in manipulating the price of a security for short-term gain. If an acquisition could be used to enhance Wall Street's valuation of a company's stock for a brief period, while speculators made a killing, that and that alone was reason for the acquisition to be made. Without a short-term equity market gain, this group had no interest in diversification. These were the nascent speculators, arbitragers, and corporate raiders.

Neither group was interested in the management of a business for the ongoing creation of value. Neither saw a company as other than a vehicle for wealth maximization by investors or speculators. Dismayed by the attitudes of students, the instructor ceased to offer the course.

A successful business is not simply a financial machine. It is a human institution that needs careful nurturing to survive and prosper. Diversification can strengthen a company when it provides protection against the ups and downs of the marketplace that might cause a nondiversified company to go into receivership.

Equity holders can, at least theoretically, protect themselves by diversifying their portfolios. But a successful business creates value by relying on constituencies other than stockholders. Suppliers, customers, employees, communities, and debt holders each play a role. These constituents are not able to protect their stakes solely by portfolio diversification in the financial marketplace. Nor, for that matter, may all investors do so. For example, employees with small stock holdings who are required to be in their company's stock purchase plan cannot diversify. The jobs of employees, the economic infrastructure of a community, and the business of a supplier or a customer are not protected by portfolio diversification. Yet the contribution of each is necessary to the ongoing success of a business. Diversification beyond a very cyclical business may be essential to preserve the business for its various constituents. Otherwise, it cannot survive in the long-term to create value.

Encouragingly, the new competition which has pushed many long established businesses into economic peril has reminded many people in our country of the significance of value creation in our businesses and of the skills of the manager who can create value. Nowhere is this renewed respect for the manager (as opposed to the investor or speculator) more apparent than in the behavior of one of the key components of the investment community: venture capitalists.

Each start-up company seeking venture capital prepares a lengthy business plan and forecasts its revenues and expenditures over several years. Products are demonstrated; patents analyzed. But surprisingly, the rules of thumb among venture capitalists about how to select which new company is going to be a winner in the marketplace depend very little on the business plan. They believe, "The numbers (i.e., the forecasts of sales and profits) don't mean much; they're too unreliable and changeable."

What then are the key rules in venture capital? "You always bet on the managers," a successful venture capitalist offered. "You either go with a manager who has a track record of success in the business; or, if he or she doesn't have a track record, then you go with someone you know and in whom you have confidence."

For many entrepreneurs who are seeking venture capital support, these rules are discouraging. If you haven't a track record, and if you don't know the venture capitalists personally, then it is going to be very hard to get financial support. An established manager with a track record of business success can take a not-so-good product or service to a venture firm and come out with financing. A person who is not a manager but who has a superior product or service can take it to a venture firm and come away empty-handed.

The capital markets want to see a well thought out business plan as evidence that a manager has done his or her homework. But investors bet on the management, not the product or service. Venture capitalists bet on the ability of a company's officers to create value.

MANAGERIAL RESPONSIVENESS

Competitiveness requires not only innovation, but also attention to implementation. Carefully conceived business strategies can be successful for a company only if they are taken from the planning stage and converted into practical realities. Even the consulting companies which prospered in the 1970s by offering strategic planning services have recently been forced by a decline in their business to infer that their clients need to do more than plan.

Doug Howell stressed productivity at the consulting firm of Arthur D. Little during the 1970s when it was not yet a popular concept in American top management circles. Early in the 1980s he served as president of Hyatt-Clark Industries, a division divested by General Motors Corporation due to high costs and subsequently purchased by the division's employees. Working at Hyatt-Clark added to Howell's conviction that productivity mattered a great deal to business success. When he left Hyatt-Clark Industries, Howell returned to the consulting world joining Bain and Company, a leading strategic planning firm. There he argued that a company cannot talk strategy today without talking productivity, because cost control is the key to competitiveness.

Insurance companies have utilized salespersons or agents since their inception. But they have never paid much attention to marketing. The rapid inflation of the late 1970s came as a rude shock as millions of consumers ceased to buy ordinary life insurance. For a brief period in 1980 several of the nation's largest insurers glimpsed the risk of financial failure down the road. A decline in inflation saved the day, but deregulation brought a rapid influx of companies into financial services. The insurance companies still had the salespeople, but did they have the right products?

A Boston based insurer set up a marketing task force and appointed as its head one of the company's brightest young executives. The task force was the genesis of a marketing department and the progenitor of a new line of financial services products for the company.

The executive who headed that task force said, "I've learned that to be successful in a competitive business environment there are two things you've got to know: The first is your customers. We have to give our salespeople products they can sell. Seven years ago our sales were 80 percent whole life policies. Today sales are 60 percent variable life and growing. And the second thing you have to know exactly right is your costs. Otherwise, you may sell the new products, but not make any money."

Two fundamentals of business—understanding customers' wants and business costs—were lost for years in companies protected from competition by government regulation or by lack of aggressive foreign or domestic competitors. The following key concepts of marketing apply more broadly now in American industry than ever before.

> *Primary demand:* the idea that the total demand for a product is generated by consumer needs, by the life-styles of people.
>
> *Product life cycle:* the notion that each product, whether a type of life insurance policy or a can opener, goes through a series of stages in which the number of competitors, advertising costs to sales ratios, and so forth differ.
>
> *Market segments:* the separation of consumers of a class of products into groups which need to be approached individually.
>
> *Product/market fit:* the requirement to make product features, price, channels of distribution, and after-sales service fit each market segment correctly.
>
> *Coping with an uncertain future:* how a manager must make decisions about products and marketing despite an inability to forecast the business environment in which the firm will be operating.[10]

[10] Martin Marshall, "Short Marketing Note No. 1" Harvard Business School, 1981.

A company's business environment has many uncertainties, including technology and economic activity, but the major uncertainty is created by competition itself: What will competitors do? To many companies in recent years competition has meant low prices; the company has had to take a loss on each unit it sells to keep its part of the total market, its market share. To lose market share in a line of products may mean the decline of that business to such an extent that the company has to write off its remaining value as a loss against other income. So to avoid big write-offs the company takes short-term losses. How do the company's employees react? They say, "We're as busy as ever, but management says they can't give us an increase in pay."

Some financial theorists argue that companies can escape the competition trap by better planning. What is needed is a more sophisticated analysis of the various investment opportunities to a company, patterned perhaps after the quantitative models of financial options developed in recent years. The key to strategic choices is how competitors will respond, and often managers do not know this. Yet, unless it is known, theoreticians cannot simulate it mathematically. The practical issue is not whether or not to invest in a new product or business when the probable consequences can be foreseen, but rather what to do when the response of existing or potential competitors is unknown.

Because the technological and economic environment is uncertain and the responses of competitors largely unpredictable, successful companies rely less on carefully conceived plans than on an adaptable organization. A company's people become the key to its corporate strategy; not that they develop it and set objectives, but that they are necessary to make it work in the marketplace by adapting it to the continually changing environment and the moves of competitors.

The best managers turn to the adaptable organization as an answer to increasing competition. They are not looking for a strategic response, a particular plan or idea, but rather for a *strategic responsiveness* built into the organization through the ability and commitment of its people.

The key business strategy question of the 1960s and 1970s was phrased, "What business are or do we want to be in?" Once the company identified the need which its products fulfilled for consumers, a series of decisions about marketing, production, and investment directly followed. This insight helped spur the growth of corporate strategic planning and the consulting practices which accompanied it.

But the question was about a corporate objective—the identification or targeting of the business the company wished to be in. Ignored was the question of how to go about being successful in that business. Unnoticed, but implicit in the question was the presumption that having chosen a target the company could, without undue difficulty, be successful. The heightened competition of recent years has given many companies losses not profits in their target businesses. In response the 1980s opened with a question to be posed prior to choosing a business to be in. "Who are we?" a company was urged to ask. How do our customers see us? Our employees? Ourselves? At the end of this inquiry, a sort of corporate identity crisis, lies the central issue of corporate strategy, no longer focused on an objective but instead on implementation. What can this company do well? What are our strengths and weaknesses? What can the company accomplish? Only after these questions have been answered does asking, "What business do we want to be in?" come to have significance.

Accompanying the question, "What do we do well?" is the corollary "What is it useful to do well?" In answer to this query more and more top companies respond, "Have depth and adaptability in the organization."

A VEIL OF SECRECY

To build depth and adaptability requires a continuing effort. Many managers have learned how to make key contributions themselves, but not how to delegate so that others learn as well. Many managers have learned how to direct and control subordinates, but not how to motivate them. Finally managers have developed the techniques of work place discipline without learning how to acquire employees' commitment to their work.

What is new in recent years is the broadening recognition among American managers that delegation, motivation, and commitment are central to business success. Key companies that have learned this lesson know how it contributes to their competitive edge. They recognize that failure to learn the lesson creates a marketplace liability for their competitors who have not learned.

"We're one of the best managed and one of the five most profitable companies in the United States," said the senior vice president of an eastern supermarket chain. "We plan for the development of our people because it makes the company stable. You have to plan so you don't get caught. A company can't wait until the last minute to have qualified people available."

What style does the company have in dealing with its managers? "Participative," he responded. "I don't want to divulge what we do because I'm afraid it would be publicized and our competitors would find out."

At a competing firm the president and chief executive officer expressed a different view. "We're not interested in planning about the people side of the organization," he said. "The country is in a recession. It's not difficult to get people now. They're motivated because the job market is not strong. We've no interest in doing more."

The contrast between these two high executives of competing companies is dramatic. The first is busily engaged in building his organization for the future. The second is content to take what the external economic environment brings him. No wonder the first executive is unwilling to share details about his efforts. Why should he risk awakening a competitor who is now sound asleep at the helm?

Yet another firm in the same business was neither awake, nor asleep, but rousing. "We're meeting more and more competition," the vice president for operations said. "We're now very committed to cost reductions. We're trying to let our employees be heard on the line. We're trying to set up a program. We're reading all we can."

Competition drives each of these managers. The first sees organizational planning as a competitive weapon, so he does it. The second does not, and does nothing. The third is awakening to the possibility and so now is searching madly for ideas and examples. Fearing his competitors will wake up to the advantage he has quietly seized, the first is silent. So it is that competition causes a veil of secrecy to descend over the most imaginative efforts of managers who are trying to gain a competitive advantage in how they manage.

In the chapters that follow we pierce the veil of secrecy allowing readers to learn of both fundamentals and new styles of management. In deference to informers, we must sometimes conceal their identities and those of their companies.

SUMMARY

The new competition comes from both domestic and foreign sources; from foreign companies importing goods or setting up facilities here, and from new domestic entrants to established industries. In the United States deregulation, diversification, and new technology encourage new entrants to many industries. Managers face a twofold challenge: (1) They must adjust the organization to fit themselves and other new people while (2) competing successfully in a very hazardous business world. Balancing these two objectives requires managers with special qualities. The adaptability of the organization will be the central variable of a company's future competitiveness. At the core of adaptability is the need for people at all levels to know what they need to know to get the job done.

Individually, new managers are good communicators. But how can this personal skill be translated into a characteristic of the larger organization? New managers have a critical responsibility to manage the flow of information they receive from above and from below to see that each end of the organization has the data necessary to do its job, not just adequately but well.

3
Escaping Business's Bermuda Triangle

Several years ago a new management team took over Midwest Insurance, a substantial company which in recent years had experienced stagnant sales and earnings. When the new management team from outside the company was brought aboard, the new company chairman was concerned about the morale and performance of rank-and-file employees. "The people in this company have really been neglected in the past," he commented. "They have been given no special consideration and have been made to feel mediocre. Their attitudes toward the job reflect this."

Midwest employed some 30,000 people throughout the country, with the largest single group (5,500) at corporate headquarters. Despite a battery of modern personnel programs, including salary administration, performance appraisal, and organizational development, the new management saw demoralization in many of the company's key units. In order to get a direct line of communication to employees, the chairman requested that a program be set up which would let employees go directly to corporate personnel with a complaint or query.

A SAFETY VALVE

After several months, this program was proposed: first, employees were encouraged to initially take any problem to their immediate supervisors; second, if employees were dissatisfied with the course of action under the first element, or did not think it appropriate to go through their supervisors, they could write directly to the program's coordinator on special forms to be issued by the company. Though employees were requested to sign the form, they were promised confidentiality. Third, employees still dissatisfied could request and receive a meeting with the chairman. It was expected that these meetings would be few enough to be handled.

The program was presented to the company's executive committee, where it ran into considerable skepticism and resistance from the entire top management team except the chairman. "This program is completely redundant if our supervisors manage well," said one executive. "It breaks out of the line of command and undermines the authority of line managers. The key communications link in any organization is the one between the employee and the immediate supervisor, and this legitimizes the employee ignoring that link."

"Managers will just abdicate their own responsibilities to communicate," offered another. "They'll say, 'If corporate wants to talk to employees let them do it, not me.'"

"We know the supervisors don't like it," said another. "Your report on your series of discussions with first and second level supervisors said they were generally negative. Some even said it sounded like a Gestapo program to monitor their activities. Others think employees will use the program to get back at them for various reasons. Why should we needlessly antagonize this key group?"

Another member of the committee objected to the program's administrative side. "We'll get superficial issues," he said, "bringing junk to the managers' attention. It'll be expensive to administer, because the coordinator will be swamped with silly complaints and questions."

"And it will raise employee expectations," interjected the final member of the group. "They'll think they can change things just by writing a complaint. When it doesn't happen, they'll be disappointed and disillusioned. This program won't help morale, it will hurt it. And when people see it doesn't work, they'll quit using it."

This meeting made it clear that the program had only a single supporter in the top management team; but since he was the CEO and wanted to give it a try, the program was implemented. When it was in place for all 30,000 of the company's employees, some 53 inquiries and requests for meetings with the chairman were received in the first three months, a level consistent with the experience of other similarly sized companies with comparable programs. The volume was manageable; the inquiries were varied. For example, Lucy Murphy wrote to the coordinator: "I wish to register a complaint about not receiving my overtime pay. As the secretary of Stephen J. Lloyd, I have worked about 60 hours of overtime during the past 3 months. My job involves staying after hours to complete typing work at least three nights a week. However, Mr. Lloyd refuses to authorize my time card to enable me to collect the overtime. He says that I should be able to finish my work within regular working hours—but I really can't do it.

"Anyway, because of Mr. Lloyd, I haven't been putting my overtime down on the time cards that I send to payroll. But, I told someone about the situation, and they said that I have a legal right to collect my overtime pay. Can you please straighten out this situation? I would like to have the money which I have rightfully earned."

Earlier the coordinator had established a small committee of managers to advise him on how to handle certain inquiries. Lucy Murphy's complaint was the first he had taken to them. "What shall we do with this?" the coordinator asked.

"We've got to find out if it's accurate," said one manager.

"How can we do that without talking to Lloyd?" asked another.

"But if we talk to Lloyd, we can't keep Lucy Murphy's confidentiality."

"If what she says is true, she has to be paid the overtime. The law requires it."

"But if we pay her, Lloyd may just fire her."

"For complaining about her overtime pay? That would be illegal."

"No, for not getting her work done in the regular work day."

"We can check that," said one. "Let's look at Lloyd's performance appraisals for Lucy. They'll say she's not a good performer."

"I don't know," answered another.

"They'll probably say she's great. Lots of our managers don't put the truth in those appraisals, especially when it's unfavorable, because the employee gets to see them."

"Well, if Lloyd has rated her as satisfactory or excellent, then he's got no basis on which to fire her for incompetence; she'd object and the government would investigate if we fired her because of the overtime complaint."

"Maybe this is just the tip of the iceberg," the coordinator offered. "Maybe Lucy is writing for a group of people."

"Perhaps we should just send out a letter to all supervisors, Lloyd included, to remind them of their legal responsibilities on overtime."

"Well, it might do some good—but Lloyd might just keep ignoring it."

"If he's ignoring it now. We really don't know yet. We haven't investigated."

"But if we go to Lloyd, he'll figure out that Lucy sent the complaint, and we won't have kept it confidential."

"Well," the coordinator interrupted, "we haven't done a great job figuring out what to do on that one. Let's go to the next. Here it is."

"I am writing this letter about the priority parking system in our parking lots. I am an exempt, professional employee, therefore I am restricted from parking in the management lot which is— as you know—quite a bit closer to the main entrance of our building. Now I realize that there are certain privileges that go along with being a manager—but I think this one is impractical. You see, I arrive at work by 7:00 A.M. every morning which is at least one hour before most people—management or otherwise. I do not see why I have to park out in 'the sticks' when I get here so early. It is really inconvenient, as well as uncomfortable on the cold and snowy days, to walk so far through an *empty* parking lot. I am requesting a change in this management parking priority policy. Let's have a 'first come, first served system.' "

"Toss that one," said one of the group immediately. "Put it in the circular file."

"Who wrote that?" echoed another. "That's the silliest thing I've heard of. Do I have to waste my time on this?"

"Wait a minute," objected a third; "I think he's right. He ought not to walk a long way just because of reserved spots. He's a contributor just like the managers."

"Are you serious?"

"Yes, I am. How would you explain the policy to him?"

"I'd tell him it's just a managerial prerogative. When he gets to be a manager, he'll get an assigned place."

"Well, I don't know," offered another. "At our place we have reserved parking, but it's because the managers go in and out of their place a lot during the day. We could explain that to him."

"You know, this may not be the only employee who is upset about this. Maybe reserved parking is sending the wrong signal to our employees. Maybe we want them to feel a part of a team; not like second-class citizens."

"Two years ago, before I came to this company," said another, "I was an assistant to the manager of a large claims office. Some of the employees complained about the reserved spaces for managers, so my boss decided to abolish them. It was to be first come, first served in the entire lot. The experiment lasted a day. That day my boss brought his new Cadillac in at 8:30 A.M. and parked between two employees' cars. That night at 6 he went to get it and found a scratch along one side where a door had scraped it. Thank God I hadn't parked next to him. The next day we had assigned parking again—with lots of room in the managers' places."

"Is there any opportunity to be found here?" asked the coordinator.

"We could publish our policy and an explanation of it," suggested one.

"We could reevaluate it and change it," countered another.

"Let's go on to the last one," said the coordinator.

"I am writing this letter as a last resort. I simply can't figure out a way to handle this problem on my own.

"I am having some serious problems with my manager who, incidentally, is married with two children. He has been my manager for the past six months. The first three months everything was fine. I was learning a great deal about the investigation of claims. And, according to my manager, I was doing a good job. Generally, I was happy with the assignment. Then, one evening a group of us went out for drinks and dinner after work. We ended up staying out rather late. While I didn't try to encourage him, my manager kept making advances to the point where it was quite obvious what his intentions were. The whole thing really upset me. First of all, I don't believe in getting involved with married men, and, second, I have made it a practice not to date men at work. I just told him flat out that I wasn't interested in any more than a platonic relationship with him and to please leave me alone. He got angry and his statements implied that my job was on the line.

"Ever since that evening, things have been going downhill. My manager has been very distant. The way he treats me now has impeded my work progress. He has virtually stopped giving me any help or guidance with my work. I have been given many very tedious and boring projects to do, and I have been excluded from several departmental meetings. On occasion, however, he makes suggestive remarks and advances."

The coordinator was disturbed to hear some snickering as his group read the letter. When he could hear a few whispered comments and some chuckles, he interjected, "This is not a laughing matter. These are serious charges. Sexual harassment is illegal."

"But we don't even know it's true. It's like the overtime complaint; it's just an allegation. Someone has to talk to her boss."

"But we promised her confidentiality."

"Maybe we should just stay out of this and see if anything else comes up."

"That leaves us very open for a sexual harassment suit. We've been informed; if we do nothing, it's as if the company condones this kind of stuff."

"If I were her boss, I'd want this investigated. If it weren't true, would you want something like this in the company's records without ever getting a chance to rebut it? Of course not!"

There was a pause. "But it's probably true," concluded one.

"How can you say that?" he was challenged.

"It reads as if it were true. No one could invent those last lines." He paused. "And a lot of this goes on—everywhere."

"My neighbor had to deal with a problem like this not long ago," offered another, "and he told me about it. My neighbor runs a small high tech firm—maybe 200 people. He has a super engineer, really important to the company. But he's a fat, kind of homely guy. Every Friday night after work he'd go out with his staff to a local bar for a couple of hours. The word came back to my neighbor that this engineer, their boss, was a little fresh; putting his hands on the women and all. So I asked my neighbor, 'What did you do?' 'I just had to do something,' my neighbor said, 'because the guy was really good and I didn't want to lose him. But I couldn't let it go on. So the next Friday night I insisted he meet me, in his office, at the happy hour. He was kind of mad because he wanted to be with his group, and he told me so. So I told him that's why I was there to see him. "George," I said, "you've got to stop touching those people." He made light of it at first. He insisted it was just playful; insisted that they liked it.

" 'I said, "No, George, they don't like it. They complained to me, that's why I'm here." I kept my face very serious. He quit laughing; then began to shuffle uncomfortably.

" 'He said, "But I really like those get-togethers. I work hard and I kind of live for them." ' "

"My neighbor said to him, 'I know, George. I know you do. But it has to stop. Your mother loves you; and I love you; but not everyone loves you.' "

"My neighbor just sat there, while the message sunk in. Finally George said, 'I don't know what I'll do on Friday nights. I get so lonely.'

" 'I know George,' my neighbor said, 'but you can't go back. Not yet. You know and I know you can't handle it. But every Friday night from now on I'll come in and spend some time with you after work on Friday. Maybe we'll go out then.' "

A lengthy silence followed in the group until the members' thoughts returned to the letter before them. "So we've got to investigate it," offered another member of the group. "The woman has a right to an investigation, and so does her boss. And the company gets too much liability if we don't look into it."

"But what about confidentiality?"

"Well, let's go to her first. We'll tell her these are very serious charges. That if she insists they are true, and can substantiate them, then we have to investigate and talk to her boss and co-workers, if they are witnesses. We can transfer her if she wishes."

"I think I'd better take this one up with legal counsel," concluded the coordinator. He waited a minute, reflecting on the meeting. "This was our first meeting, but it's pretty clear why we needed some program like this. I really can't imagine either of the two women taking their complaints to their supervisors and letting it stop there, since the supervisors are the problem.

"Probably most of our supervisors aren't behaving this way, but we'd better start some meetings and training to make sure. Most of our employees' concerns should go to their supervisors, just as you generally favor, then up the line of command. But we need this safety valve for difficult situations."

FINDING OUT WHAT IS GOING ON

The contrast between ways of doing things at the top and at the bottom of large organizations has never been greater. In recent years there has developed considerable openness, flexibility, and informality of communications and relationships among the management teams of many of our large companies. People contribute to the problems of the moment without regard to specific lines of demarcation between their functions. Individuals acknowledge that they are part of a team, working for common goals, and while personal ambitions, jealousies, and contests appear, as they do in any human organization, in most places these conditions do not dominate relationships.

At the bottom of the organizations, where large groups of clerical or production employees are gathered, a very different climate exists. In most companies bureaucracy is in full charge. People are largely confined to a narrow range of tasks, working under close supervision, and without the openness and flexibility which exist in the upper managerial ranks.

Among managers communications are interactive, involving give and take of discussion between people of different levels and functions. At the bottom of the organization communications are one way, generally from the top down by newsletters, memos, videotapes, written and verbal directives. In part, because people want and benefit from openness and interaction in communications, performance and satisfaction are far weaker at the bottom of the organization than at the top.

In the larger middle stretches of an organization, in the ranks of middle managers and professional employees, there is a great black hole; a Bermuda Triangle, into which information flows from both ends, only to disappear. Into the triangle from the top come not only the objectives of top management, whether at plant, division, or even corporate level, but also the business rationale for what is required. When costs are squeezing profits, plans come down for cost reductions. They are rationalized by the expected savings from each part of the plan and connected by the role of each part in an overall scheme to cut excessive costs plant- or organization-wide. Out from the triangle to the work force go a series of disconnected, seemingly arbitrary directives, devoid of explanation, purpose, or interconnectedness. The spirit is gone; only the letter remains. The work force is given so little information that it is neither able to make sense of what it is to do, to contribute any ideas of its own, nor to willingly and imaginatively apply itself to the task at hand.

Upward from the employees flows information about attitudes, expectations, and production problems only to disappear into the triangle. Flowing upward primarily from the mass of middle managers come reports of results on a series of disconnected dimensions. The triangle causes remarks like these:

"What is going on in international lending?" asks the executive vice president of a major bank. "I know what the numbers are, but what is really going on? Why are the numbers like this?" Or as in the situation at Midwest Insurance, "What is happening in the work place that causes employee morale to be so low?"

Do the managers in the triangle see themselves as having a role in communicating the reasons and needs behind corporate directions to rank-and-file employees? By and large, no. They have neither the respect for the rank and file, nor an understanding of how better knowledge at the work force level could enhance quality, output, and efficiency.

Do the managers in the triangle see themselves as having a role in communicating employees' concerns to their bosses? By and large, no. Either they think their bosses do not want to hear "that stuff," or they say, "That's what the union or the personnel office is for." Furthermore, they do not think they receive answers from their bosses about employee concerns or job-related questions. So they cannot handle employee concerns.

Employees do not see either the union or personnel people as good communicators for many purposes. A union's method is too formal; it often lacks informal influence on management. Often remote and distant, it may use a political filter in deciding whom to assist. Its scope is usually limited to complaints about contract violations. Unions are effective when they select certain key issues and go after those; they are often extremely effective on issues that matter to employees as a group and to the union as an institution. But a vast body of day-to-day work related issues is not covered by the union's activities.

Similarly a personnel department has limited scope, limited informal influence, and its own concerns to press. It is not an appropriate device for ordinary work related matters either.

Because of the Bermuda Triangle, the organization as a whole does not do a good job of listening. The objectives of management are lost to employees; the concerns and contributions of employees are lost to managers. The triangle receives, but it does not transmit.

Communications must be personalized to be effective. Top management can gain some goodwill by occasional facility visits, but this is not very important. The real payoff is in the accessibility of facility-level management to the work force, so that a personalized rapport is developed.

Today's generation is a television generation. It reads, but uncomfortably, unless the material is simple and story oriented. It finds as much reality in the celebrities of television and motion pictures as in personal contacts with family, friends, and coworkers. Perhaps paradoxically as society grows larger and more bureaucratized, individuals place more value on a personal touch— which is what television provides—personifying and personalizing communication as if one on one.

At the workplace, however, television's one-way communication is inadequate. Employees have lots to offer about their jobs and working conditions. They want an opportunity to express themselves, even if they do not always take advantage of it when offered.

Personalization builds loyalty and commitment. It gives employees recognition from management, and alerts managers to what is occurring in the workplace. Hewlett–Packard Company, which insists its managers personalize, has popularized the concept by labeling it "Management by Walking Around" (MBWA). A stratagem to eliminate the triangle is for the MBWA manager to get out of the office, away from written reports and other managers, and out onto the floor of the plant, sales office, or research laboratory, to spend time with and talk to the people. If there were no Bermuda Triangle, MBWA would not be necessary.

Unfortunately, in many situations not even MBWA is a sufficient response to the triangle. Harvey Vaughan managed the biogenetic research laboratories of a major pharmaceutical company. Long a practitioner of MBWA, Vaughan was confident of his contact with the scientists and technicians who reported to him. One day, to his surprise, he received an anonymous letter directed to his boss and copies to six of his subordinate managers. While not directed at him personally, for two full pages the letter criticized the promotions and assignment processes in the laboratories.

A series of management meetings followed. The company's chairman suggested borrowing an idea from the management of a large bank of which he was a director. When the bank's chairman had received an anonymous letter complaining of racial discrimination at the bank's headquarters, the handwriting and fingerprints of all employees had been investigated in an attempt to identify the writer. The effort failed; the letter was disregarded, and nothing more was received from the anonymous writer.

Vaughan and his boss felt the chairman's suggestion was likely to do more harm than good, and gently deflected it. Instead they thought long and hard about whether the complaints were justified. Vaughan also worried about the letter as evidence that he was out of touch with the employees. "We've grown," he commented. "I used to have all my people in a single, one-story building. Now we've spread some groups out to three other nearby buildings, and I rarely get to them. Also, as I think about it, when I walk around I tend to stop and chat with the same people over and over. I may not be seeing lots of the people."

In the end, Vaughan chose to file the letter, waiting for further communications from its writer. He also decided to set aside time in his office and an hour or two a week in the cafeteria during which he was available to employees. Walking around helped, but wasn't enough. An opportunity to be approached was important, too.

When Reginald Jones was chairman at General Electric Company he instituted a novel way of getting feedback on his own performance. While most managers are willing to evaluate those who work for them, they are not willing to be evaluated by their subordinates. Such an evaluation, however, is a very important part of upward communications. What employees and middle managers think about how the boss handles his job is usually lost in the organization's Bermuda Triangle. Jones was too good a manager to let this occur, but not even Jones could expect his subordinates to come into his office to criticize him candidly to his face.

The corporation's top officers held an annual meeting to review business performance and the performance of top managers. On the final day an informal dinner was held. Jones retired to his hotel room and did not attend the dinner. But he designated as its host a well-respected long-term officer of the company; a sort of elder statesperson whose integrity was acknowledged. The ground rules for the dinner were for participants to engage in a frank, no-holds-barred discussion of the corporation's performance under Jones, and of Jones's leadership. No comment was to be attributed to any individual. Everything was to be off the record. No one was ever to mention the dinner to Jones except the elder statesperson.

The morning after the dinner Jones met for several hours with the dinner host to go over the previous evening's discussion. No names were mentioned, but the full critique of Jones's leadership, strengths, and weaknesses, was presented to him. It takes a strong person to subject himself to personal criticism, and to attempt to learn from it. Jones was selected by his peers as America's most admired chief executive.

MAPPING INFORMATION FLOWS

Seven thousand people work in a facility belonging to a large defense contractor outside a major northeastern city. Six layers of management exist, starting with a corporate vice president and ending with first level supervisors who direct the work force. The top of the management structure is open—there is easy access for individuals up and down and across functional lines. At the bottom communications go up or down the chain of command; employees cannot carry their problems to others, often including their bosses, and there is a lack of information and no idea how to get it. In between top and bottom the Bermuda Triangle swallows information, but disgorges virtually none.

A staff planning group looking for ways to enhance productivity addressed the issue. A chart was prepared as a first step in identifying problems in communication. Information was divided into four categories: general information about the business (How are we doing? What is today's opportunity or pressing problem?); information about how to do the job; information on how the individual fits into the process in which he or she is working; recognition of the individual's own contribution. Next, the plant's work force was broken into four categories: top management, project or department management, first and second level management, and production and clerical employees. A matrix was prepared crossing types of information against categories of the plant's work force. The task force then put an x in each cell where a group of employees was receiving information. A great many empty cells directed attention to how much information should be provided and by what devices.

For each employee in the triangle (i.e., except at top and bottom) a communications analysis could be prepared. First focusing on the superior: how much information comes from my superior to me and in how timely a fashion? How much information goes up from me to my supervisor, and in how timely a fashion? Then focusing on the subordinate: how much information goes down from me to my subordinate, and how timely is it? And from my subordinates to me, how much comes up and how timely is it?

By getting managers to think through how information flows up and down, and what was being lost, the plant management made its first stab at breaking information loose from the Bermuda Triangle.

In many companies, informal lateral communications in middle management are being facilitated by use of networks of microcomputers. At the government relations office of a large company, staff managers are continually visiting different company locations. For years the office has been troubled by reverberations from location managers when first one, then another executive from corporate descended on them, unaware that the previous week a counterpart had been there. Attempting to find out who had been where, and to coordinate visits by phone calls, had turned out to be very expensive, time-consuming, and imperfect.

Recently the company computerized the calendars for its staff executives. Now an executive who plans to visit the company's Houston location simply calls up from the computer a list of recent visits to Houston by any other staff executives.

ACTIONS AS WELL AS WORDS

Communications are much more than words or data. The most significant communications are actions which—as the old saw has it—are more important than words. Many companies today are trying to persuade or induce employees to accept new technology. There are understandable apprehensions on the part of some. Managers should be able to set an example, but sometimes it does not work out that way.

Helen Sullivan was 54 and a senior secretary at a large industrial company's headquarters in the Middle West when she first used a computer terminal. She was the first secretary in the company to use electronic mail; the first to give up a typewriter and go to word processing; the first to interface with the corporate communications data bank. So effective was Sullivan and so influential as an example to other employees that she taught courses about the use of the new office technology.

Eight years passed; she was 62 and as excited about the new equipment as ever. Then the 1982 recession brought on a corporate staff reduction. Her existing job was eliminated and off she went to interview for a new job in the same building. In the outer room at her new boss's office she saw a computer terminal. So she told him what she had done and could do on the equipment. He responded that he does not use it; that its capabilities have been oversold. "Just bring a notepad for dictation and we'll get along fine," he said to her.

Sullivan went back to the personnel department. "I've had so much fun learning the new technology in the past eight years," she said, "that I can't go back to the old systems." With that she left the company.

In contrast, J.B. Green Company had a prosperous though small business providing market data in book form to mail order companies. In the early 1970s the company went to optical character recognition for processing orders. The company's customer list was computerized in 1976. In 1980 an interface was developed between the company's market data base and its phototypesetting equipment, so that the printing of its books was essentially computerized.

The early 1980s brought the microcomputer, and the first possibility of small customers using market data for computerized analysis. J.B. Green had been a pioneer in applying new technology to its own internal production processes. Could it be a pioneer in applications to its product?

The company's president purchased two microcomputers in 1982. Immediately members of the company's staff began to work with the equipment. Applications of the data base to customers' needs flowed quickly out of the already computerized internal data collection and handling processes.

J.B. Green Company had no problem communicating the technological change under way among its customers to its own staff. Actions spoke louder than words. Years of being a pioneer in its own business use of new technology led naturally into a pioneering role for its customers. "I couldn't have stopped my people if I had tried," Green's CEO commented.

RISING ABOVE SUBJECTIVITY

A major problem with communication between managers and those they supervise is the inability of many people to distinguish between individuals and their actions. Thus, when a person performs poorly, it becomes a reflection on his or her personal qualities of competence, intelligence, and potential. While performance and ability are sometimes related, they are also often independent.

Managers who cannot distinguish today's poor performance from tomorrow's possibilities are often unable to bring themselves to criticize a subordinate's behavior. As a result, the subordinate does not know what the problem is.

In a typical case, a manager will tell a subordinate at an annual salary review that he or she has done all right, but then give a very low salary increase. The subordinate becomes both angry and confused. Angry at a stingy reward for satisfactory performance; and confused about what is wrong with his or her performance. In extreme cases managers cannot confront the employee at all. So they simply rate performance as satisfactory, give a moderate pay increase, and hope they will be promoted out of the situation or the subordinate will quit or transfer.

A motto at some corporations, "Be tough on standards," is a way of insisting that managers not let their distaste for personal confrontations prevent them from pressing for performance from subordinates. "But," the motto sometimes adds, "not on people." A manager is to uphold standards, not criticize people. The issue is what people do, not who they are. Behavior counts, not personality or personal qualities. The motto is very constructive. If followed, it forces a manager to try to preserve standards, and frees the manager to deal with employees as they change over time.

Standards remain high, to be established by policy and example, to be measured by audit and observation, and to be reinforced by recognition and reward. But this is only part of a manager's task. The other part is to develop and motivate people. More complex than standards, people require different types of treatment. People need leadership and encouragement as well as measurement and reward. A person who is performing poorly at the moment is nevertheless a good person, and one with opportunity in the future.

During a class at the Harvard Business School, a large company's CEO described just such a situation encountered by the company's top management team. A key executive had had a bad year. The CEO proposed to cut his bonus to almost nothing. Another top executive of the firm objected. "If he's been good for us for 16 years, he was good for us last year. He should get his full bonus."

"I disagreed," the CEO said. "I firmly believe that people go through crises in their lives. They get divorced; they go through a mid-life crisis; their effectiveness falls off."

Neither executive persuaded the other, and in the end they compromised. But the CEO, while seemingly the harsher of the two, was more faithful to the motto: Be tough on standards, not on people. The bonus was the reward for meeting standards; it was not the senior executive's personality that was at stake. The CEO's counterpart on the bonus committee couldn't separate the person from his performance.

As Alfred P. Sloan, the architect of General Motors, said, "It is imperative for the health of the organization that it always tends to rise above subjectivity."[1] This is nowhere more important than in evaluating performance and communicating the evaluation to people in the organization. Subjectivity must be avoided in how performance is appraised—not only your friends do a good job. Subjectivity must also be avoided in communication with people about their performance—poor performers are not necessarily inept people.

A TIGER'S NEW STRIPES

Can an already established manager somewhat set in his or her ways learn to do a better job of motivating and inspiring those with whom he or she works? In general, the answer is maybe. Because the lesson involves the behavior of managers it is a

---

[1] Harold C. Livesay, *American Made; Men Who Shaped the American Economy* (Boston: Little, Brown, 1979), p. 238.

sensitive subject, not readily learned from lectures or briefing books. Some do learn quickly, almost as if it were second nature and the manager was only waiting to be told that his or her natural inclinations were proper behavior. The majority are far slower— the old ways have too strong a hold.

In the late 1970s when General Motors Corporation began to expand its efforts to improve relations among managers, the work force, and union representatives in its plants, it took into account the peculiarly difficult problem of changing behavior. Ordinarily when the company embarked on a new program each plant manager received a briefing book setting forth, tab by tab, the purpose and content of the program. Meetings were held at each plant, the program was parceled up into pieces, and each functional manager was given a piece to do.

But for this new effort at changing human relationships there was only the shortest briefing book. The plant manager was told that he had an obligation to have a program, and the company gave it label, but the briefing book did not spell out content. Instead, a variety of resources were offered—books, articles, seminars, visits to other plants and other companies—from which manager and staff were to fashion their own unique effort.

"We couldn't tell them what to do," Jim MacDonald, GM's president, said later. "It didn't do any good to give them orders. We tried to get them into seminars and meetings where they heard story after story about how things could be changed. Some didn't believe it, but we kept them coming until finally a manager would catch fire, 'I didn't know you could do that,' he'd say. He'd see the possibilities and go off to do something for himself."

SUMMARY

Communication within a company is crucial. Today most companies have a kind of Bermuda Triangle into which crucial information seems to disappear or get scrambled. People at both the top and bottom have too little or erroneous information. To alter this, managers must make special efforts to amplify and transmit the information they receive. Through better and different kinds of communication, managers can affect the competitiveness of the company. High performance is made possible when employees understand what should be done and have enough information to accomplish it. Managers also have to develop a context in which people will choose to make their maximum contribution.

4

Employment Security: Think Of The Opportunity

J. E. Frankum, vice president for transportation of a long established airline, studied a report prepared by his company's training staff. The airline was losing market share to new competitors. Layoffs had begun. Soon people with less than ten years of service would all be gone. Interviews revealed that customers complained about the poor attitudes and service of the company's staff. He had asked his training staff to investigate the problem. "In broad terms," their report began, "the service problem lies in a caliber of service that is efficient but lacking in warmth. It is a matter of employees performing well technically but with a matter-of-factness which reflects no genuine enthusiasm and conveys no honest desire to serve."

As evidence of the problem the report cited a lack of employee enthusiasm and a lack of small courtesies to passengers; inappropriate or less than standard personal appearances and carelessness; as well as the more standard measures of morale—absenteeism, lateness, and high turnover. Frankum read on in the training staff's report, "There is an overall sense that employees do not feel that they are part of the organization in terms of being involved in business matters or in having supervision listen to and act upon their recommendations. . . ."

He was pleased to see that the report was not simply a litany of complaints about employees but reflected the company's basic philosophy that morale problems were ultimately management's responsibility to resolve. The report showed a belief in employees who were neither inherently lazy nor irresponsible. It pinpointed the basic causes of the problem: "The vast majority of employees, regardless of job title, want to perform well; they want the satisfaction that comes from success; they want to do what is right. . . ." But the report concluded, "The environment to tap the motivation to do well is lacking. . . ."

Frankum thought about the issue. How does a manager make people want to contribute to the enterprise? Companies in intense competition need employees who go beyond technical competence, which is comparatively easy to teach and monitor, to strive for the highest level of personal service to customers. Such effort is needed although it is beyond the technical confines of a job description. It cannot be obtained by edict, but must be volunteered. "But," Frankum mused, "do employees volunteer effort and commitment out of security and involvement, or out of insecurity and risk?" He could push his company in either direction. Which was the better way to go?

AN ISSUE FOR TODAY

Job security will be a major issue of the coming decade. Unions have raised it as their number one priority in response to the massive layoffs in heavy manufacturing during the 1981–82 recession. The issue of "fairness"—that economic policies designed to end the recession and regain competitiveness should demand equal sacrifice from all sectors of our society and work force— even commanded public attention in the Reagan–Mondale presidential contest. Employment security is a fairness issue to much of the public.

New managers also have reason for concern. During the most recent recession many companies were forced to lay off managers in large numbers. Some of our most successful companies have achieved higher productivity and quality with fewer managers (see Chapter 11). This generation of managers also faces fierce competition for top jobs from its large peer group. Employment security may become a necessary trade-off for managers as well as the managed because of the relative lack of promotional opportunities within the firm.

United States companies have traditionally taken three general approaches to the issue of employment security. The majority of companies make no implicit or explicit offer of employment security to employees and respond to economic hard times with layoffs among production workers and managers. Their responsibility is limited to meeting the minimal requirements of the law. Layoffs are ordinarily made with very little advance notice. Union contracts and seniority provisions sometimes require advance notice—averaging no more than one week.

A second group of companies takes a more active role, but still does not offer full employment. Layoffs are avoided unless absolutely necessary and often support for retraining and/or relocation is offered either through the company, through the company's support of government safety net programs, or some combination of the two. Companies adopting this stance are usually motivated by a mix of humanitarian concerns and the fear that if U.S. companies do not voluntarily assume the responsibility for easing the transitions of laid off employees, public support for legislative requirements to do so will prevail.

Managers are also motivated by other public relations concerns and the very real need to correct the public's perception about some economic fundamentals. In the public's mind, for example, corporate profits make up a large proportion of sales and the necessity of layoffs seems small. A recent poll, for example, showed that the public estimated that the average manufacturer's after-tax profit margin was 37 percent.[1] In 1982 the correct figure was

[1] "Business Bulletin: A Special Background Report on Trends in Industry and Finance," *Wall Street Journal*, 3 November 1983, p. 1.

3.8 percent.[2] Companies and their managers have good reason to be concerned about their image with the public when popular beliefs are so inaccurate.

United States companies are vulnerable to criticism that profits are put before people even if the average profits are not as large as the public imagines. The media show a particular interest in the subject. Mike Wallace recently reported on a segment of "60 Minutes" describing the history and effect of closing General Electric's (GE) metal iron plant in Ontario, California, after fifty years of operation. The plant was profitable, but not profitable enough and GE anticipated that if the plant was kept open, dwindling profits would soon turn to losses. Al Kennel, GE's local spokesman, explained that GE was getting out of the metal iron business in large part because their marketing people told them that consumer preferences were moving quickly away from metal to plastic and that converting the existing plant to production for the new market would take too long and be too costly.

The 850 employees and some members of the community saw the situation from a different perspective. The local mayor anticipated that 2,000 employees would eventually lose their jobs in the community because of the ripple effect of the plant closing. He suggested that GE was making a profit but could make more by moving production abroad to lower wage countries. GE, on the other hand, said that labor costs were not the issue but that they already had a plant in Singapore and outsourcing could lead to inroads in foreign markets.

General Electric held firm to its decision. As Boston College Professor Barry Bluestone put it, "given the rules of the game, they are conducting themselves like statesmen. . . ." Efforts by the union to find a buyer for the plant or to buy it themselves, and even an offer to take a pay cut failed to make the continued operation of the plant viable from GE's point of view. The displaced employees were given six months' notice of the plant's closing; some workers were shifted to another GE plant and a state-run

[2] *Ibid.*

job relocation program was set up at the plant to ease the transitions where possible.

Finally, as discussed earlier, a few companies have voluntarily committed themselves to full employment policies. They go to great lengths and expense to keep this commitment. During the 1970s IBM was affected by two recessions. By the end of the first, 12,000 IBM employees had been transferred; of these, 5,000 were trained for new careers.[3] By the end of the 1974–75 recession, 5,000 more employees had been reassigned and nearly half of these were retrained.

Full employment practices are the exception rather than the rule among U.S. companies. Survey results show that only about 1.5 percent of large American companies have no layoff policies.[4]

Conventional wisdom has it that only very large companies have the resources to maintain a full employment policy. But many small, family run companies, based on a paternalistic philosophy, have also committed themselves to employment security and avoided layoffs. Managers of these companies know that layoffs are expensive. These costs include "severance pay, higher unemployment compensation taxes, continuation of health and other benefits for a period after the layoff, administrative and legal costs, the expense of rehiring and training workers when demand increases, outplacement fees—adding up to a staggering financial burden that substantially reduces whatever gains the company would make by cutting back the work force."[5]

SECURITY OR INSECURITY: WHICH IS THE BETTER MOTIVATOR?

What motivates an organization's people—security or insecurity? Managers must address themselves to no more fundamental ques-

---

[3] Theodore E. Grosskopf, "Human Resources Planning Under Adversity," *Human Resources Planning* 1, no. 1 (1978): 47.
[4] LDG Associates' random sample survey of 228 large U.S. companies in 1983.
[5] James F. Bolt, "Job Security: Its Time Has Come," *Harvard Business Review* 61, no. 6 (1983): 115.

tion. It is fundamental both because motivation is a key to people's performance in an organization and because unlike many other problems in management, this one calls for an either/or decision. Often effective managers are those who are best able to balance conflicting pressures—to get just the right mix of contending objectives or means. But employment security is harder to balance; an employee cannot be both secure and insecure at the same time. He or she is one or the other. The issue is, which is better?

A company must make a decision about this matter. Either employees should have little confidence in their employment tenure, knowing that a business downturn or the closing of a plant or division could cost them jobs; or they should feel confident that the company will make every reasonable effort to keep them employed. The need for a choice is dictated by the advantage the company hopes to gain. If it believes that employees are motivated by insecurity, then it must wish them to know that they are insecure. If they are confused, then the motivation will be lacking.

If the company believes that employees are best motivated by security, then it must wish them to believe they have security, otherwise they will not be motivated. The company does not benefit from confusion in employees' minds about this issue. A company might, of course, try to mislead employees by promising no layoffs when it has no such intentions. But in an economy as cyclical as ours, its true intentions will soon be known—with the final downturn in business.

Further, a company which promises security but because of an extreme decline in sales is unable to provide it, may yet gain loyalty and motivation if its efforts to retain people are in good faith and extensive. Employees understand the marketplace perhaps better than managers believe.

Just as a company must decide whether or not it wishes to try to motivate people through insecurity or security, a manager in a smaller circle must decide similarly. Although the manager cannot ordinarily alter company policies, security or insecurity can be stressed in dealing with people who report directly to him or her. Like the company, an individual manager cannot avoid the issue and hope to be effective because motivation is one of the key managerial obligations.

So the question becomes, Which is the better policy? Is insecurity and fear of job loss a better motivator than employment security and personal confidence?

THINK OF THE OPPORTUNITY

Hard times have a way of motivating people. When unemployment rates in the United States went above 10 percent in the early 1980s, many managers noted that the attitudes of people toward their jobs began to change. Employees seemed to be grateful to have a job. They attended work more regularly; they accepted direction more willingly; they performed tasks with greater effort and care. Insecurity, it seemed, was an effective motivator.

Hence it is surprising to find several very successful companies with a reputation for high employee performance foreswearing insecurity as a motivator. Among them are large and long established firms like IBM, Hewlett–Packard Company, and Upjohn Company and recent start-ups like Tandem Computers and Apple Computer, Inc.; and most of the large Japanese companies. These firms by practice do not lay off employees in times of economic downturn, or at least adopt layoffs as a last resort.

Sony Corporation has had a plant in San Diego for many years. Several years ago the company encountered a sudden decline in sales. Soon the San Diego plant was piling up inventory, and then had to begin reducing production. Where were costs to be cut?

The American managers of the plant requested permission from headquarters in Japan to begin work force reductions. They received a refusal. They renewed the request, pointing out that sales were way down and that significant losses would soon appear on the bottom line.

To this, Akio Morita, the founder of Sony, replied, "Think of the opportunity."

"What opportunity?" the American managers persisted. "We are going to be drowning in red ink."

"Think of the opportunity," Morita repeated. Then he explained. "If we keep the American work force with us through these difficult times, then they will understand that we are really committed to them. And they will be committed to us."

There was no layoff. The company absorbed losses for a while until business recovered. In the next few years the San Diego plant performed very well, in some instances even outperforming the company's plants in Japan—the first foreign facility of Sony to do so.

A VENEER OF COOPERATION

Undoubtedly high unemployment and the risk of unemployment cause an attitude change toward more cooperation in many employees. But is it more than a veneer, as people try to keep their jobs? When the business cycle turns around and the risk of joblessness declines, people are inclined to return to previous, perhaps less cooperative, patterns of behavior. On the other hand, concern about losing jobs has often caused employee behaviors which undercut a company's efficiency. Assignments, tasks, or jobs are stretched out to provide employment for an individual; little commitment or loyalty is given to the company because employees are uncertain about when their employment will be terminated; employees seek to do only those things with an immediate reward because long-term payoffs are made uncertain by the risk of job loss; finally, employees may resist technological change for fear it will eliminate their jobs.

These unfavorable results of insecurity are not readily apparent in a time of high unemployment, but the behavior may simply be concealed. Nor are these observations restricted to blue-collar workers who have received more press attention. They extend equally to clerical, technical, professional, and even managerial positions.

Samuel Hayward was a middle-level manager with a large oil company. The company's understanding with its employees had been that managers had employment security. A few years ago, however, the company was acquired by another large firm, not in the oil business. Soon, layoffs of managers at the oil company began.

Hayward's comments about the layoffs are illustrative of the conflicting pressures on him, which in turn have an impact on the company. "When they laid people off, it sent a shock wave through the organization. People wanted to slow down, to get back at the company. They also wanted to do less to stretch out their jobs. I've always been a company person—always worked very hard—but I felt the same way," he said. "Still, I've got to be careful, because if I don't work, or if they think I'm not putting out, then I might get sacked." He shrugged. "There it is. Now I'm working because I'm afraid not to—I'm working out of fear. If I get an offer from another oil company, I'd take it. I'm looking now," he finished.

Employment security can reverse many of these patterns. It can encourage people to develop and reveal methods that enhance productivity, since they know they won't lose their jobs as a result. Security can allow them to put their full commitment and loyalty into a company, since they know the investment is long-term. Security allows people to plant seeds of ideas, competence, and effort to be reaped later in recognition and benefits at the same company. Tasks need not be stretched out; time need not be spent on looking for other job opportunities. Security can help a company have a far better employee.

The willingness of employees to accept, use, and support rapid technological changes, now so vital to the competitive position of many companies, also may be affected by employment security. How receptive are employees to new technologies? The evidence is mixed. In some companies there is little concealed hostility; in others grudging acceptance; in still others active support. Support seems most common where there is employment security. In a recent survey a company with both a no layoff policy and rapid technological change found the overwhelming majority of its employees actively welcoming technological change. Was employment security a reason? They thought so.

WHERE EMPLOYMENT SECURITY IS NOT A MOTIVATOR

Employment security can provide better employee attitudes and behavior—but not automatically. The connection is not direct and mechanical, but indirect, subtle, and influenced by other factors—as are all human causalities. Employment security has been provided in several instances in the United States for many years without the resulting advantageous employee behavior described earlier.

For example, government employees have had job security. But there is little evidence of enhanced attitudes and behavior as a result. College faculties have had tenure, but again with limited, at best, gains to the employer. And under collective bargaining agreements many thousands of employees in industrial companies have received job security as a result of seniority. Even in the deep recession of 1981–82 when hundreds of thousands of industrial workers were laid off, others with long service remained secure in their jobs.

Did security cause employees in government service, on college faculties, and in unionized industrial firms to give large personal commitments to their jobs, to welcome new technology, to advance productivity enhancing ideas, and to contribute in a wide range of other ways to the success of their organizations? For some individuals the answer is certainly yes; but for many, probably the majority, the answer is no. Given employment security they looked not for a greater contribution to make, but for a way to do less. And often they found it. Employment security became not an opportunity to contribute, but rather a shield behind which to conceal poor performance.

Perhaps it is the experience of governments, colleges, and unionized firms with job security that has made managers in many private companies suspicious of it as a motivator.

PRECONDITIONS FOR EMPLOYMENT SECURITY

What do IBM, Hewlett–Packard Company, Upjohn Company, and others know that enables them to turn employment security into a motivational plus, and employee motivation into a competitive advantage in the marketplace?

They know two very important things: First, they are aware of the preconditions necessary to make employment security an advantage to a company and not a disadvantage. Second, they know the difference between employment security and job security.

What are the preconditions? People in a firm must understand that there are *quid pro quos* for employment security: flexibility and adaptability. A firm can be successful enough in the marketplace to provide employment security only if its employees are prepared to be flexible in accepting assignments, in learning new technologies and new skills, and in geographic location. The companies that provide employment security do not do so without their employees understanding their obligation to make it possible. Adaptability to new conditions, circumstances, missions, supervision, and organizational structures is required from them.

The big mistake in public service, colleges, and unionized industrial facilities has been to grant job security without obtaining these quid pro quos in return. The result is poorly performing organizations with high costs; in the end taxpayers and consumers have proven unwilling to pay the high taxes and prices necessary to support these organizations with large numbers of people in secure jobs. Very few have benefited. Even the unions which helped to tie job security to seniority without a quid pro quo other than minimal levels of performance have been injured by the result. Noncompetitive companies cannot provide much employment for very long.

The problem, however, is not only the union's creation. Job security in the public sector, in colleges, and in unionized private industry is largely a reaction to management failures. When managers are unwilling or unable to let employees contribute to their jobs, are unable to distinguish true performers from their personal or political favorites, are unable to control their prejudices, or are too busy with other concerns to know whom to reward and whom to discipline—then job security is imposed on them. It is crucial to recognize the difference. In these instances job security is imposed on management in reaction to poor managerial performance in the past. It is something granted employees in opposition to management. No wonder there is no quid pro quo.

In some ways public employees and/or unions imposing job security on managers is self-defeating, since this neither promotes better management nor contributes to an organization effective enough to provide long-term security. This is because an organization which intends to provide security for all or most of its employees, as opposed to a small, senior remnant, must be very well managed to do so.

This is the other major precondition of a successful employment security program. Considerable planning and self-discipline are required of management. The easy way to provide security is to grow faster than employees are added, but this is not possible for most companies in the long term. Instead, security is provided by growing at a chosen rate which can be sustained in the long term; by transferring people in discontinued operations to growing ones; by retraining people in new skills so that they do not become obsolete; by working out relocations where possible for those who must transfer.

These are expensive propositions, requiring considerable staff planning and also expenditures on retraining and relocation. It is remarkable what full employment companies are able to do to preserve jobs for their employees. IBM, for example, has been known to freeze hiring by large groups of its facilities until a few persons displaced by a plant shutdown are offered equivalent positions elsewhere in the company. In effect, IBM managers were told, "You can hire anyone you want, so long as he or she is from the plant we just had to close." In another incident the company merged two sales offices, but kept both open for months until all employees who would not be needed in the surviving office found jobs elsewhere in the company.

Planning is crucial. When orders come in fast, unless something is done, employment will rise to a level that will require layoffs when the inevitable slowdown arrives. To avoid this, buffers are used. Subcontractors are obtained, or temporary employees are hired. Then when the downturn comes the reduction in employment goes to the subcontractors or to the temporaries. It would be nice if all reductions could be avoided, but this is not possible for a single company to accomplish in a boom and bust economy such as ours.

As important as planning is, self-discipline is more significant. Managers have to accept inconveniences in the name of employment security. It is inconvenient to have to hire only from people surplused at other facilities in the company, to find subcontractors or turn away growth, to hire people temporarily, to retrain rather than hire outside applicants, and to bear the costs created by each of these activities.

But as Mr. Morita of Sony pointed out, there are also opportunities here. A company that learns to plan well for employment security learns to make very good use of its assets generally. People are retrained in technical skills, but they already know the company, its procedures, and how to get things accomplished. This is often a great advantage which saves the company other training costs (see Chapter 14). Facilities also can be recycled, saving on construction costs and gaining not only employee but community loyalty for the company.

IBM managers talk of a location in the south of France that has been in operation for 20 years and gone through several transformations during that time. Twenty years ago it was an electromechanical manufacturer. A decade later it had moved into the transistor market. Today it is a semiconductor plant. Most of the same people are there although it has gone through two major market repositionings and retoolings. How was this accomplished? The company spends almost 9 percent of its entire compensation budget on training.

EMPLOYMENT SECURITY—NOT JOB SECURITY

Probably the greatest discipline required of managers at a company which offers employment security has not yet been mentioned. It is a somewhat peculiar discipline—a mirror image—an ironic requirement. The managers must be so self-disciplined that *they do not* take business actions solely to preserve jobs. Plants must not be located where the people currently are, if to do so is a noncompetitive move in the marketplace. Costs cannot be inflated just to preserve employment. The marketplace has to take precedence. Otherwise the company will fail in the long term and employment security will be a mirage.

This is the point at which employment security as a policy places its most forceful demand on managers. Poor managers cannot run an effective employment security practice. The careful balancing of marketplace needs with planning for human adjustments is too complex a task. One or the other must give and employment security will always tend to give first, for a company that places security above competitiveness will not long survive.

For this reason full employment companies do not confuse employment security with job security. People are not offered security in their current jobs, but in a succession of assignments that over time add up to a career in the company. No company can afford the rigidity of mind that seeks to preserve certain jobs and to keep certain individuals in them. Job security thought of in this sense is opposed to the flexibility and adaptability necessary to make an organization competitive. This is so basic a point that even many collective bargaining agreements recognize that some jobs may be eliminated due to economic circumstances. Bargaining agreements provide that senior employees may "bump" to other jobs to preserve their employment status (i.e., rather than be laid off). But often the sequence of bumping gives the company inexperienced people in most jobs, at a time when costs are high, sales low, and experience would count for a great deal. These systems also place an unreasonable burden on a company if its market position is vulnerable to competition. What full employment companies offer is employment security, contingent on the flexibility and adaptability of the employee and his or her willingness to accept or find a position in which to make a significant contribution.

IS EMPLOYMENT SECURITY ONLY FOR THE SUCCESSFUL COMPANY?

What makes it possible for a company to follow a full employment policy? Often it is argued that companies like IBM, Hewlett–Packard, and Upjohn can provide full employment because they are growing and successful. The implication is that companies with less success and in more volatile industries cannot afford such a luxury for their employees.

Is this an accurate judgment? Both IBM and Hewlett–Packard are in the information services business. So are many other companies, but few as successful as these two. The industry itself is not enough to make a company succeed. Rather the policies of the two companies, in particular their full employment policies, appear to contribute to their success as well as reflect it. Similarly, Upjohn has been successful in an intensely competitive industry, its policies contributing to its success.

Simply put, the question involves how to read causality. Are these companies employment security companies because they are successful? Or are they successful in part because of their employment security policies? It appears that there is a reinforcing causality at work. If so, then the view of many managers that their businesses are too volatile for employment security may be mistaken. No matter how volatile the business climate, planning and self-discipline can preserve a core work force which is granted employment security. If the firm is to be competitive, this should be done only if the quid pro quos from employees are clearly understood and if the company can develop the managerial competence to make employment security a reality.

SECURITY OR NO?

The relationship between productivity and employment security seems direct to companies practicing full employment. One company ascribed reduced costs for a decade to its full employment policy; reductions that "would have been impossible without productive and committed employees. And much of their commitment stems from the security they know is theirs through our practice of full employment."[6]

Should a manager urge his or her company to formally announce an employment security policy? Some managers recommend that the company should make no formal statements to employees or to the public, but rather live out the policy, hoping it will survive product and business cycles, technological changes, and all the other shocks and readjustments that are part of a competitive business environment. Silence on the matter is a viable route though not necessarily the best one. Even if the company is silent, employees will know through actions whether the company makes an honest effort to avoid redundancies. Word travels fast and a rigid policy is not really the objective. In the absence of a formally announced policy, there will be no need to break promises if layoffs become necessary despite a company's best efforts to minimize or avoid them.

The practice is what is important. Some companies, rather than remaining silent on the subject, state that full employment is a business objective or goal. They announce that they will make use of downgrades, freezes, and so on, using layoffs only as a last resort.

---

[6] *Ibid.* p. 116.

A combination of methods is used by those few companies committed to full employment with or without a formally enunciated policy. Hiring freezes are immediately instituted if projected manpower requirements indicate an imbalance with product demand.[7] The tools of full employment can include reassignment of employees to other locations within the company; "buffering" of manpower shocks through managing overtime; vending or subcontracting; and temporary, part-time, or reduced hours. Incentives for early retirement, outplacement services, and even loaning employees to other organizations provide additional means to shift personnel while keeping them productively employed.

Many reasons compel companies to move toward full employment practices where possible to win greater commitment from managers and managed alike and to more effectively make use of their human resources in the long run. If companies are to experiment internally with less structured, more freewheeling environments, employment security may provide the glue that holds people to this rapidly changing and responding workplace.

A commitment to full employment is not without its costs. Planning at the corporate level must be closely tied to these efforts. And planning is expensive. Coupled with the cost commitment must be discipline by top management as well as those below them. This discipline will involve a commitment to thinking through the problem of what to do with employees who need to be moved to other types of work or to other locations. It is in many ways easier to show them the door than to work with them to find a place for them to contribute. A commitment to employment security where possible, most likely will help keep a company competitive.

OPPORTUNITY THINKING

Regardless of where a company or a manager stands on the issue of employment security, keep in mind the approach of Sony's

[7] Much of this discussion is drawn from Bolt, *Harvard Business Review*, pp. 115–123.

chairman. Looking at what appeared to others as nothing but a problem, Morita had the good sense to ask his managers, "Where is the opportunity?" and to encourage them to "Think of the opportunity."

Whatever the situation, this is a manager's first principle—to ask, "Where is the opportunity?" It is amazing how often that question leads to the discovery of something valuable.

SUMMARY

High commitment and performance are necessary for competitiveness in a company. But what motivates people? Do insecurity and fear of job loss motivate people, or is the opposite, employment security, the better method? A company has to choose between two competing means and act in accordance with one or the other. On a smaller scale, a manager has to make the same choice. In today's environment tremendous opportunity exists for managers to improve motivation and performance by treating people as ongoing citizens of the corporation rather than expendable parts. But there are quid pro quos for employment security without which it may backfire. Used correctly, some degree of employment security can harness people's energy to the organization in a way that has been crucial to the success of top competitors.

Where are the key people of the future to come from? The outside labor market is an uncertain course. Most companies have to develop top talent by themselves.

5

Nurturing Stars

Jack Simpson went into the executive vice president's (EVP) office with a confident step. His own boss had just been promoted, creating a vacancy at the division vice president level. Jack, who was assistant division manager and in charge of its largest product group, was certain he would get the job. His career had been one of rapid advancement. Rarely in a position for more than eighteen months, he had moved through a succession of successes. In his own mind the proof of his unique competence was that the people who followed him in a job always turned in weaker bottom lines than he had.

The interview, however, took a very different tack than the one Jack had anticipated. The first comment the EVP made was in the form of a question. "Name three people," the EVP asked, "who are your level or higher in this corporation because of their involvement with you." After an uncomfortable pause during which Jack tried to decide if the executive was serious, he answered, "I can't name one."

"Jack," the EVP said, "you've done good work for this company. The things you've done personally have been done well. Units you manage have a good record. But they don't have a good record after you leave. The limiting factor on our company's growth potential is good managers. No responsibility is more important than finding and developing good people. Numbers are not the issue; the quality of people is the issue. My key criterion in evaluating managers is their ability to evaluate and develop people."

Walking to a flip chart, the EVP drew a rough matrix. One side he labeled "the individual contribution of a manager"; on the other "develops subordinates and the organization's capabilities." Turning to Jack he pointed to the upper left hand corner of the box. "You're here, Jack," he said, "I want better balanced people." (See Figure 5.1.)

"And that," the EVP concluded, "is why this promotion is not going to you. You've been too busy looking up the ladder to develop people for this company."

Leaving the office in a turmoil of confusion and disappointment, Jack smashed one fist into his other hand and blurted out to a surprised bystander, "Why the hell didn't they make that clear to me five years ago?"

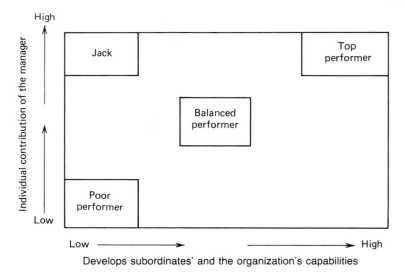

Figure 5.1

SPEND TIME ON PEOPLE

General Electric Company (GE) has a justly renowned management training facility at Croton-on-Hudson some 50 miles north of New York City. As people advance in GE's managerial ranks, they often spend a few weeks in Croton-on-Hudson taking courses which prepare them for wider responsibilities.

"The new challenge for these people as they start to move up in the company," one of the directors of Croton-on-Hudson told a new instructor, "is that they have to start managing managers. They have to start thinking about the capabilities of the managers who report to them and about how the combination of the capabilities of individuals makes up the capability of the organization. They need an organization focus on managing the company's managers."

Ordinarily, the time for a manager to start developing other managers is before the new managers are even on board. A manager may also inherit a going organization; thereafter, he or she is able to select the persons who are brought into it. Among managers there is a controversy over how this is to be done. Should people be hired to fit the job opening, or should people be hired for their long-term ability to contribute to the organization?

The vice president for operations at a large service company put it this way:

"To have a pool of people ready isn't realistic. It just doesn't work that way in a service company. We don't have the resources to keep managers on until we need them. If a company is grooming a person for a new job, he's not doing what he is supposed to be doing."

Ron Falks, the chief executive officer of a small manufacturing company, made a similar point from his experience. "I've built two companies from the ground up, then sold them. I am just now selling the second, and haven't decided if I'll do a third. I didn't do any management development in these companies, but not doing it works only if you sell the company when it gets into the $5–10 million range. As the company grows larger, you have to develop people. I sell it first, and so I leave the problem of building management capability to the buyer."

In a speech to students at the Harvard Business School, Jack Welch, chairman at General Electric, answered the argument about management development from his company's point of view.

"The issue is one of balancing the short term against the long term. I know that some people say American management is too short-term oriented and doesn't take account of the longer term. I reject that argument for our company. The essence of a manager's function is to balance the short term against the long term. We do it every day in countless ways."

Management development is one of the most important ways in which General Electric provides for the future while still meeting the day-to-day crisis of managing businesses. The contrast with Ron Falks's position is dramatic. Because Falks will not make the effort to develop people and will not spend the time and resources, he has to get out of each business he builds just as it becomes ripe for significant expansion. The investment the acquiring company makes is not only in dollars, but also in managerial talent to make Falks's former business go as it gets bigger. The acquiring company has to make this people investment because Falks could not or would not do it.

With an eye on the future of an organization, Clifford Hardin, vice chairman and director of research at Ralston Purina Company during the 1970s, advised other managers: "When you are bringing young people into your organization, try to select only those of top quality—people you think will be capable of rising rapidly in the organization. When that philosophy is expressed before an executive audience, someone usually objects, 'But we don't need that many high quality people. We have a number of routine jobs that don't require world-beaters.' My reply is that if you consistently go after quality people, you will make enough mistakes in judgment to take care of the routine job slots. You severely limit the potential of your organization when you let yourself accept people who are just good enough for the opening at hand, but probably cannot go any further."

Also, Hardin suggested, "Other things being equal, a person will be a better executive in middle age if that person has had some real decision-making experience before reaching age 30. Educators have known for years that there is a time when a child wants to learn to read, and if he is taught then, he will learn better than at any other time in his life. There is a time to learn athletic skills and languages, which, if missed, will make the learning process more difficult later. For most people, decision making is learned best in the 20s and 30s. A person does not have to be president of the organization to gain this kind of experience. Usually, there are many places in an organization to which a person can be assigned where he or she can have decision-making experience."[1]

Reg Jones of GE echoed Hardin's views in a 1982 question and answer session with members of Harvard's Advanced Management Program. Jones told his executive audience about two keys to developing managers: First, spend time on people. During the decade in which Jones headed GE, he had spent more time with the vice president of executive manpower than with the head of any other function in the company, including finance, marketing, and corporate planning. Second, give people general management responsibility early, so that they can develop managerial qualities and capabilities.

At GE Jones made a deal with the young tigers in charge of the company's new businesses. "You stay with your schedule," Jones told them; "you meet your commitments, and your budget, your investment funds are inviolable, regardless of boom or recession." Thus, the young managers got their opportunity to grow their businesses and, in so doing, to develop managerial skills. GE gets both a business and a key managerial resource for the future; there is time synergy here.

Key executives are at the heart of business activity to a far greater degree than most managers or the public recognize. Instead,

[1] Clifford M. Hardin, "Business Management; Lessons from Experience," (Center for the Study of American Business, Contemporary Issues Series No. 7, Washington University, St. Louis, 1982), pp. 3 and 5.

most people assume the quality or novelty of a product or service concept is the key to business success. Most top managers, however, recognize that far more excellent business opportunities based on new products or services exist than people who can be relied upon to turn the opportunities into successful businesses.

Despite GE's outstanding management development efforts, Jack Welch has often observed: "At GE our biggest shortage is one of effective managers, people to whom we can entrust a new business and know that it will be handled well."

A successful firm recognizes the importance of top-quality, well-trained managers to its future. For example, in second tier companies a new business venture is usually evaluated essentially as: "If we do this activity, can we keep costs squeezed down sufficiently to make a profit?" This is a very important question, of course, but a top tier company takes a somewhat wider perspective: "If we do this activity, will it provide enough surplus to compensate very talented people, who can make this business grow and keep it competitive in the future?"

The difference in the two perspectives is that the former asks only if a short-term profit can be squeezed out. The latter looks for a profit that will keep good people focused on the business to keep it performing well. The former is a static focus on short-term numbers; the second is a dynamic focus on long-term competitiveness. Both require profitability, but the former sees that as an end in itself; the latter, as a means to long-term commitment to the business. These somewhat subtle differences in approach to business choices distinguish top performing managers from second tier managers.

Writing about America's investment banking industry, Mike Spence, now Dean of the Faculty of Arts and Sciences at Harvard; Samuel Hayes; and David Marks pointed to this long-term perception of profit as a means to attract and retain good people. "Throughout the history of investment banking, without unusually talented people to keep the banks flexible . . . even established houses—like that of the Seligmans—could fall on hard times. . . . Their strength lay in their ability to put together a group of investors

... more effectively than anybody else. As a result they could ... remunerate the talented professionals who managed the services on which both profits and client loyalty depended."[2] To put it differently, while lots of people could put together a deal and make a little money, the firms which grew into the great investment banking houses understood that a surplus on one deal was only valuable if used to support top-quality people who could successfully put together a series of deals.

A top executive of one of the nation's leading oil companies criticized the education of managers which rewards those who give quick answers to business problems rather than those who, while taking a broad conceptual approach, raise new issues and find relevant materials. In the oil business generous cash flow— more than $4 billion per year in the executive's company—is forcing managers to make hard decisions about where to make investments. Should a substantial part of their receipts be put into exploration for more oil, or should the company diversify into new businesses? Choices of this nature do not require quick answers to narrow problems, but rather numerous thoughtful views and creative ideas about how to approach such a broad range of choices.

On similar grounds Europeans criticize American managers for what might be called managerial myopia. After four years of assignments in the United States, a German manager said, "In my company's American subsidiary, the American managers are so committed to working long hours at operating problems in the business that they have no time to broaden their perspectives. They don't read; they rarely keep up with the news from abroad. They have no context of general knowledge about the world in which to contribute to broad business decisions. They are very ignorant of Third World countries, for example, which is one reason why European countries often do so much better in selling

---

[2] Samuel L. Hayes, III, A. Michael Spence, and David Van Praag Marks, *Competition in the Investment Banking Industry* (Cambridge: Harvard University Press, 1983), 12–13.

to those countries. If I were in Germany and didn't keep up with world events better than my American colleagues do, I wouldn't last on the managerial team."

The Japanese put their own unique twist on the contribution of talented individuals to the company as a whole. Rather than encouraging gifted managers to exploit their talents directly in operational decision making, their supervisors urge them to use their extra margin of intelligence to smooth out interpersonal relationships and assist slower members of the group in their performance.[3]

An important method of developing managerial talent is to provide challenges. An old management rule of thumb, not in favor in recent years but perhaps staging a comeback today, is to give a person more responsibility than the person believes he or she can handle. The person then either grows with the responsibility or must drop out. When the purpose of this strategy is to develop human capabilities, it also has a role in creating better managers. When its purpose is to force a person to break under the strain, it is neither useful nor appropriate.

A significant part of challenging managers in recent years has been to develop their understanding of the advances now occurring in technology. A top officer of a large industrial company commented: "We have wanted our managers, whatever their functional expertise, to have had enough hands-on experience and careful instructions to be sensitive to other people in the company. Now [in 1983], we want to add technology. Our managers in whatever function need an understanding of the new technology and how to manage it. In product development our engineers are saying to their managers: 'You don't understand; you're asking for an impossibility.' And in other areas it's the opposite; managers are being told that remarkable things can be done by the technology, when it isn't clear that that is the case at all. There are lots of technological charlatans out there. So we want our managers to understand the implications of key technologies for our company,

---

[3] Kenichi Ohmae, "Myths and Realities of Japanese Management," *McKinsey Quarterly* (Summer 1981): 12.

its people, and the society. We are increasingly dependent on technology to keep us in business and ahead of our competitors."

The business schools are attempting to play their part. For several years some schools have required MBA candidates to use microcomputers in their studies. And in 1983 Harvard Business School introduced microcomputers into its middle management programs for some 250 American and foreign executives. The participants in these programs were nominated by their companies generally because of their potential for advancement in the company, and because their previous careers have ordinarily been somewhat narrow in focus so that a broadening educational experience was needed.

During the first 1983 program, 90 percent of the participants indicated that they had no previous experience with a microcomputer; and two-thirds said they were apprehensive about using one. A computer was placed in each student's room. One student asked to be given a room without a microcomputer for a roommate. He was told that Harvard had no rooms without microcomputers. Throughout the fourteen-week program participants utilized the devices. In the evaluations of the program submitted by participants at its end, not a single reference was made to the computers. Like telephones, they were no longer things to be dreaded, but instead ordinary devices to be used as desired, and then entirely taken for granted.

WHOM TO PROMOTE

Terry Fashig had a vacancy to fill in his technicians' unit at Universal Products facility in Minneapolis. The head technician in the unit was transferring to another location. Fashig's preference was to promote Martha Greenisle, a technician in his unit, to the position; but first, in accordance with company regulations he had to give notice of the vacancy to other employees.

The notice was posted for a week, during which two technicians applied for the job in addition to Greenisle. One of the applicants was Roger Fairfield, a long service employee who had worked under Fashig's supervision in the unit for the past ten years.

Fashig had no doubt that Greenisle was the correct choice for the job. She had entered the unit only two years earlier, when she first joined the company, but had previous experience in the unit's type of work. She was pleasant, hard working, and ambitious. Over time, she would probably advance into Fashig's own position.

Fairfield, in contrast, was near the end of his career at the company. He had few leadership skills, and was not as familiar with new processes as Greenisle. Fashig suspected that Fairfield saw the promotion as an opportunity to do less work, by not taking his responsibility to lay out and schedule work very seriously. In an interview with Fairfield, Fashig first confirmed his concern about Fairfield's purpose, and then tried to persuade him not to seek the job. He failed.

Fashig was free to promote whomever he wished, so long as the person chosen had formally applied for the position by signing the notice he had posted. In principle, Fashig could promote Greenisle. Further, the company's policies encouraged him to pick the best-qualified candidate.

Still, Fashig hesitated. He had heard other employees discussing the promotion and saying that by right it ought to go to Fairfield. After all, he can do the job, the employees agreed, and he had been at the company far longer than Greenisle. There was even, Fashig realized with shock, some insinuation that were he to promote Greenisle, something other than merit might be behind his choice.

In similar past situations, Fashig had tended to choose the longer service employee for a promotion. He tried to balance the right of the long-service employee to get first crack at opportunities, and the right of the company to receive the best efforts of its employees. For years Universal had been a successful company easily able to accept a slower pace of work and less contribution in a job, where such a choice presented itself. Aggressive younger employees would wait for their turns, Fashig had decided. To promote the less senior employee was sure to cause reverberations among other employees which Fashig preferred to avoid.

In this, Fashig was like many other managers. Surveys of line managers in hundreds of large firms show that when vacancies are posted or otherwise made visible in an employee unit, managers tend to select the senior applicant for the job; often admitting that in so doing they passed over better prospects among less senior people. Choosing the less capable but senior candidate was justified, managers said, to preserve harmony in the workplace.

Now Fashig was less certain. The company was not doing as well; competitors were eating away at its profit margins. Costs were being reduced by cutbacks, and Fashig and other managers had become concerned about their own jobs. For the first time in years, Fashig was conscious of the contribution his own operation made to the company; and for the first time in years he wanted that contribution to be the best possible. It was getting harder to provide the best; his staff had been reduced, his budget cut, and the workload edged up. In this environment, he needed the best contribution in the head technician job. That meant Greenisle, and Fashig decided he was going to make that selection, explain it to the work force, and then try to ride out whatever dissatisfaction occurred.

TESTS VERSUS THE RECORD

In 1978 Susan Polson was working for a telephone company. She had joined the company in 1970 with a B.A. in engineering, and by 1978 had had four different management jobs, each in engineering in the net department. She was now in a middle management position and was on her way to Atlanta to spend three and a half days in the company's advanced management potential assessment program. There she joined a group of other middle managers recommended by their bosses as people of high management potential.

During those days Polson participated in six major assessment tools, each designed specifically for the program. Two sessions involved group exercises and four individual activities. She was observed in these efforts by a professional staff of psychologists and by assessment teams of higher level managers from the company.

In the first group exercise each of six participants represented a city council member at a meeting to allocate a multimillion-dollar federal grant to upgrade services in the city. In the second group exercise Polson was one of a six-person board of directors of the Ajax Fund, a small mutual fund investment company. The directors managed the fund's purchase and sale of corporate securities.

Thereafter Polson completed each individual exercise. First she acted as assistant vice president for traffic generation of a railway, working through a mound of letters, reports, memos, and other written materials involving decisions on a variety of complex issues. At the end of this exercise Polson was interviewed by a person acting as her boss in the fictional railway and asked to explain why she had handled each memo, letter, and report as she did.

Next, Polson was asked to develop a program for stress management requested by the president of another fictional company. Her program was presented orally at the end of the exercise as if to a group of executives from the company.

Between these exercises Polson took a series of written tests. She was asked to finish incomplete sentences; to study a series of pictures and write a story about what was happening, telling why and what the outcome will be; and to complete the company's own intelligence test.

Lastly, Polson had a personal interview with a member of the assessment center's staff. It was her only opportunity to discuss herself, her experiences, her record in the business, and her talents and objectives.

Polson had gone to the center flattered at her boss's nomination, but somewhat apprehensive. She left it exhausted, relieved, numb, and with grave doubts about how well she had done. Several weeks later she was invited to a meeting away from her office with a psychologist from the assessment center. She was first told the good things in her performance, then the bad, and finally given a bottom line rating. Polson was judged to be a poor prospect for promotion to higher level managerial jobs.

She was angry and upset. "In all my working years I have never been put in as pressure-filled a situation as that . . . the group exercises were more game playing than anything else . . . no other source in my life has given me the negative feedback they did, so I can't help but question it. They ought to look at my record on the job," she seemed to be insisting, "not at the play-acting."

Any promotion is a crucial matter, for promotions, even at low levels, channel people into the pipeline of managerial resources upon which a corporation draws as it fills vacancies or staff positions. And a promotion selection is a complicated matter because different priorities must be met. This is nowhere more evident than in prioritizing the data on which a person is evaluated for advancement.

Large companies today ordinarily have three sources of information about a candidate for promotion: First, the record of the individual's performance in the positions he or she has held up to now. Second, the results from a battery of tests of various types, including exercises evaluated by trained psychologists or managers (this is particularly the case for promotion in upper operational positions). Third, those people in the company who have worked with the individual have personal judgments about his or her suitability for advancement.

But what priority is to be given to these three sets of information in deciding on advancement? To a degree, the answer would seem to vary with the perspective taken. Managers hiring people to report to them would ordinarily rely first on their own judgment of those persons (particularly if the managers had prior working experience with them), second on the performance records, and last on the results of formal testing. In part this is because the manager's first concern is to get a contributor onto his or her team in a specific job.

From the company's point of view, priorities are a bit different. Since the company's long-term interest is to advance people who have the potential, it may place far more reliance on formal testing which is intended to identify long-term potential. Formal assessment ordinarily determines suitability for promotion to a position at least two grades higher than that for which the person being assessed is currently being considered. Second priority is probably given to the individual's performance record. The personal knowledge of the manager who is likely to be the candidate's supervisor in the next assignment is not unimportant, but is less so than the other factors.

Finally, the candidate's perspective creates yet a third order of priority: First is the candidate's performance record. "What I have done." This is an unambiguous measure based directly on the candidate's personal qualities; most candidates believe it is more job-related than formal testing. By and large testing seems less subjective than personal knowledge of hiring managers and so usually receives second priority.

Candidates for advancement are often leary of being judged by managers who are hiring for a position because of demographic differences which affect personal judgments. Younger people worry about life-style, dress, and attitudinal distinctions which may cause older managers to be critical. Black or female candidates may fear prejudicial judgments from white male supervisors. (These observations are based on discussions with large numbers of MBA candidates and active managers, and reflect the median responses. Of course, there are important individual exceptions to each generalization.)

Table 5.1 provides a summary listing of the priorities applied in determining the suitability of a person for advancement from each of three perspectives.

An effective promotion system needs to accommodate all three perspectives. The hiring manager has responsibilities to fulfill and needs to have a dependable team. The candidate needs to believe the system is objective and unbiased. The organization needs to have its long-term interest in the candidate's career considered at each junction of advancement.

Corporations have broader responsibilities than the hiring managers and should have different priorities. The company needs

Table 5.1
Priorities Determining Employee Suitability for Advancement

Think of How You Value and Use:	From Vantage Point of		
	Hiring Manager	Organization	Candidate
Performance	2	2	1
Formal testing	3	1	2
Personal knowledge	1	3	3

to develop managers for higher positions and also to meet affirmative action requirements. Hiring managers do not ordinarily have these same objectives; instead they face a much more short-term need for a person who can contribute near peak as quickly as possible.

There are only two ways to deal with this disjunction: Companies may try to train managers to internalize the longer-term corporate goals, or they must intervene directly in the promotion process. The best managed American companies do both but at different levels in the corporation. At the level of the top 1,000 or so managers they intervene directly in the promotion and selection process. At lower levels in the organization they try to instill in hiring managers their responsibilities for developing people and for affirmative action.

WHO OWNS THE POSITION?
WHO OWNS THE PEOPLE?

For the first 15 years of Cheryl North's employment with a large industrial company she had virtually complete freedom in whom she chose for her management team. She was responsible for the performance of her unit, and it seemed only right that she should choose the people who would contribute the most. She ran a tight knit team and believed that the way she chose and worked with those who reported directly to her was a key element of her success as a manager.

When she was promoted to divisional vice president, however, things began to change. She noticed that other people in the company were asserting claims to a special relationship with people who reported directly to her.

When she spoke about it with one or two of her staff, they were noncommittal. Each had been hired into the firm by someone other than North and kept a tie to the manager who had hired him, perhaps expecting that if his mentor had an attractive opening, he would be chosen. Also each was flattered by the interest which high level managers in the company were now expressing in his career, just as North had herself been flattered when she first received such attention several years before.

"Who the heck owns these jobs?" she complained to herself; "and who owns these people?" There were in fact two claimants for ownership of the positions which reported to her, North realized: herself and the higher management of the company. And there were several claimants for ownership of the people who reported to her; herself, higher management, the manager who had brought each individual into the company, and the individual. The question of ownership resolved itself into very direct issues in both instances: Who was to fill a vacancy in a position which reported to North? Who was to manage the careers of people who were moving up in the company's hierarchy?

Identifying high potential people is a key element of any corporate directed promotion process. A large financial services firm has an effective process for doing this: Managers are asked to identify among their subordinates persons who could move up two levels, or who have the potential to become a vice president in the company. The nominating manager must specify why the individuals have been identified and what he or she is doing to develop the high potential people.

Further, the nominating manager must defend this judgment before a table of peers. Is the manager consistent in the people identified? "If you have a tough job, whom would you give it to?" peers might ask. If the answer is someone other than the high potential person, they will want to know why. "What criteria are you using to identify people? How are you measuring performance on these criteria?"

Several years ago the chief executive officer of one of the nation's major insurance companies decided to take a more significant role in the careers of the up-and-comers in his organization. Assigning the responsibility within his staff, the CEO had a survey done of how three major industrial companies managed executive development. A proposal was prepared for the executive committee and approved. Then the top officers selected five key positions in the corporation and identified those positions as now belonging to the company as a whole, not to the functions or subsidiaries in which they were located. The best potential managers were then rotated through the positions. The first executive committee meeting to review up-and-comers identified 22 people; in six months 18 of those people advanced into a planned development track. The executive committee now meets two days each year to review the 600 key executives in the company. Functional and subsidiary managers bid for the best of these people on the basis of offering challenging assignments. Through this device high potential people are identified and rotated and their careers developed.

At another large insurance company the process of corporate level ownership and control of high potential employees has progressed so far that one 21-year-old in the finance department who has been with the company for only one year has been identified. Already corporate level executives are acting as if his career belongs not to his manager, but to the organization as a whole.

FAST TRACK TRAP

Because of its management training effort and the commitment of top executives, GE has a reputation as a first-class developer of managerial talent. So respected are GE managers that the company has become a recruiting ground for other organizations seeking topflight executive talent. In consequence, the network of GE alumni in other American companies is now large and well respected.

General Electric's management development activities are based on two key notions: The first is, as Jack Welch, GE's chairman, puts it, "the winning play every time is the right person in the job." To be able to take advantage of opportunities created by changing technology and customers' needs, a company must have a source of top quality executives. The second notion is that it is usually an error for a company to leave the selection and promotion of people to fill managerial jobs to the unilateral discretion of the hiring manager. Executive jobs are stepping stones in the development of managerial talent needed by the entire organization, so the entire organization should participate in deciding who goes into those jobs.

Corporate level intervention in the career development process of up-and-coming managers is necessary because of the problems created by ambitious managers trying to develop their own paths to the top. Sometimes high potential people become impatient at their rate of advance; they fear they have been forgotten or intentionally passed over when others are promoted. The result may be valuable managers who watch the scoreboard and not the game—who cease to be vitally involved and committed to their current assignments.

Furthermore, movement across businesses and functions may be important for an individual if he or she is to avoid the fast track trap. That is, the rapid advance up the hierarchy in a narrow function or in a single business may leave the ambitious executive high up the corporate ladder but plateaued by specialization and not acceptable in a general management position.

In practice, companies often find it difficult to move executives across different lines of business, especially where industry experience is necessary to be successful. While it is difficult to achieve, companies are anxious that ambitious managers not spend time and energy trying to leap internal boundary lines in the effort to broaden their capacities. Instead, the company prefers that they look for opportunities in their own division or function, while leaving to top corporate management the task of identifying high potential employees and moving them across the groups on an exceptional basis. The company thus assumes the responsibility for moving the high potential employee around, placing a block here and one there, and slowly advancing that employee toward the top.

One young manager from a large industrial company articulated a problem with this approach. "Our company gets lots of good people. Some are identified, but not told; they leave. Still others are good, and waiting to be identified."

What is the best way to judge how good a manager is today? How can those who need to know identify where he or she needs assistance in developing talents? At a large defense contractor a talent inventory has been in use since the 1970s. Some 15,000 people have been assessed as part of its operation. In this unique and imaginative program multiple assessments are made of each manager's capabilities by supervisors, peers, and subordinates. Each of the seven assessors uses a standard instrument, and each assessment is anonymous. The assessment is made on these five dimensions (established by a randomly selected group of managers):

Analytic capability
Respect for subordinates' abilities
Human relations
Initiative
Acceptance of responsibility

After an assessment has been completed, the supervisor discusses it with the employee and the two agree on two or three objectives for the individual's development in the next year or so.

Formal education programs, inside or outside the company, play an important role in executive development. But how is a company to get its up-and-comers to take education seriously? Job pressures and the seeming remoteness of much education from day-to-day practicalities may turn off executives.

When members of the senior management group at a large bank came only intermittently to an in-house executive program, the bank's new CEO developed a novel method of indicating his displeasure. After the program ended, the CEO held a breakfast to discuss the content with participants; only full-time attendees were allowed to come. Others who had attended part-time called him to explain their absences and to ask to be allowed to attend. They were refused. But the CEO told them that an in-depth breakfast evaluation of future programs would be held, since he viewed the development effort as crucial to the bank's future, and that after the next session he expected all managers to be at the breakfast.

One of the most effective devices for advancing a manager's capabilities is also one of the simplest. At the headquarters of a large computer company a visitor sat down in the office of an upper-middle manager. "I'm sorry I couldn't meet you elsewhere," the executive told him, "but I'm sitting in today for both my boss and his boss, both of whom are traveling. They're getting their money's worth from me today," he said, reaching for his phone and taking another call intended for his boss. "Roger Johnson," he said, "what can I do for you?"

STAFF FUNCTIONS AND LINE RESPONSIBILITY

The principal responsibility for developing managerial talent cannot be assumed by a corporation's central staff, nor should it be. The responsibility must be with the managers who supervise people on their way up. Managers have the obligation to work with these people to establish performance goals, to assist and coach them in achieving the goals, and to evaluate their performance in doing so. So crucial is the supervising manager's role that many key companies eschew assessment centers and other devices as diverting attention from the central role of the supervisor.

What well managed companies have in common is a recognition of the importance of the management development process. But they differ considerably in the type of support they give supervisors in accomplishing the identification and training of new managers. A manager at Hewlett–Packard Company commented: "There is no prescribed career developing or progression pattern. In a lot of companies, you can sit down and literally do a flow chart. If you want to get to point F, you do A, then B, then C, then D, and E and you're ready for F. You can describe each job. It's not at all true in this company. When it comes time to promote, we try to look for the best people. There are many examples of unusual progressions at HP. There are many paths you can follow to any particular end.

"For example, in my first eight years, I guess I had about seven or eight different jobs and four different functions. A couple of them were lateral moves, some of them were promotions. It's not necessary to get a bigger title or to jump a level in the pay system to be given new responsibility. I feel very positive about that."

Not only does Hewlett–Packard feel this is the best use of people, but the constant cross-fertilization across functions aids the coordination of the design, manufacturing, and distribution processes. This attitude toward promotion, however, requires different kinds of mechanisms for identifying candidates, since the candidates often are not within the same area of the company, nor along some common "preparation path," nor even within the same specialty area. Some of the devices that play an additional role were described by another Hewlett–Packard manager:

"There is a lot of very purposeful mixing of people. One way is through the division review process. In addition, we spend a fair amount of time talking to people, having communications luncheons, things like that. There are a fair number of social and quasisocial gatherings like the beer busts and picnics.

"We use a lot of task forces—it's an important vehicle we use for getting things done in the company. It's a way we get along with a relatively small staff. We sometimes call this real people involved in solving real problems. First of all, it gets work done. As a matter of fact, it is a very, very important part of the way we do business. But it also gives a lot of visibility to people."

Open discussion of hiring needs also helps to identify candidates for job openings. A group vice president commented:

"We just recruited a national sales manager who reports to our group marketing manager. I solicited far and wide. We had several serious internal [within the group] candidates and I looked at them. But I also contacted Operations Council, told them about the opening, the kind of person we were looking for, the kind of experience we wanted. I got 8 or 10 inputs back from that.

"I already had a half dozen people in mind outside the group that I had heard about during the quarterly review process. You don't always get to meet the person, but you hear a little about the individual from the person's boss or boss's boss. That doesn't sound like a big deal, but you do it every quarter and the repetition sinks in. In addition, every year the Operations Council spends three days together during which it ranks all company executives as a single group.

"I also let it generally be known that we were looking for a national sales manager. It was the world's worst kept secret by design. Two people picked up the phone and called to say they'd be interested, could we talk about it. We depend on giving people a lot of visibility."

At GE an executive management staff (EMS) is attached directly to the office of the chairman and is organizationally separate from the company's personnel function (which is called the corporate relations staff and reports through one of the company's two vice chairmen). Established in the late 1960s the EMS not only provides early identification of individuals with top management potential but also provides experiences to enhance their growth and breadth of knowledge. The EMS oversees some 5,000 executives; the remaining 395,000 employees of the company are the concern of the corporate relations operation. The top 600 employees in GE receive very close attention from EMS; the remaining 4,400 less so.

The EMS is a small organization whose members work closely with top line executives, but independently of them. An executive personnel consultant from EMS is attached to each of the seven sector executives at GE. The internal consultant is charged with knowing the top executives in each sector personally, assessing their career potential, providing for their development, and preparing lists of candidates for vacancies that develop. An executive with an opening in the top 600 positions is required to get a candidate slate from EMS and select from it.

The consultants reporting to the EMS, and hence to the chairman, provide GE's top officers with access to the entire pool of available top management talent across the corporation as well as an objective viewpoint. No mere computerized inventory this; instead GE top managers have direct access to the professional judgment of a small group of persons about the executive talent available, based on the professionals' personal knowledge of the individuals concerned.[4]

Other companies provide support, but in less sophisticated fashion. At a large transportation company managers who are hiring for executive positions are given the results of a two-hour telephone interview conducted by a psychologist with each candidate for the position. The questions asked the candidate are open-ended, requiring him often to explain his answer. "It depends," a candidate may answer, "on whether the situation is this way, or that." When asked to clarify a question, the psychologist usually refuses, forcing the candidate to muse outloud about what the question means. The better managers at this company often share the results of the psychologist's analysis with successful candidates, helping them to see their own strengths and weaknesses as viewed by a professional observer.

PROMOTION TO THE VERY TOP

Probably the key decision made about promotion in any company occurs when the CEO must be replaced. The potential pitfalls are many; for example, the CEO may pick a person who is in

[4] Stewart D. Friedman and Theodore P. LeVino, "Strategic Appraisal and Development at General Electric Company," in C.J. Fombrun, N.M. Tichy, and M.A. Devanna (eds.), *Strategic Human Resource Management* (New York: Wiley, 1984), 183–202.

style and appearance just like the CEO, and yet lacks the human qualities. The CEO may pick a hard charger who will continue to try to make all the decisions personally just as the CEO did as operating manager. Or the CEO may pick a person who fits the company's people perfectly, but cannot handle the external relations required of a CEO. Journalists' accounts and private discussions of failures in transferring top leadership are so common that one wonders if errors are more common than successes.

Robert Marshall, chairman of the board, president, and CEO of a growing instruments manufacturer, reached for his ringing telephone. "Hi, Rob, it's Jan Lever. I'm calling to fill you in on the response to our ad for a CEO in the *Wall Street Journal*. It appeared about a month ago, and you would not believe the number of resumes and letters I've received. At last count there were over 700!"

"Incredible. I hope you're still willing to go through them for me."

"Oh, sure, but it will take a while before I send you the ones that look most promising. Reading all these materials is a huge job, even with the clear guidelines you and I worked out before we placed the ad. I don't really know when I will be finished, and resumes are still arriving daily."

"Well, I appreciate all your work, Jan. I'm not in a hurry, and I don't want to put undue pressure on you or our staff. Just proceed as rapidly as you can, and if you want to send me some of the replies before you've checked them over, go right ahead."

Marshall replaced the telephone, then after a moment picked it up and dialed the corporate secretary, who had been the corporation's controller until about a year ago.

"Helen," he said, "You know that ad we placed? Jan just called to tell me she has over 700 replies already, and they're still coming! What does that suggest about American industry? Here we have a small company looking for a top executive, and hundreds of people in powerful positions in very large corporations are anxious to apply for the job. Frankly, I'm amazed."

With the assistance of his personnel department and a recruiting firm Marshall culled from the responses some 40 individuals who seemed especially well suited to the position. Marshall eventually interviewed eight of these final candidates, and after review and discussions, he decided to offer the job to Sal Marsulla. Marsulla had recently left his post as president of Cranston Equipment Corporation, a company that made plastics and packaging machinery. Marshall commented, "Sal not only had an engineering background, he had a master's degree in manufacturing engineering–machine design. He was a Navy man, and had held responsible managerial positions. He was in the right age bracket. He had no ambition to acquire equity—so many of the candidates were understandably ambitious for aggressive control and that was not what I wanted. And there he was close by in Ames. I didn't want the responsibility of taking someone away from a job and moving him here and having him not turn out. There were also plenty of candidates who were unemployed but would have required moving, although I didn't talk to any that seemed to fit. I opted for the easy way out."

Before making Marsulla an official offer, Marshall arranged for him to meet Phil Denton, an industrial psychologist whom he had previously consulted on another matter. Marsulla and Denton spent about three hours together, and Marsulla came away feeling that if the interview and the few written tests he had been given had gone well, the job was his. His intuition on this point was correct, and Marshall asked Marsulla if he would become the company's president.

Officially Marsulla became the company's chief executive officer. Marshall's role as chairman was mostly that of monitoring, checking to see that operations or engineering were running smoothly, rather than actively participating in those functions. Marsulla was surprised to learn that Marshall's monitoring was often at a very detailed level. Marshall might want to know why a particular man was chosen to work the first shift, and another the second. "Rob looked at every invoice; he had his hands on everything," Sal commented.

Yet Marshall's intended goal in seeking a new CEO for his company was to remove himself from day-to-day responsibilities, so that he could "look over the shoulders of others and see what needs strengthening." He wanted to spend more time in the field, making clearer to the manufacturers' representatives the advantages his company's products provided and how best to sell them. Marshall intended no immediate retirement from active functioning; he wanted a president and CEO with whom he could work harmoniously, but who would be able to take over as chairman also should it become necessary. But within six months of Marsulla's arrival, Marshall was beginning to have some doubts.

"I think Sal is dedicated, hard-working, interested, and animated," Marshall observed. "But I'm not sure he has the ability to sit down and resolve. There's a big question mark: is he going to be an executive? Does he have the ability to analyze strategy and consider action? I may have made a mistake."

Perhaps the most carefully thought-out transition of recent years was conducted by Reginald Jones at GE. As described by Jones on April 15, 1982, to an MBA class at Harvard Business School, and amplified to this author, Jones's process had two broad steps. First, he set about to identify and get to know the seven major candidates for his job, all from within GE.

Unannounced, Jones held a confidential session with each candidate in which he posed the question: "You and I are in the corporate jet. It goes down and neither of us survive. Who should be the next CEO at GE? Jones commented, "Some tried to climb out of the wreckage, but I said, 'No, no—you've got to pick someone other than yourself.' "

Months later a second interview was conducted in which Jones asked a similar question and listened as each candidate gave a now carefully considered response. Jones was learning about the chemistry of his top management team.

As he narrowed the list of candidates, Jones shifted his focus from the selection of a successor to the implementation of the decision. The company was handed over to Jack Welch only after a lengthy period in which Welch had become the clear favorite to succeed Jones, and a top management team had been put in place which was fitted to Welch. Because Jones had chosen a person not closely similar in style to himself, he spent the extra time and effort to allow others in the company to see that it was a selection made for what Jones saw as challenges which would confront GE in the future. Three years after Jones stepped aside and Welch became chairman, it was evident that the company had been successfully transferred to Welch's leadership.

What were Jones's principles in selecting his successor? Two have been mentioned earlier, to pick someone unlike yourself, and to make a selection that fits the challenges of the future. Several others can now be added. First, know the candidates inside and out. Failure to do so was Robert Marshall's big mistake. His selection had all the superficial appearances of a good fit, but Marshall knew Marsulla too little to see the pitfalls ahead. Marshall had no version of Jones's airplane interviews to help him get to know the candidates in depth, and he suffered for the lack of it.

Second, put a team in place. No individual is a good bet to run a large company alone. A carefully selected team adds important dimensions and qualities to what an individual can bring to a top job. Most major U.S. corporations which are successful in the long term are run by a team of top executives. This does not mean that there is not a boss; but it means that there is not an autocrat. Third, in order to choose a team that will function well, the CEO who is choosing a successor must know the chemistry of the key people. Ordinarily it would not be wise to choose three of the top six candidates for a team to fill out the company's top officers. There is too great a likelihood that jealousies and resentments among them will poison the atmosphere. A better choice may be the top candidate and two others further down the candidate list, who are prepared to accept supporting roles.

Finally, do not try to continue to run the organization after you have stepped aside. This, too, was one of Robert Marshall's errors. All executives are reluctant to relinquish control and influence in organizations to which they have contributed much of their lives. This is true not only at the CEO level, but at many points in a manager's career—leaving an office, a plant, a division, or a subsidiary.

How can an enduring contribution be made? Some try to leave their imprint on the policies or procedures of an organization, in its products, services, or strategy. Yet these things cannot be cast in stone, for as the business environment changes, they will be made obsolete. Policies, products, services, and strategies will each require modification as the marketplace changes and competitive challenges are met. If the company's new management is rigidly bound to the policies of the past, it is very likely to fail in the future.

A better contribution is left by exiting managers who can turn over their responsibilities to people whom they have helped develop and in whose judgment they have confidence. These new people will be able to make the modifications in policies, products, services, and strategies required by the marketplace. They ensure the survival of the company by being well-trained and competent. The exiting manager has not left tablets of stone which seem permanent but are perishable in reality; instead, he has left responsible and adapted people to keep the organization going. It is through good people that the exiting executive has perpetuated a contribution to the organization.

SUMMARY

Managers have their skills tested in identifying and bringing up-and-coming managers along. Although the development and application of objective standards for selection has been a major preoccupation in the 1970s, the 1980s and 1990s will demand a delicate blending of objective and subjective evaluation criteria. Getting the right person for the right job is a key element in making a success of any competitive strategy. A further component of a company's ability to succeed will be the ability to use compensation to nurture these stars.

6

Motivating Through Compensation

Always a topic of considerable interest to managers, compensation is frequently controversial as well. Many of the readers of this book are in medium or large organizations and are subject to a formal pay system. Some are probably satisfied with how they are faring under the system; others may be very dissatisfied. In either case, readers are thinking of themselves as the subjects, whether beneficiary or victim, of the pay system.

This is too limited a perspective, however, for aspiring managers. Up-and-coming executives in any organization must quickly supplant this perspective, or at least supplement it with a different viewpoint. From the perspective of themselves against the system, general managers must turn to a perspective of the system as their own. Specifically, rising executives must be able to see the compensation system primarily as one which they manage, not to which they are subject. They must make it work for them with regard to those who report to them—rather than being principally concerned about how it affects their own pay. They must be able to see themselves in charge of the pay system; not it in charge of them.

Until a person can get on top of the pay system, so to speak, he or she will not be able to be an effective general manager. Key questions to ask in selecting people for higher responsibility are: How do they see themselves? With which role are they able to identify? Can the candidate think like a manager, or not?

A compensation system is in place to serve a purpose for the organization and the people who are in charge of it. If a person wants to be one who is involved in running the organization in an important position, then he or she must possess a detached view of the company's pay policies, independent of their personal impact.

This is not to say that the compensation systems in place in American companies are the best or most appropriate ones. Some are good; some not. This chapter is concerned with problems in pay systems and attempts to improve them. But the correct perspective for the reader is as a manager in charge of a pay system; not as an employee subject to it.

Today's best managers want compensation systems that contribute to several objectives: The compensation system must attract and help retain good people, who are a key resource of the business. Also it must be under control and administrable so that personnel costs do not get out of hand. It should motivate people by providing incentives to get the desired behavior, and to reward those whose performance is outstanding. It must also play a role in allocating investment, because labor costs in any operation are routinely compared with capital costs to determine if any investment of additional capital is financially wise.

For all these purposes to be fulfilled simultaneously, several requirements must be met. The system must be correctly designed and should be subject to continual review to be sure it is yielding the results desired. Also, the system must be administered correctly. This responsibility of line managers requires them to have the system and its contribution to the company's business purposes in perspective. Each manager must understand the system, support it, and internalize its requirements. If managers cannot be committed to the system, it must either be explained in a persuasive way, or junked in favor of another which can gain respect and support. Managers must communicate the system to other employees, and administer it fairly. Managers who have not internalized the system can neither explain it satisfactorily to other personnel, nor get their trust in its administration. Managers must learn to think like partners in the firm, understanding and making the system work because it belongs to them.

Frequently managers do not think of the system as their own, but rather as an alien imposition which belongs to headquarters or the personnel staff, and which interferes with their own management style. Wishing to provide substantial pay rewards to their own teams, managers become like wind-up toys sent to headquarters by their own subordinates to milk the system for the subordinates' gain. In practice, managers are acting against the company.

Faced with this all too frequent situation, many companies have abandoned most of the objectives for compensation mentioned earlier. Rather than helping to attract, retain, and motivate good people, it is enough for the system to avoid creating big problems. "We don't know what we want from compensation in our company," said a top executive, "but we know what we don't want—big problems." Rather than focusing on pay as a motivator, this company focuses on its potential for stripping people of motivation. "Give everyone what the other person gets is the strategy, and hope no one is so angry as to cause a ruckus." Because pay can only demotivate—the guiding principle is sameness—sometimes mislabeled equity. But is sameness enough for a pay system to deliver in today's competitive environment?

PAY VERSUS CHALLENGE

"Frank, there's no question about it. We're out of line. Way out of line. The situation is real. It's hurting us, and I have two resignations here to prove it."

John C. Boyd, senior vice president of finance for Megalith, Inc., paced across his office in agitation. Near the door stood Frank C. Nicodemus, Megalith's vice president for human resources. Long-time colleagues in this successful multinational firm, the two men were continuing a debate begun much earlier, when Boyd had attempted to raise the salaries of his key managers by 25 percent.

"You told me last June that these people were too young and inexperienced to be worth the money," Boyd continued. "And I told you we'd have to pay based on their competence, not their seniority. Now it's October and two of them have given notice in the past month. They're half of the team I brought in here to bring the Finance Group out of the Stone Age, and they've been absolutely vital to the development of the group. And now they're both leaving—to get salaries I wanted to pay them months ago."

Boyd turned and shook his head. "Frank, I know that what's done is done, and we're not going to get Lonny and George back. But what if my other key people take off, too? Where would that leave us? I've got to have more room in the salary schedule to take care of the exceptional people who've made this group click!"

Boyd paused, and Frank Nicodemus responded. "John, you'll remember I showed you that all four of your key people were right at the top of our scale. Megalith's compensation system isn't something we've arbitrarily picked out of the air; every year we check the schedule against trade associations' published data, and we adjust it to make sure we're about average—that we're competitive with the best in the labor market. To make exceptions to a well-grounded scale would be both hasty and rash. It would raise hell around here, throwing everything out of balance.

"We shouldn't overpay those people just to get them to stay," Frank Nicodemus continued. "The two managers who left took broader gauge jobs at their new companies. If they want more to do, let them go outside. We can replace them at our current cost."

Behind the argument between the two executives lay a period of several years in which the company's business had rapidly expanded into the international market. To meet a complex financing challenge, the company had built its finance department from 110 people to 630, growing at 50 percent a year for several years. Recently, however, growth had slackened off to the 5 percent range, and the operations of the department had become routine.

The four bright young managers the executive vice president had brought in to build the department were bored, and two had left. Should the company retain the other two by offering them large enough salary increases to keep them from going elsewhere?

The more Frank Nicodemus studied Boyd's request, the more he became convinced that it was inappropriate. Studying the results of an attitude survey taken in Boyd's department, Nicodemus was startled to see that Boyd's top seven managers, including the two he was now concerned about losing, did not register dissatisfaction about their pay. Asked the question, "Considering the work you do, how would you describe your present compensation?" They replied that it was slightly better than satisfactory.

But they were not at all happy with the organization in which they were working. "To what extent are the goals in this organization truly challenging?" they were asked. The answer given was "only to a very little extent." "Relative to its competition, this organization is . . ." brought the reply, "Not a leader, but a follower." On another set of questions the top managers working for Boyd rated compensation high, but organizational vitality and management style low.

"The problem here," Nicodemus told Allen Witfield, Megalith's president in a private meeting, "is not the salary program. Our surveys show it is adequate compared to other companies of our type and size. The problem is Boyd. He's been building his empire over in finance, but he hasn't got much for the people to do. They don't feel challenged and they don't think Megalith is a leader. So some of them are leaving us."

"What do you conclude?" Witfield asked him.

"That Boyd isn't much of a manager. Also, I think Boyd should be able to replace those people. If he can't, then he hasn't been paying attention to developing his lower level managers."

"You're kind of hard on him, aren't you?" Witfield asked.

"I like Boyd as a person, and I think he's good at his function. I don't think he's very good at managing his people, and I don't think we ought to upset the salary program to bail him out. If we gave the raises he has asked for to his other two favorites, then we'll have to make adjustments for lots of other managers in other functions. The system has to be kept equitable."

"Are the people Boyd is talking about really as good as he says they are?" Witfield asked.

"Yes, they're good."

"That's what I think too. You know them, don't you?"

"Yes."

"So do I. I don't like to lose such good people."

"Well, on the other hand we can be pleased," said Nicodemus, "that Megalith can survive the loss of talented people like them. Any company has to be able to replace key executives; we can't afford to have irreplaceable people. Boyd hasn't done the best job developing his younger managers, but there's enough talent there to fill in. A company is strong when it can replace good people."

"Yes," Witfield responded, "but wouldn't we be stronger if we could retain them? Aren't you in danger of just rationalizing our loss? There is truth in your view, Frank, but there can also be a pitfall. A company may experience a continual loss of excellent people, always somehow filling their positions, and delude itself that it is the stronger for this turnover, when in fact it is simply bearing the cost of executive development for its competitors. Also, the view that everyone is replaceable may blind the company to the special value of some people."

"Allen, you've got a point," Nicodemus responded. "But all companies will experience the loss of some key employees in the course of business, and should be able to replace them. To attempt to hold people at all costs is expensive and can be counterproductive."

"What, after all, is John Boyd's failing, Frank?" Witfield began. "You came in and told me he was an empire builder, a poor developer of people, unable to challenge his managers, and a threat to the company's salary program. You base this on attitude survey data, and I don't challenge the data. They're useful to have. And I pay attention to them. But the question is how you interpret them.

"We agree that the people leaving us are very good. Maybe we can't reward top performers well enough in our salary system. I know that we have to choose to some degree between having people at the same levels getting the same pay, which is only fair, and being able to pay for outstanding contributions."

Witfield continued to think out loud. "If we tie our salaries to performance, then we have to live with the problem of some of our people getting less than others in the same job and thinking it is unfair. But if we tie our salaries to job classifications, how can we use money as a motivator?

"We're in a very difficult position. Our salary system is carefully designed to be fair by paying people in the same job the same pay, and tagging the rate of pay to what other companies like our own pay their people. The system is fair on inside comparisons; and it is fair on outside comparisons.

"But, we have some very good people in finance, thanks to John Boyd who recruited them, and they're leaving us. You know, finance isn't the conservative straightforward function it was a few years back. Now it changes every day. There are new financial instruments, new lenders, new kinds of deals. Boyd and his people have kept up in the past, and I'm not sure we can do as well if his key people leave."

"We have to let people leave," Nicodemus interrupted. "If we don't, people will invent offers to force us to raise their salaries in an effort to keep them. When people leave and we promote others into their positions good things happen. We demonstrate the strength and depth of the organization, and we know that opportunities exist for advancement."

"Yes, but it's very unfortunate to have really good people leave us and take their talents elsewhere, especially if it's to our competitors. Good people are hard to find. I can't find fault with Boyd for trying hard to get us to keep key contributors. I'd be angry if he didn't."

"Perhaps the way to look at this is to see that the two guys who left are sending us a signal about Boyd's organization," Nicodemus suggested. "They're voting with their feet and saying it isn't challenging at Megalith anymore. Maybe what we ought to do is talk to Boyd about what is going on in his function. Is it slowing down, and why?"

"Yes," Witfield agreed. "That's a good point. But what do we want him to do?"

"Perhaps he could take on some additional responsibilities and reorganize to let his key people have more challenging jobs. If he doesn't do that, I don't think money alone will keep them."

"I agree," Witfield said simply.

"Do you want to talk to Boyd about it?" Nicodemus asked.

"Yes, but that isn't all there is to the matter, is it?"

"Why not?"

"Will challenge alone keep them? Won't they want to be paid more, too? You know, Frank," Witfield continued, "I think compensation may be the most rigid, inflexible thing we do. We have such a complex system, we try to fit pay to job fairly among so many different situations that we can't make adjustments for the unexpected.

"When people who are major contributors leave, we discount complaints about pay and act as if they would remain for more challenge. In effect I think we are offering challenge as a substitute for pay. We are almost asking people to work harder so we don't have to pay them more. I am increasingly worried that our compensation system is wasteful of our key human talent. It doesn't contribute to our keeping top performers, but to losing them.

"Boyd got a bad review as a manager because he asked for more money for his people. But all he was doing was calling attention to the company's loss of real talent. And the response you propose is say to him 'Give those who remain more to do so we don't have to pay them more.'"

"Well," conceded Nicodemus, "if they do more, then we could pay them more."

"How?"

"If the job has more responsibilities, it can be paid more."

"But not for increased performance in the same job?"

"Not beyond where we are."

"Well, I don't think challenge alone is enough." Witfield concluded.

PAY AS A REWARD

Challenge is sometimes available to employees in large measure and from unexpected sources. In early fall of 1981 the Congress passed President Reagan's tax cut package, the Economic Recovery Tax Act. According to one provision of the Act, companies with depreciation charges in excess of their profits could, by a device labeled safe harbor leasing, transfer those deductions to other companies in order to offset taxes. Excess depreciation could be sold or bought. A new market was created.

However, conforming to the technical requirements necessary to make the transactions legal was not easy, and matching buyers and sellers required some effort. Also, the Congress had provided that the opportunity to transfer depreciation for tax purposes would expire in only a few months.

At the credit subsidiary of one of America's largest companies financial specialists went to work. They devised appropriate legal language, found sellers of depreciation, and bought enough so that for fiscal 1982 their parent company paid no federal income tax despite substantial operating earnings. Further, by being first to "cream" the market, they were able to pay only 30 cents on average for each dollar of depreciation. With a tax savings to the company of some 50 cents per dollar of depreciation obtained, the company netted 20 cents per dollar in taxes saved for each dollar of depreciation purchased.

In only a few weeks in the fall of 1981, some eight people working tirelessly and intelligently, saved the parent corporation more than $100 million in taxes. How were they to be rewarded?

The challenge alone had been exhilarating. But the credit company's top managers hoped for a more tangible reward for its people. The parent company applied its uniform salary and bonus system to the credit company. A bonus was worked out, averaging some $3,000 per employee for the eight key contributors.

Figuring that each person had on average made the company more than $10 million in tax savings, the affected employees were less than satisfied with the bonuses. Comparing their earnings with what Wall Street firms would pay for similar performances made them even angrier. By June of the following year, three of the eight people had left the credit company for other positions.

Should the parent company have been more generous in its bonuses? Yes, if it wished to retain the people. But did it? Wouldn't other people in the same positions have done as much? Can a credit company replace those who left without undercutting the future performance of the credit company? These are difficult questions to answer. They are hypothetical and cannot be answered other than by supposition. But the very indeterminacy of the matter forces a manager to think carefully about the company's position.

The only answer is to try to balance concerns about equity in pay with concerns about rewarding performance. The same parent company that failed to reward its credit company people adequately has managers who handled a somewhat similar incident far more successfully. A plant manager had an engineer who reported to him. By perseverance and a bit of genius the engineer was able to resolve a technical problem no one else had been able to solve. By so doing the engineer made the company a lot of money.

The manager had no way to give the employee a financial reward commensurate with the contribution. However, the manager wrote the engineer up for a first level management citation and awarded a $1,000 bonus. He took the proposed award to his boss, another step up the management chain. "Why did you write this fellow up for a management award?" he was asked. The first level manager explained.

"Why $1,000?" he was asked.

"That's all I can approve," he answered.

"How much can I approve?" his boss asked.

"Twice that."

His boss took the written form, crossed out $1,000, wrote in $2,000 and signed it. The first level manager was asked by his boss to take the authorization form up one more level to his boss's boss for approval.

"Why are you giving this employee a management award?" he was asked. He explained. "Why $2,000?"

"That's all my boss can approve."

"How much can I approve?"

"Your assistant says double that."

So his boss's boss scratched through $2,000 on the form and wrote in $4,000 and signed it.

Several weeks later the engineer received from the company a certificate recognizing his contribution; he received from payroll a bonus of $4,000; and he received from his manager a copy of the award request form with the amount raised twice and the signatures of his own boss, his boss's boss and his boss's boss's boss. Done in this personal and sensitive manner, combining a limited financial award with individual recognition for his contribution was sufficient to retain a valuable employee.

A LOT IS GOING ON

Compensation is sometimes said to be an area in which nothing is happening in business. This is a serious misapprehension. It is true that salary programs have become complex and somewhat rigid. But employees' expectations about compensation have been changing rapidly. The systems have been rigid, but the context has shifted dramatically.

In the 1960s Americans came to expect that each year they would receive pay increases sufficient to give them a steadily improving standard of living. In the 1970s successive oil crises and inflation forced people to lower their expectations. No longer could they necessarily expect to do better each year, but still they expected pay increases to at least keep pace with inflation. In the early 1980s pay increases fell behind inflation. Again expectations had been lowered, but employees were still insistent on increased wage levels that at least exceeded those of the previous year. When inflation rates fell dramatically in the 1980s, increases in compensation fell even faster. In consequence, as conditions and expectations have changed, managers have had to continually invent new explanations for an unchanging system of pay administration.

Managers are looking for more flexibility in paying people. Most employees receive an annual increase in pay, though many also receive quarterly increments (often as a result of cost-of-living allowances provided by union contracts). Taking advantage of the flexibility often available in a small company, Perfusion Services, Inc. (a supplier of equipment and technicians for open-heart surgery) decided to provide pay increases in small amounts every two weeks. The continual increase in pay, though amounts varied, seemed to motivate people more than the annual pay adjustment.[1]

Some companies, however, have found the flexibility demanded by today's marketplace cannot be supplied by a single pay system, no matter how frequent the increases. Diversified larger companies, in particular, have not been able to answer all the expectations of people in different businesses and geographic areas with the same compensation system.

In high technology, for instance, personnel in California have insisted on being paid with a piece of the action—in particular, they have been attracted by complicated stock options. In 1849, during the gold rush, Californians saw their neighbors finding nuggets in streambeds. No one wanted to work for the general store any longer. People abandoned their jobs for the mines. In the 1970s and 1980s Californians saw their neighbors finding fortunes in the stock of high technology companies and wanted that opportunity themselves. In order to retain high tech employees in California, many companies have had to develop compensation programs featuring stock option plans.

Managers and engineers in high tech companies are not the only people who will only work for a piece of the action. Entre-

[1] Ellen Wojahn, "A Raise in Every Paycheck," *Inc.* (February 1984): 110.

preneur Kemmons Wilson, a founder of Holiday Inns, Inc., commented on his recent business ventures that he had to take key people as half-and-half partners. "It's the only way I know," he told a reporter, "to get people to work."[2]

In financial service companies bond and currency traders have in recent years become major contributors to corporate earnings. Successful traders are much in demand, and receive very high salaries. Unable to accommodate these salaries in established systems, companies have established separate pay systems for traders. Managers find themselves receiving salaries equal to one-half or one-third of the commissions received by traders who report to them. In order to respond to complaints from other employees who are not so well paid, top executives have to say in effect, "If you can do the trading, go to it—then we'll pay you what successful traders get."

Large banks now employ people not only in regular commercial banking functions but also in managing investments, in handling corporate mergers and acquisitions, in bond and currency trading, and in support functions like data processing. To a degree each of these areas has its own unique character. Facing so much diversity, the banks are having to abandon the effort to have only a single compensation system. A money center bank now is likely to have at least five distinguishable systems: one providing salary alone, another hourly pay, a third pay by work accomplished, a fourth stressing commissions, and a fifth combining limited salary with potentially large bonuses. Employees of the bank earn widely disparate amounts of money, based partly on their functions and partly on the pay system in which they participate.

A few years ago, a large eastern magazine publisher purchased a motion picture company. With the company came a group of producers and other executives accustomed to the Hollywood life-style. They expected that the company would provide homes in Beverly Hills, Rolls Royces, and similar perquisites, not available even to the company's top management in the East. After several

[2] John R. Dorfman, "New Tricks," *Forbes* (16 January 1984), 110.

months of resistance the company bowed to entertainment industry practice and granted Hollywood perquisites to the key executives in its motion picture subsidiary. Asked if managerial people in the company's publishing business insisted that they should also have these advantages, the company's CEO answered, "Yes, though I tell them no, and just try to keep all our publishing people out of the Los Angeles area."

Widely divergent pay levels and methods of compensation in different industries are forcing diversified companies to create multiple compensation plans because a single plan cannot cover the range of practices involved. This new complexity in pay is altering the nation's concept of fairness or equity as it applies to compensation: from sameness for people working for a single company in similar jobs, to differences which reflect outside market forces.

"What do you want out of the compensation system?" the publishing company's CEO was asked by a confused executive, "external equity or internal consistency?"

"Consistency is nice," he replied, "but I've got to keep each business competitive in its own marketplace. Some of our divisions have to go down in pay levels to meet the competition. Others have to go up. In those businesses competitive pressures are forcing us to look for people able to perform well, and to pay them whatever and however necessary to retain them."

FLEXIBILITY IN COMPENSATION

Once it is acknowledged that pay systems must be more flexible than in the past, the question arises: how flexible? Does flexibility in a pay system help to motivate people in their jobs? No, says a very influential school of thought. People have a hierarchy of needs, of which only the more primitive (food, clothing, and shelter) are readily satisfied by pay. Higher level needs include self-actualization, personal recognition, and individual growth. These needs are not met well by pay.

It follows that financial compensation has only a limited role. Necessary to satisfy certain needs, it is inadequate to meet others. In particular, pay cannot motivate people to better performance, because it does not answer higher level needs. Furthermore, people are conscious of each other's pay levels, and have strong feelings about fairness. If Mary is paid less than Joe, but feels she should get the same, then she may be angry, resentful, and unwilling to perform well on her job. Pay is serving not as a motivator, but as a demotivator.

The conclusion is that pay is a negative item in a company's policy: it can cause trouble if it is inequitable, but it cannot do much to motivate performance. This is a powerful argument which has affected the motivational efforts of many American managers and the way they think about compensation. However, it has certain limitations.

A higher level need of human beings is for status. To many people compensation level is a measure of status. "George is very successful," usually means George gets a big salary. "Sam is an important figure," usually means Sam has a lot of money. Long after food, shelter, and clothing needs are satisfied in a rudimentary fashion, additional dollars contribute to a person's need for recognition of status and success.

Also, as Thorstein Veblen pointed out almost a century ago, many Americans are conspicuous consumers. They measure their importance by the showiness and expense of the items they buy.[3] It is hard to believe that this has changed much from Veblen's time. Hence for most people, pay is essential in satisfying a key higher level need.

As Allen Witfield of Megalith pointed out previously, some managers believe that since challenge allows people to fulfill higher level needs for growth and self-actualization, challenge can be made a substitute for compensation, rather than an accompaniment or supplement. People do need challenge to meet higher level needs; they also need money to meet higher level needs.

---

[3] Thorstein Veblen, *The Theory of the Leisure Class* (New York: A. M. Kelley, 1975). (original copyright 1899).

Finally, the concept of pay having to meet a primary standard of fairness has gotten mixed up with the conception of fairness as sameness. In fact, the argument that pay is not really able to motivate people but can only be a demotivator has a lot of force. Americans traditionally believe that compensation should be tied closely to the content of the job a person is doing at any given time. The origin of this view is the principle of equal pay for equal work. Thus what Americans think of equity is determined by whether people in the same jobs get the same pay. Avoiding the disincentive aspect of pay means paying people in the same jobs the same amounts.

Many managers are experimenting with other standards of equity. These include whether people with long experience with the company should be paid more than those with lesser experience, and whether pay should reflect the quality of a person's own performance over time.

Economic research suggests that in the United States experience and performance on the job are more important in establishing pay scales than we ordinarily think. The experience and expertise which an employee gains on the job are referred to by economists as part of human capital. Studies have indicated that senior people earn more than less senior people in many companies, even when jobs are the same or closely similar.

Some companies also pay people according to the quality of their personal contributions over time, as evaluated by their supervisors. Thus people in the same jobs can receive very different rates of pay depending on the quality of their sustained performance. Fairness is not tied totally to job content in our country, because experience and quality of performance also affect attitudes toward pay.

The Japanese have gone further than we in reducing the importance of job content as a major factor in setting pay scales. Rather than job content, the salary of an employee depends on length of service with the company and the broad type of position he or she has. Managers are paid more than blue-collar or clerical workers, as are engineers. But among blue-collar employees the detailed job task is not very important in determining pay; nor are different tasks significant in determining pay among clerical workers, or engineers, or among managers.

Nakao Yoshito is an executive employed by a medium-sized Japanese chemical company. He is paid a salary and twice a year receives a substantial bonus. Ordinarily, the bonus is not variable with the company's success or failure in the marketplace. This is the ordinary practice, though many American writers insist wrongly that Japanese bonuses vary annually with the profits of the firm. Should his employer have several bad years, however, Yoshito understands that bonuses might be reduced. Several years ago Yoshito worked in a factory. Now he is in sales. His pay did not change when he changed jobs. His pay is attached to him, not to the job he is in. His earnings are determined by his length of service with the company, his ability, and his performance.

Twice a year Yoshito and his supervisor set goals for his work. As each six month period ends, he is evaluated on his performance and the amount of his merit pay (not his bonus) is established. His salary level is not related to his performance, but to his length of service and broad classification, management.

Once every two years Yoshito is evaluated by 15 different people using a form containing some 28 items. Among those who evaluate him are his boss, his peers, his secretary, and customers. This evaluation is not used for salary purposes, but to influence his career development (where does he need improvement?) and also to help determine the level of his merit pay. In sum, Nakao Yoshito is paid by three different methods: salary, bonus, and merit pay, of which only salary—and that to a minor degree— is closely related to the specific job to which he is assigned.

We will see in Chapter 7 that some American companies are now groping toward a concept of pay that is more and more independent of job content.

WHY PEOPLE WORK

Why do people work? It may seem strange to come to this question after so lengthy a discussion of compensation. While following most thinking about compensation, up to this point we have assumed that the reasons people work are similar for a broad majority of people. The controversy is over what those reasons are. Is it for money, for status, or for self-fulfillment?

Even a cursory examination of human nature reveals that people work for different reasons. An informal survey conducted among several hundred young managers (men and women with technical and humanistic backgrounds) found the following primary motivations listed for work, with the percentage distribution as follows:

For enjoyment, prestige, satisfaction, or achievement	32.5%
Power and influence (the right to decide and take action)	26.3
Pay (to achieve a very comfortable level)	16.3
To make a contribution or fulfill a duty	15.0
For long-term advancement	4.8
For the excitement of competition and challenge	3.8
To develop oneself as a person	1.3
	100.0%

Whether or not this list and these percentages are accurate for broader groups in our work force can certainly be debated. At this point the question is whether or not a compensation system could, or should, be targeted to individual motivation. That is, should compensation be broadly defined to include both pay and nonpecuniary rewards and opportunities? And, can compensation be so individually directed that it could motivate the performance of individuals in an organization by permitting each person to be rewarded according to his or her own set of values?

Some companies are trying to do this. Daniel Meager runs a very successful small company which provides services to remote television installations for companies and public broadcasters. He uses a fleet of trucks operated by part-timers, and has a professional staff of technicians. "I identified the best people in this area in this business and persuaded them by one thousand and one ways to work for me," he commented. "Flexibility is my company's major source of leverage. Because we're small we are able to stay free of government regulation (the laws apply but no one takes the time to look at us), and free of unions, stockholders, and of any boss.

"The key to getting people with technical or managerial talent is to give away a piece of the equity. They want to be part of the company's ownership. The key to having part-timers who will provide good service to customers is to pay them a good hourly wage, and give them a bonus. They don't expect long-term employment, so they don't care about equity. But I need them to treat customers well and to help attract new business, so I pay them a bonus for each new account and for each renewal.

"Flexibility allows us to tailor-make rewards on a spontaneous basis to whatever turns the particular employee on. One truck driver drove 36 hours straight from Chicago to Florida so that we could make a deadline. He was a hero, so I gave him three days' vacation immediately with his wife in Florida at company expense. Another key employee got in a dispute with his landlord, so the company's law firm helped him out.

"Sometimes in a small firm you don't have money in the cash box, so you can't give people trips or other rewards easily. So one time we provided training for people who wanted to go into their own businesses. They did a good job for us, then left us. But they're cooperators, not competitors. There are weaknesses, too, in being small," Meager confessed. "I can't offer big benefits, especially pensions, and there are no established career paths. I have to depend on employees taking initiatives themselves to help their advancement."

To a surprising degree the better managed large firms also try to attain flexibility in dealing with the varying motivations of employees. IBM practice demonstrates the various aspects of compensation given sales representatives. The company provides a salary, commissions on sales, bonuses for achieving targets, awards for outstanding performance, and wider recognition through membership in clubs composed of top performers. Awards and clubs combine personal recognition with financial rewards.

When asked to list the major incentives to work for this company, however, several former employees went far beyond pay and individual recognition:

Salary: competitive with other firms
Prestige: this is the industry leader
Security: a no layoff policy
Benefits (pension, and so forth): competitive with other large firms
Environment: top notch people, team atmosphere, good management—sales representative relationships
Promotion: from within only
Training: ongoing throughout career
Management policies: availability to employees, awards for suggestions
Performance plan: promotions available, salary increases based on performance
Power and influence: sales is the management track in the company; credibility with customers because of the company's reputation

Two wide-ranging systems of compensation are pecuniary and nonpecuniary. In both the small TV company and IBM, management was consciously providing flexibility and multiplicity in rewards. One of the two ways to interpret these efforts is to say that each company is trying to meet the hierarchy of human needs in each of its employees. Another is to say that each company is trying to meet the divergent motivation of different people by providing a range of potential rewards. To a degree both companies are attempting to tailor their compensation to the differing psychologies of different people.

The best managers are aware that to be able to motivate people they must be responsive to the hierarchy of needs and also to the divergent motivations of different people.

SUMMARY

Compensation remains a powerful motivator but it has been downgraded and misunderstood. The new managerial generation is competitive and wants financial success. It is not a counterculture group eschewing material rewards. Traditional thinking about compensation downplays motivation and emphasizes avoiding problems by a certain sameness. Just as people can be motivated by the promise of employment security, compensation systems can be administered to motivate people. The challenge is to be flexible without being unfair.

It is possible to break out of the straitjacket of rigidly applied systems by developing systems that are more responsive to individual contributions and motivations.

7

Pay For Performance And Personalized Pay

The story goes that during Yogi Berra's playing career as catcher with the New York Yankees, he was so good at talking to batters on opposing teams that Yankee Manager Casey Stengel called Berra his "inside man." Whatever Stengel wanted to know about his opponents' strategy or capabilities, Berra wormed out of batters at the plate. As Berra's reputation got around to other clubs, their managers made strenuous efforts to muzzle batters. In one World Series, the Dodgers' manager threatened to fire any batter who spoke to Berra at the plate.[1]

Not only in baseball do managers try to preserve secrets from the competition. And in some companies the penchant for confidentiality extends even to the company's own employees. Tom Canavan was one of LEP Corporation's engineers, currently in charge of a project in LEP's semiconductor division. Recently he had been making major contributions to a new technology, and he was concerned that he might not be fairly paid for his efforts. So Canavan told his supervisor he thought his pay at LEP was

[1] Red Barber on "All Things Considered," National Public Radio, December 16, 1983.

131

a little low, but he wasn't sure, at least as compared to his peers. He didn't know what the other managers at his level were making.

"Tom," the supervisor said, "I'm prepared to talk to you about your own salary, but not about anyone else's. That would be an invasion of privacy. If you don't think you're paid enough, I'll tell you why your rate is where it is, and what you can do in terms of performance to get an increase."

Because his supervisors ranked him as an excellent performer, Canavan was not satisfied with the conversation. He knew he was doing a good job for LEP, but wasn't sure if he was being paid fairly. It was not difficult for Canavan to find out the rates of pay of some of the other engineers in his unit. He knew the company's salary ranges for people in his classification because he had recently been in a managerial position, heading the project, and had made salary recommendations for other employees in the same classification as his own. But he had not seen everyone's salary, and he was unsure especially about two or three of his colleagues who were very effective engineers. Less talented people were willing to talk fairly openly about their salaries. But the best people were secretive.

The company encouraged the secrecy, refusing to disclose to Canavan the level in which an employee was classified, the salary range for the classification, or the salary of any other individual. It was excessive secrecy, in Canavan's view, and it was causing him to mistrust the company and even contemplate departure.

What was most surprising to Canavan was that other LEP employees did not seem to share his distrust of the company's pay policies. He thought LEP had no reason to keep so much from employees. If the pay system was fair, then it should be open. If it was not open, then it could not be fair.

PAYING FOR PERFORMANCE IS FAIR

LEP's top managers are aware of the suspicions which confidentiality about salary engenders in some employees and outsiders who hear the system described. They are continually monitoring their employees' attitudes toward the salary system to see if Tom Canavan's reservations become more general. It is interesting to them that the highest level of pay dissatisfaction is encountered in the engineering units, where people move in and out of managerial positions frequently and there is, in consequence, more openness about the pay system. In other areas of the company, where pay confidentiality is stronger, there are fewer complaints. And until complaints are more widespread, LEP is not likely to abandon secrecy; there are strong business reasons to retain it.

Surprisingly, pay is not an easy thing to get managers and potential managers to carefully think about. The problem is the personal reaction people tend to have to discussions about pay. The questions that come more readily to mind are: Am I being treated fairly compared to my peers? How much can I earn? How do I get more?

These questions are each from the perspective of a person who is in the pay system; not from the perspective of a person managing a pay system. Since managers have a dual role, being in the system and also in charge of it, they have a special responsibility to understand it from both sides. Unfortunately many readily take the employee's perspective; only after years of experience do they assume the manager's perspective.

The management perspective about pay includes questions such as these: How can I use compensation to motivate employees? Can compensation costs be kept within reasonable levels? Do I want to reward performance by individual employees, and if so, what features of a pay system contribute to this?

Like many other companies today, LEP is anxious to be able to reward in a special fashion its employees who make the most significant contributions. For years it has attempted to refine methods for doing so while retaining control over both costs and morale. Pay is perhaps the most sensitive element of any company's relationship with its employees, since the opportunity for dissatisfaction is enormous. Further, managers often tend to be relatively lax in administering a pay-for-performance system, so that too many people may get high ratings and generous pay levels, threatening to drive the company's costs up.

Whether or not to pay for performance is a question that causes concern at numerous companies. Many people believe that distinctions among employees based on performance are too difficult to explain to others, and are certain to cause morale problems. In consequence, although many companies have a performance component for management's pay it is far less common for other employees.

LEP has not been troubled much by doubts. Rather than reevaluate whether or not to use pay for performance, LEP has tried to develop the best system for its implementation. The result is a surprising blend of openness and secrecy. The company has refused to recognize a conflict between fairness in pay and a premium for high performance. Indeed, LEP tries to instill in its employees the conviction that recognizing an individual's contribution in his or her salary is fair, and that a pay system which fails to recognize differences in contribution is unfair.

To LEP's way of thinking giving rewards to people commensurate with their contribution expresses a peculiarly American sense of fair play which had its beginning with the Pilgrims. During the Pilgrims' first winter in Plymouth Colony (1620–21), the elders who governed the colony tried to divide stores equally among all families. In the summer, noticing the unequal contribution of individuals to the colony's provisions and the dissatisfaction created by equal distribution, the elders decided to forego equal distribution. In effect Plymouth Colony proceeded from one philosophy to another.

At all times, the elders worked from the basic presumption that all the immigrants were full members of the colony. "We are all in this together," their promise ran, but the conclusion changed. Initially, the elders had reasoned: "We're all in this together, so we should each get the same." Now, under the press of adverse weather and soil and of the need for great exertions to build a foothold in the wilderness, they reasoned: "We're all in this together, so we should honestly recognize each other's individual contributions and efforts and reward each accordingly." To the Pilgrims in 1621, rewarding individuals for their own contributions was fully consistent with the unity of the colony. As a team of persons embarked on a difficult task, they felt it was the best way to elicit the uncommon effort which survival required.[2]

The Pilgrims were in competition with the elements, a great wilderness, Native American Indians, and nonEnglish Europeans. Centuries later LEP found itself in competition with other companies, foreign and domestic; like the Pilgrims it sought to balance the need for unity and teamwork with recognition for the disparate contributions of individuals.

The theme of concern for individual contributions echoes repeatedly in American history. Thaddeus Stevens of Pennsylvania, perhaps the Civil War's most inveterate opponent of slaveholding, said in a speech to Congress in support of the proposed Fourteenth Amendment to the Constitution that "no distinction would be tolerated in the purified Republic but that arose from merit and conduct."[3] There were to be no distinctions based on race, creed, or place of national origin in the nation after war had purged it of slavery, Stevens proclaimed, but distinctions between individuals arising from merit and conduct would still be defensible.

Believing that distinctions among people based on performance are in the essential spirit of American life, LEP has tried to build a general system of recognition and reward around individual performance. To accomplish this managers are urged to take performance appraisal seriously. Without accuracy in this fundamental building block of a performance system, properly deserving (or undeserving) people cannot be identified. A merit pay system which is based primarily on favoritism or on the chance that an employee has a greater salary opportunity elsewhere and may leave, is worse than no merit pay system at all, for it will, over time undermine employee morale and inflate company costs.

[2] William Bradford, *Of Plymouth Plantation 1620–1647*, Samuel Eliot Morison (Ed.) (New York: Alfred A. Knopf, 1970), 120–121.
[3] Richard B. Cheney and Lynne V. Cheney, *Kings of the Hill: Power and Personality in the House of Representatives* (New York: Continuum, 1983), 68.

Furthermore, to reinforce the merit principle, not only pay but also other aspects of advantage at the company are on the performance basis. Thus promotions, transfers, and assignments all reflect to a degree the individual's quality of contribution at LEP.

This is uncommon in American industry. In many companies merit pay plans stand alone, without secure foundations in the performance appraisal system. "Our managers don't like the personal aspects of performance appraisal systems," say executives of a large company which reports that its divisions have over 30 different merit pay plans.

Also, the merit principle often applies only to pay, but to no other aspect of employment causing top performers to wonder why they are valued financially by the company, but apparently in no other way.

But there are very significant pitfalls in managing pay for performance. It is crucial that what gets rewarded is truly performance and not favoritism. Also some substantial uniformity of pay among people in similar jobs who are at the same level of performance is necessary. In this sense a pay for performance system is not one in which fairness is abandoned, but a more complex equity has to be applied. It is no longer sufficient for the employee to believe: "I'm in the same job, and I get the same pay; that's fair." Now the employee must say, "I'm in the same job, I perform at the same level, and have been doing so for a while; I should get the same pay as someone else in a similar position, but different pay from a better performer who's been here longer."

So paying for performance is a complex undertaking. To make it work LEP has had to develop four key components for its managers' use.

First, managers must have available or develop legitimate individual measures of performance for each employee; even if the employee is part of a team working on a project, the manager has an obligation to single out his or her individual contribution. The manager must be close enough to employees to be able to evaluate their contributions.

Second, managers and subordinates must have an explicit understanding about what the subordinate is expected to do; not detailed instructions, but a definition of achievements for which the subordinate will be recognized as outstanding. This understanding needs to be reached by the manager and subordinate together, and modified as required by changing circumstances. It is an informal, tacit contract between manager and employee upon which both can rely.

These first two elements establish performance goals for each employee, and a means by which the employee's achievement of the goals, or failure to achieve them, will be measured.

Third, because LEP has many employees, it must see that people in similar positions are treated similarly. Jobs have to be appropriately slotted with other jobs of comparable difficulty, skill, and responsibility. The accurate description of the job is the responsibility of a supervisor; its appropriate classification among other jobs is the responsibility of staff persons. Also, a budget must be prepared for salary increases, so that persons in similar jobs who perform at the same level are given similar pay increases. By and large, each manager is given a chart which indicates the appropriate salary increase for a person depending on his or her job, and sustained performance level. LEP is not willing to recognize unusual bursts of outstanding performance by salary increases, preferring instead to reward a one-time contribution in a special awards program. Salary increases are reserved for sustained high performance.

Finally, as a whole the system's effectiveness depends on the employees' conviction that it is being equitably administered. Each employee must see that both the individual managers and the company as a whole take seriously their obligation to make the system work. Jobs that are incorrectly classified; individual performance that is measured wrongly, or not measured at all; or pay increases that reflect favoritism not real performance will, if common enough, result in so many people like Tom Canavan who distrust the system that it cannot operate effectively.

AVOIDING FAVORITISM

Favoritism is an especially difficult problem to control, since by its nature both the manager practicing it and the employee who benefits have an interest in keeping it concealed. Other employees may suspect, but have little evidence that it is occurring. The suspicion alone is often enough to ruin the fragile trust upon which a company and its employees depend.

LEP encountered a difficult experience in favoritism at a West Coast plant. As in many manufacturing facilities, production employees were anxious to have the extra earnings created by opportunities to work overtime. John Williams was the plant manager when employee attitude surveys began to show a rapid increase in reported dissatisfaction.

What was particularly confusing to Williams was the message that a primary cause of the current discontent in the plant was the method of awarding overtime. Williams had himself taken care to be sure that the company had a policy that prevented favoritism. Was the policy being neglected?

Company policy provided that a record be kept of the overtime worked by each employee each month. When overtime assignments were available, the employee with the lowest accumulated overtime in the month was offered the first opportunity to work overtime. Only if that employee refused to work was the opportunity offered to an employee who had already worked more overtime. Although in an emergency the company might assign overtime on an involuntary basis, the policy was one of voluntary overtime and of distributing overtime opportunities equally among the employees.

In the next few days Williams verified that the policy was not being neglected. Each shift foreman had been keeping a list of overtime worked by each employee. And when an opportunity to work overtime arose, the foreman did go first to the employees who had worked the least overtime.

In one instance Williams watched Jacob Phillips, the second shift foreman, fill two overtime assignments. First Phillips determined that he needed two employees to stay over on Friday evening for several hours. Then he consulted the overtime list. It was late in the month, yet Oscar Peterson and Roland Black had worked no overtime and were at the bottom of the list. Phillips went to Black first.

"I've got about four hours of overtime for tomorrow night," he said. "Do you want to work it?"

"Darn!" Black answered. "I'd like to; I need the money, but I promised the kids I'd take them to a ball game. If I had known earlier, I'd have set another night for the game, but I can't change it now. Isn't there some way you can give me more notice?"

"Sorry," Phillips said, "but I wasn't sure we'd need the work until today."

Phillips's discussion with Peterson had the same result. Since both low men had refused the Friday night overtime, Phillips went back to his list. It was not until he reached the top of the list that anyone was willing to accept the overtime. The first person to accept was Sally Wallace.

"Sally," Phillips said, "I have some more overtime available for tomorrow night. Do you want it?"

"Sure," she said. "You know Joe and I don't go bowling except on Saturday nights. You'll be there, too, this Saturday, won't you?"

"Yes," Phillips replied, "we'll be there. And I'll put you down for the overtime."

Williams couldn't see anything wrong with how Phillips handled the overtime opportunity, and he seemed to do it this way each time. Perhaps there is no problem, Williams thought. But a few days later when he talked again with some of the more loyal employees they insisted there was still a problem. "Some people are making a lot of money because they are getting all the overtime," he was told, "and the rest of the people are mad about it."

LEP staff from different plants met with employees from Williams' plant at sporting events, community occasions, and bars. Repeatedly they heard about a system of favoritism which stayed within the letter of the company's rules, but went far outside the spirit. This is how it worked. Early in a week when supervisors saw the possibility of overtime being required on the weekend, they privately cautioned their friends among the employees to hold the weekend open, in case overtime was available. Often employees did not hear of the overtime until Thursday or Friday, when it was formally scheduled. The supervisors went to the highest person on the overtime list, just as required, but usually that person was busy. The supervisor then worked his way down the list, getting refusal after refusal, until he got to his friends who, having been forewarned, had kept the weekend free to work. By this simple, informal process, supervisors were allowing their close associates among the employees to enhance their earnings far beyond what less favored employees could achieve.

Williams's remedy was to require the plant manager to review the overtime distribution in each area, to flag uneven distribution, and to investigate its source. With higher level management watching their activities, supervisors ceased to engage in blatant favoritism.

A PRACTICAL REASON FOR CONFIDENTIALITY

Many companies believe that openness is a good policy that helps the company preserve employee good will. The assertion is that secrecy engenders suspicion and causes employees to waste time trying to get information about how other employees are treated and how management decisions are made. This is probably true where a company's systems for assigning work or compensating people are poorly managed.

But lack of confidentiality can also cause problems. In particular, it encourages employees who are not the best contributors to complain to managers about the favorable treatment given those who are. The nuclear service arm of a large electric company recently converted from a system of salary confidentiality to one of openness. The result was chaos. The 20 percent spread in pay between top and average performers has narrowed dramatically.

Unable to persuade employees that other employees should receive higher pay, managers could not resist the pressure to give the same pay increases to almost all employees.

Perhaps in a perfect world, managers and subordinates could be perfectly open with each other not only about their own relationship, but everyone else's as well. But the real world makes this very difficult. For one thing, often employees do not know in detail about other employees' performances. The less repetitive the task, the more initiative taken, the greater the range for creativity, the greater the payoff for individual execution, the less likely one employee is to know in depth the expectations about and performance of another employee. Thus, in an open system if one employee complains about another's pay the supervisor must often give out extensive information about the performance of the other employee—and this can seem to be a violation of privacy to the person being talked about. As a rule managers do poorly in rewarding true performance when there is a great deal of openness in the process. This is true of salary differences based on performance and of the selection of people for promotion (see Chapter 7).

A general rule of thumb is that openness about a salary system causes the differential which managers actually pay outstanding performers over average performers to decline by half. Specifically, a company which successfully maintains pay confidentiality can expect to have top performers earning between 10 and 20 percent above average performers. A company which not only maintains confidentiality, but also is able to get managers to work out performance targets with employees and to measure the results carefully, may achieve a 30 to 40 percent spread. Openness, as a practical result, cuts these differentials in half. Hence the practical business reasons for confidentiality.

NO FORCED DISTRIBUTIONS

A pay for performance system that utilizes confidentiality as an important element is not thereby an immoral or improper system.

Although few are now conditioned to think this way, a person's salary may legitimately be considered an aspect of personal privacy, information not available to others. Furthermore, a pay for performance system allows a person to influence his or her own pay level through quality of performance; it also fulfills the important goal of treating the employee fairly.

But we must always return to the obligations which managers must meet in order for the system to be perceived as fair by employees. In order to control costs, many companies force each manager to meet a certain distribution of top performers, excellent performers, satisfactory performers, and so forth. This is a "forced curve," in which some employees are required to be at the lower end of the performance rankings. Exceptions may be provided by individual managers on an unusual basis; but the forced curve is reasonably tightly adhered to. The reason for the forced curve is to control costs by limiting the expected upward creep of performance ratings.

At LEP there is no forced curve. Each manager is instructed to rate those people who report to him or her according to actual performance. A curve which forces some into the lower rankings, even though they may have done excellent work, is believed to be incompatible with the fair treatment the company tries to accord each individual employee.

How then does LEP control the upward creep of performance ratings? The major method is to hold managers who have large units of employees reporting to them to distributions of performance ratings based on large numbers. Thus, a plant or division should show a curve similar to the forced curve other companies use. (Generally in the United States today outstanding and excellent performers combined are about one-half the total distribution.) Where performance ratings are creeping up, on balance, the plant or division manager goes to the managers who report to him or her to be sure that they and their subordinates are assessing people's performances realistically.

Other companies use additional devices. A large New York City bank tries to avoid performance creep by requiring that whenever a person is promoted, his or her initial performance appraisals must be no higher than the satisfactory level. As explained to the employee, this policy reflects the employee's need for time to learn the job.

PERSONALIZED PAY

Most compensation systems in large companies in the United States today are so rigid and bureaucratic that it is surprising to find so many elements of flexibility in LEP's system. Managers may award performance appraisal ratings without reference to any fixed curve. Managers are able to give larger salary increases to top performers, and are permitted (even required) to keep salary ranges and each individual's salary confidential.

Finally, for the top 1,000 managerial jobs LEP has done away with salary ranges altogether. Sound business reasons, which had their roots in human behavior and attitudes, caused this change. The salary ranges, which were informally known to the managers involved, were interfering with career progress and planning. Managers were seeking advancement to the specified job levels and the upper extremes of the salary ranges, rather than concentrating on their own contributions and performance, and the overall return to the corporation.

Instead of job levels, LEP now has "peer groups," covering division presidents, vice presidents, and top functional managers respectively. For these people, pay increases are based on the supervisor's evaluation of the individual's performance, without numerical guidelines. Instead, the criteria are broadly stated in terms of the quality of the manager's performance and whether or not he or she is "paid well" compared to people at similar levels in other companies. There is a great deal of flexibility even in what may be termed a "personalized system of pay administration."

Will personalized pay spread down the ranks in U.S. business? For decades companies have developed compensation systems to treat people alike—in order to ensure that managers do not exercise favoritism in granting pay increases. Even managers' actions in pay for performance systems are tightly regulated by a central personnel staff that issues quantitative guidelines for increases for people depending on their performance level and current place in a salary range.

At LEP top management has developed such confidence in its highest managers that they are now given only the broadest guidelines and are expected to treat each of their subordinates individually, in a personalized manner. Perhaps in the next few years enough American managers will become competent in the development, evaluation, and appraisal of individual contributions that personalized rather than bureaucratic pay decisions can be extended to many more business organizations. In the old days personalized pay meant favoritism—tomorrow it can mean recognition of individual motivation, contribution, and performance.

SUMMARY

Sameness is not necessarily fairness in compensation. Today people want to be recognized for their individual contributions. This, to them, is fair. Managers have much latitude to administer pay both to encourage and to recognize individual performance and contributions. It may be possible to abandon altogether compensation systems that deal with people as members of a group and instead move toward a system that makes significant differentiations between people. In the present environment this may be essential to retain employees who are crucial to the success of the firm.

The conventional wisdom of management is that as certain businesses mature, less qualified people are best suited to manage them. Thus the company saves on compensation because lower quality people are less valuable. But is this view justified in today's very competitive environment?

8

Evading The Business Maturity Trap

When John Boyd at Megalith, Inc. was told that he could not give pay increases to hold his key managers, he was also told that he did not really need them. The growth of his division was largely over; sales had leveled off and the corporation's planning staff saw his businesses in a new light. Instead of being areas into which the company was prepared to put investment dollars, his division was now expected to provide cash for investment to other ventures. Boyd's division had been moved into a "harvest" phase.

"Your product lines are mature," the corporate planners told Boyd. "We look for little growth. Your job now is to do everything possible to cut costs, by rationalizing production, delivery, and service, and to do it with a minimum of investment. Yours is a profitable division, and we want to use the surplus funds it generates to help the company acquire a portfolio of businesses that have the potential for high growth in the future."

Since his division's mission in the corporation's overall strategy had been altered, Boyd was told he did not need the same type of high performing managers he had previously employed. Actually, it was good that the young tigers had been lured away to

145

other companies, since they would surely have been unhappy in the changed environment.

In a mature business, executives could not be offered the chance to move up the corporate ladder, except quite slowly. In place of new ideas and innovation, a persistent devotion to cost cutting and efficiency building was required. In place of leadership spark, administrative steadiness was required. Boyd's top people would have been misfits for these jobs. The division's businesses were now mature, unexciting; they no longer required a cadre of ambitious individuals. Instead a small group of steady managers was enough; a few smart people and a mob of drones could make the division go as well as its mission in the corporate strategy required.

Boyd was able to see the bent of mind which caused the planners to talk to him this way. There was a certain logic to their arguments, and he was not surprised that both Frank Nicodemus and Allen Witfield had adopted the planners' point of view. Boyd's division no longer had top priority in his company, cash and human resources were put to better use elsewhere, and his own role and that of his managers had turned to one of caretaking.

FALLING BEHIND IN PRODUCTIVITY

Boyd was not the only high level executive, in his own or in other companies, being given a caretaking assignment for a business his company now considered mature. "We're in the textile industry," an executive of a medium-sized company said, "which is considered a sunset industry. There are lots of people available, most of whom can do the unexacting jobs we need done. We don't anticipate problems getting people like that."

A survey taken for this book late in 1983 of division-level managers in more than 200 large U.S. companies found some 24 percent which had been given an objective of maintaining the division's market share, rather than attempting to grow. Not only their established objective set these businesses apart from others in corporate portfolios, but also the way the mature divisions were managed.

Divisions to which companies had assigned rapid growth objectives were more likely to plan for the long term, as well as for the next year. Mature divisions were not likely to have forecast their staff requirements ahead, nor to have inventoried talents or skills; expenditures on training and development were very low; and plans for replacing key managers if they left the company were minimal. All divisions with a rapid growth mission were interested in the performance of their people and the impact of the organization's style and quality on the motivation of its people. A large group of the mature businesses expressed no such interest.

Apparently, when a division was assigned the status of a mature business, its management became a backwater; poorer quality people were assigned to the business, and it was no longer managed for the long term. A top executive of a large electronics firm described the situation in its mature businesses as follows: "Out of the several hundred people we have in key manufacturing areas, only 10 percent were trained or had degrees in manufacturing; and over 60 percent of the managers had been with the company 25 years or more." Asked why, the executive said, "It's because we put the people in these businesses on a cost return basis, rather than on a visionary planning basis. We put the managers under too much pressure to meet a 30-day financial target."

In mature manufacturing businesses managers accepted high rates for the financial payback on new equipment, so little new equipment was brought in; new products were allowed to proliferate in the production mix; plants grew in size until the largest became virtually unmanageable, less because of technical than human and social considerations, and little was invested in the human side of the organization.

As Wickham Skinner, a perceptive long-term student of operations management describes it, the pressures to lower costs seemed to drive companies into making products and parts rather than obtaining them from suppliers; into creating high volume but special production processes; into building few, but large plants with locations dictated by transportation. But these choices contributed directly to "complexity, inflexibility, lack of focus, and problems in control and manageability."[1]

Top managers and corporate planners believe that mature businesses placed in a harvest, or cash-producing, mode by the company do not need very good human talent. Yet ironically, as those placed in charge followed the line of least resistance supposedly mature businesses, whose profits could be siphoned off to support other activities of the company, were soon caught in intense competition and lost money rapidly.

Nowhere is the failure of American business to carry out an overall strategic concept more apparent than in our heavy manufacturing industries. Twenty years ago a large part of the world market belonged to U.S. firms and most had a firm grip on our domestic market. Apparently secure from competition except among themselves, U.S. companies switched to harvest strategies. The efficacy of using less imagination and less energetic managers to run these businesses was accepted. Productivity stagnated.

In 1967 Japanese manufacturing had labor productivity averaging 39 percent of the U.S. level. By 1981 the Japanese level was 98 percent of the U.S. level and it surpassed the U.S. figures in 1983. These are not the rates of change in productivity, in which the Japanese have surpassed us for many years; but the absolute levels, upon which the survivability of industries and also the general living standards of our population depend.

In automobiles the Japanese began at 42 percent of the U.S. level of productivity in 1967, surpassed the American level in 1979, and by 1981 were 20 percent ahead of the American companies. This means that in 1981, American autoworkers would have had to earn only four-fifths of Japanese pay scales for labor costs per unit of production in both countries to have been equal.

In steel the comparison is far worse for our country. By 1981 Japanese labor productivity was 115 percent, more than double

---

[1] Wickham Skinner, "Manufacturing Strategy in Mature Industries," *Journal of Business Strategy* (February 1980): 6.

the U.S. level. For labor costs per unit of production (a key measure of the competitiveness of companies in the two countries) to have been equal, American employees' pay rates would have had to have been less than half those paid in Japan. In a sense, this is all American workers, supported by American technology and management, could expect to earn on a fair trade basis.[2]

These statistics are based on Japanese sources, and may be overestimates. Our own government's numbers are lower, but show the same trend. By 1980 Japanese labor productivity in iron and steel was estimated at 41.5 percent over our own and Japanese labor costs per unit of output at 37.5 percent of our own. American steelworkers, less productive for whatever reasons than their Japanese counterparts, earned twice as much (in dollar terms) per hour. But rising productivity had nonetheless paid off for Japanese workers, who in 1964 had earned not half of the U.S. steelworkers' average pay (as in 1980) but only one-sixth.[3]

Attempting to harvest their steel businesses, American companies diversified in oil, financial services, and other growing businesses. But the mature businesses did not perform as expected. Instead, each became subject to such fierce competition from abroad, that losses rather than cash surpluses became common. In steel and in other businesses as well, a strategy of harvest could not be left to take care of itself. It had to be implemented carefully and by good managers, just like strategies of growth.

GROWTH-MATURITY-DEMATURITY CYCLE

What is the concept of business maturity? Simply put, a business first passes through a stage of rapid growth, then levels out for a long period of slow growth, stability, or slow decline; this phase

---

[2] Estimates from "White Paper on Labor," Ministry of Labor, Tokyo, 1981, published in *Pacific Basin Quarterly*, No. 10 (Summer/Fall 1983): 3.

[3] D. Quinn Mills and Malcolm R. Lovell, "Competitiveness: The Labor Dimension," in *United States Competitiveness in the World Economy* (Cambridge: Harvard Business School, 1984): 436.

is labeled maturity (see Figure 8.1). In this phase a company tries to retain market share, while putting profits into other pursuits. Efforts to gain market share—to grow—are believed to be foolish, both because they require investment of resources which could be more profitably used elsewhere and because they might spark price competition from the other companies in the business.

But the last 20 years have demonstrated that what is one manager's mature industry is another's opportunity for rapid growth. In industry after industry in this country where the whole market has grown little, new competitors have grown rapidly, gaining sales and market share from established companies. In steel, autos, copper, electrical machinery, textiles, apparel, footwear, and lumber products, foreign producers have entered the American market to grow rapidly at the expense of established American firms. In construction, communications, airlines, trucking, and financial services, new domestic competitors have gained at the expense of established companies.

Apparently mature industries are not mature at all if maturity means that nothing of business significance is likely to happen there. To explain this phenomenon in the auto industry, three

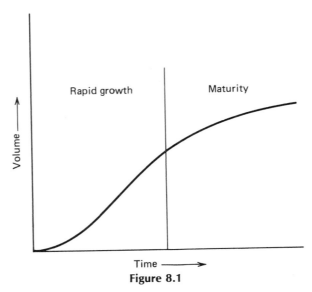

Figure 8.1

scholars developed the concept of dematurity.[4] At the core of their concept was the observation that any of several events or circumstances should propel an industry from maturity into dematurity. For example, a new technology could reduce production costs dramatically, giving an advantage to the producer who invested in the technology. The semiconductor provided the basis for a new group of entrants to the data processing industry. A less expensive set of labor policies could also provide an umbrella under which new competitors could emerge, as nonunion operations provided an opportunity for many new construction companies to become established. A change in external circumstances might prompt basic changes in an industry's product, so that new firms could gain an advantage by producing a better product than those of established firms. For example, in the U.S. auto market, the gasoline price increases of the 1970s brought into prominence the smaller, front-wheel-drive vehicles that foreign manufacturers had developed.

The problem with the maturity model, it seems, is that it did not provide for these kinds of major changes. It had assumed a product or set of products with slowly changing features, produced by processes which slowly tended to greater efficiency (the so-called learning curve). Without major discontinuities, or anyone anxious to exploit them, the maturity model and the harvest strategy which accompanied it served well enough. But in the 1970s and 1980s a swarm of entrepreneurs, some in large companies and others on their own, were anxious to exploit any opportunity to turn someone else's mature business into their own high growth company.

For today's managers, the more accurate long-term way of thinking about a business is not the trend to the maturity model of Figure 8.1, but instead the cyclical model represented in Figure 8.2, in which periods of growth are followed by periods of stability, only to give way at some point to renewed growth.

---

[4] William J. Abernathy, Kim B. Clark, and Alan M. Kantrow, *Industrial Renaissance* (New York: Basic Books, 1983): 15–29.

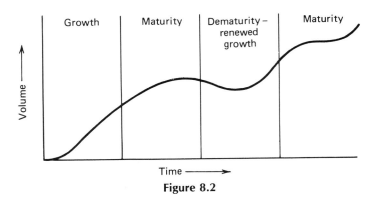

Figure 8.2

Alternatively, the process may be thought of as a circle (see Figure 8.3) in which phases of growth give away to maturity over time, then maturity gives away to dematurity. This in turn allows rapid growth for those companies exploiting the technological or market opportunities which emerge in the dematurity phase.

Top performing managers must know where their businesses are in this cycle, and fashion investment and marketing to that phase. They must recognize the onset of dematurity, invest in the new technology and people necessary to exploit the changes, and push the organizations into growth at the expense of other competitors. Only in this way can their businesses succeed.

Recognizing the phase of the business and taking the necessary actions to exploit its opportunities is not something the caretaker

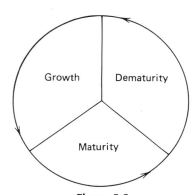

Figure 8.3

manager can do. Nor is it something that can be left exclusively to corporate planners far removed from the circumstances of the business itself. Planners will eventually recognize the change in phase of a business, but often too late to respond successfully to the competition. The cash cow has got to be preserved, not lost to competition. This perception turned the 1970s cash cow into the 1980s core business.

WHAT IS OUR BUSINESS? WHO ARE OUR COMPETITORS?

Because a business goes through recurrent phases, it is never fully a sunset business; at least not if it is understood correctly. Even the classic counterexample, the buggywhip manufacturer, is not an exception. At the dawn of the automobile age it would have seemed certain that the buggywhip manufacturer was in a sunset business. What was the business? If the manufacturer thought of it only as buggywhips, then the business was in a virtually final phase. But if it was a transportation accessory business, then it was in reality in a dematurization phase and about to break into decades of rapid growth. The transportation business neither matured nor disappeared; it blossomed. But change accompanied growth. Some manufacturers saw this and adjusted; some failed to see it and disappeared.

"What business are you in?" the CEO of a heavy equipment manufacturing company asked the executive in charge of the company's heavy drill business.

"We're in the drill business," the executive responded irritably. What the heck is this about, he thought to himself.

"No, you're not," the CEO suddenly exploded, "You're in the hole business. Our customers don't want drills, they want holes. They only buy drills to make holes. If our competitors can think of a better or cheaper way to make holes, they'll buy from them. You go think about that!"

Products such as drills go through a life cycle that has an ending. Products mature, decline, and disappear. Businesses, properly understood, never do. A business is the meeting of a certain need. The methods by which the need is met change, sometimes rapidly, imposing costs of adaptation on business. All successful businesses go through a succession of products; an unsuccessful business rides a single product to its inevitable decline and disappearance.

How can a manager keep alert to the possible dematuration of a business? A first technique is to watch the competition. This is something at which both American and foreign firms have become adept in recent years. Newly manufactured products are quickly bought by competitors, dismantled, and if possible, copied. Similarly new services are quickly copied.

The real task is to correctly identify competitors, because today they come from unexpected directions. When a company watches only the traditional competition, it may be unaware of the new. For example, who is the competitor of a nationwide bus line? Greyhound found that it was not only Continental Trailways, but also start-up, low cost airlines that brought the cost of flying between major cities down below the price of bus tickets. Greyhound was forced into a strike and other severe measures to reduce costs.

Regional banks' first competitors were other banks in the same region. A few years ago they became money market funds; then the deregulated thrift institutions; then the large money center banks; and now Sears, Roebuck and Company. The money center banks once watched only each other. But today innovations come from the financial subsidiaries of industrial companies, such as the General Electric Credit Corporation.

If top management does not see the onslaught of dematuration in a business, its employees may. John Boyd of Megalith had a warning, but failed to recognize it. His best managers were leaving in part because they saw his business slipping into an also-ran position. He was, however, too blind to recognize this and allowed himself to be satisfied with their insistence that too little pay alone was at the root of their dissatisfaction. Had he probed more deeply, as did the interviewers from the consulting firm, he would have discovered that his managers knew what the competition was doing, and that his organization had slipped from leadership.

"We're a mature industry," the vice president for operations of a heating equipment company commented. "We're high on investment in people; good managers are our biggest need." This is a very different concept from that of fitting unimaginative people to the mature business. Only with good managers can the signals of a switch toward dematuration be perceived. Only with good managers can the slow moving mature organization suddenly be revitalized to take advantage of an opportunity.

The mature phase creates its own problems, however, by seeming not to provide opportunities for helping people advance. Where is the challenge? The opportunity for pay increases? The opportunity for promotions? They are not easy to find, but some companies are providing them.

Even slow growth companies open new offices, branches, distribution centers, retail outlets, or plants. These provide challenges and broader experience for existing managers. In diversified companies which find few synergies among their businesses, the movement of people can provide both a challenge and a unifying tie. A metals company which has in recent years acquired a legal services firm, an insurance company, and an oil operation finds moving managers among the divisions provides opportunities to bring new perceptions and a heightened awareness of the overall business climate to their organization.

HAVE A BUSINESS—NOT A PRODUCT

The failure to distinguish a business from a product has as its counterpart the failure to recognize what separates a successful modern corporation from a single business. Venture capitalists are like start-up manufacturers with a product that can be sold rapidly to attain large revenues and good profitability. One of the largest venture capitalists insists that a start-up have the potential for $40–$50 million in volume in four to five years. At this point the company can be sold to the public, and "harvested" for the venture capitalist, who ordinarily takes profits at this point.

The public investors, however, often have bought not a business but a single product company. When that product hits the maturity stage, which may be quickly in an industry with rapid technical evolution, the company slows down. If the product is superceded, the company may fail, leaving investors with large losses in their investments.

Only innovation can keep a company going. Asked how his large computer company assessed the competitive strength of new entrants to their business, an executive answered: "We watch their research and development budget. Do they have enough engineers at work on next generation products? Anyone can have a good single product, but that isn't enough to worry us."

Successful companies are never single product companies; nor are they ordinarily primarily manufacturers. Distribution and sales efforts are as important as the products a company offers. The top performing industrial companies today do far more than provide products. They assist the consumer in meeting the basic need at which products are directed.

For example, most major industrial companies now provide options and opportunities to customers for financing their purchases. So much is this the case today and so many profits have been found in the financing, that from a profitability viewpoint, many companies are financial service companies with an industrial attachment. IBM has long been described as a sales organization with a manufacturing division. General Motors Corporation has evolved into a financial services organization with a manufacturing base. But this is too simple a view.

The most successful modern organizations combine sales, customer financing, new product development, and manufacturing in a mixture so integrated that any missing component is a serious omission. Manufacturing companies, those which think of themselves in this limited fashion, are reluctant to look to retailers, financial service companies, or research laboratories for ideas on how to manage their operations. This is a form of management myopia, of failing to understand the business they are in, for the products they manufacture are only a part of what attracts the consumer and ultimately contributes to their revenues.

Whether in a single business or a multibusiness firm, the successful executive today has the attributes of the best general managers. Any managerial style said to be appropriate to the mature business but not to business generally, is dangerous to its survival. Caretaker managers tend to be undertakers; and the few dollars saved by employing them are gained at the risk of the vitality of the business itself.

BREAKING OUT OF MATURITY

How do companies avoid the maturity trap? The most important means is self-discipline: forcing themselves to watch competitors and to listen to their own people for signs of dematurity opportunity. Most important is developing the habit of mind that denies long-term maturity as a concept and guide to management, and that searches continually for change. Recent years have presented more opportunities than most, though not all businesses are bursting out of a maturity stage. The art of management involves correctly assessing the readiness for a shift from maturity to dematurity in each business. Breaking a business into the dematurity stage can be done in several ways.

Via Technology

Technological advances are continual today, offering significant opportunities. The microchip made possible the personal computer, which revolutionized data processing and bids to revolutionize management and administrative tasks. Biogenetics has spawned new generations of products for human health and for animal husbandry. Both the microchip and genetic engineering are in start-up phases, and will have applications in many fields of human need. The search for applications of technology is a central way to break open a mature business.

Many companies are placing their bets with large research and development budgets. Allied Corporation is betting on a system of enhanced research and development which is closely tied to marketing's perceptions of customers' needs.[5] General Electric Company is betting that the computerized and robotized factory of the future can make GE's own products more competitive by driving down manufacturing costs, and that it can be sold to other companies, creating a vast new business for GE. IBM is looking to more flexible manufacturing processes to control costs while meeting the proliferation of products in today's information processing marketplace.

Technology often does not serve very well as a road to profitability. While a business may be revitalized through new technology, other companies may rapidly apply the technology, removing the advantage of the pioneer. Apple Computer, Inc. was the first to develop the personal computer, but many other companies rapidly followed suit, including IBM, whose marketing prowess stripped Apple of much of its early start advantage. Black & Decker Company appeared in the marketplace early with "smart" hand tools—those with a microprocessor controlling the speed of blades and drills—then Sears with its marketing strength followed with considerable success.

Via Marketing and Price Cutting

A surprising number of American companies remain product driven—relying on their sales force and distribution channels to dispose of whatever engineering and manufacturing chose to produce. With the increasing force of competition in recent years, this strategy has become hazardous.

To break out of a stagnant business some companies are relying on new marketing channels. The discount clothier has opened

---

[5] "Allied after Bendix," *Business Week*, 12 December 1983, 76.

up the hitherto mature world of the department store, forcing the large chains to cut margins or to lose market share. So provoked are the chains by the new competition that at the industry's trade association meeting in 1983 the chairman of an established chain attacked discounters for their practices and threatened to reply in kind.

Similarly, the stock brokerage business was opened to discounters. The bull market of September 1982–August 1983 disguised the seriousness of the challenge as record trading volume earned profits for established Wall Street firms. In that year of a bull market Merrill Lynch Pierce Fenner & Smith, Inc. added almost 6,000 employees and participated in a bidding war for salaries of top performers.[6] But when the market leveled off in the fall of 1983, then tumbled in early 1984, the established firms found their costs far too high to compete successfully with the discounters.

Business maturity is a fleeting stage. Technology, external events, and consumer preferences continually offer opportunities to break out into a dematurity stage. Careless managers with little ambition or imagination will not recognize the opportunities. No company can afford them.

SUMMARY

Throw out the old idea that some businesses do not really need top-notch people because the businesses are mature. In today's competitive environment few companies can adhere to this philosophy and survive. Products mature, but a business properly defined does not. So-called business maturity often turns out to be a temporary phase that ends with the loss of market share to new competitors. High quality people will be central to the success of attempts to preserve mature businesses against new competitors.

[6] "Brokerage Firms Spiraling Cost," *Wall Street Journal*, 3 February 1984, p. 25.

9

Holding Key People
And Protecting Yourself
If They Leave

In 1980 a large conglomerate acquired a promising young semiconductor company. Headquartered on the East Coast, the conglomerate was a $20 billion a year business noted for its strict financial and managerial controls. One of many informal, laid-back counterculture companies in California's Silicon Valley, the semiconductor company was doing barely $50 million in sales per year.

"How can this acquisition work?" financial reporters asked of the conglomerate's chief executive officer. "You're mixing oil and water."

"Not so," the CEO insisted. "We've given the semiconductor company far more autonomy than our other divisions. They'll keep their own officers and management style. The only thing they have to do is continue to grow as they've been doing, and conform their financial results to our reporting system. And we've given them an unlimited draw on our financial resources—something we've never done before. We've told them that whatever capital they can use, they can have. The more the better for we have tremendous confidence in their business."

"What do you get out of it?" he was asked.

"Our company needs a window on semiconductor technology," he replied. "We think it is going to revolutionize large parts of our business, and we think these are the best people in the semiconductor business."

The conglomerate paid tens of millions of dollars for the small company, and set out with high hopes for the acquisition. A year later the chief executive and founder of the semiconductor company took off for a job as chief operating officer of a much larger and long established company. The conglomerate was not unduly troubled, since his successor had also been a founder of the company, and was widely believed to be the creative genius behind its success.

Unfortunately, the successor was not only a person of considerable self-confidence but also possessed an unbounded sense of his own superiority. He had become quite contemptuous of the executives at the conglomerate, and upon becoming CEO at the semiconductor firm did not hesitate to voice his feelings. When his verbal abuse began to be directed at the conglomerate's chairman, a confrontation was not long in coming.

The blowup resulted in the discharge of the semiconductor company's CEO. Unfortunately for the conglomerate, he had prepared well and took with him all the small company's chief engineers. The conglomerate was left with only the shell of the company it had acquired at so high a price.

David Packard, one of the two founders of Hewlett–Packard Company, was asked by entrepreneur Jim Pinto of Action Instruments what he thought was the key to running a successful business.

"People," Packard replied simply, "people."[1]

Packard was himself an excellent example of how important a single individual can be. Packard had initially worked for a

---

[1] Joel Kotkin, "A Call to Action," *Inc.*, November 1983, 88.

large company in the 1930s, but found its bureaucracy too confining. So on a shoestring he and Bill Hewlett founded the company that bears their name. A key to their success has been their ability to attract and retain excellent engineers. In the 1980s, more than 40 years after the company's founding, Hewlett–Packard remains the best respected company among faculty and students in American engineering schools, a reputation envied by such excellent companies as IBM and General Electric Company. Part of Hewlett–Packard's success is due to the effort they put into recruiting engineers; they are one of the few companies who use staff engineers rather than personnel professionals to recruit at engineering schools.

RESTRICTIVE COVENANTS

Getting good people is difficult enough; keeping them is a challenge that not only large companies but also small ones experience. The loss of key people can be an expensive annoyance to a large company, as it was to the conglomerate mentioned at the start of this chapter. But it can be a devastating blow to a small company.

Sandvac is a small plastic molding company established 15 years ago as the American subsidiary of a German chemical company. The company's technology is proprietary, and for several years it had no competition in the United States. However, as its market expanded, other companies developed similar processes and entered the marketplace against Sandvac.

Unable to protect its position by patents on its no-longer-unique technology, Sandvac came increasingly to depend on manufacturing know-how for its competitive edge. Cost effectiveness was gained by keeping the all-too-finicky equipment running as much of the time as possible. Sandvac soon developed maintenance and management techniques to squeeze as much operating time out of the equipment as possible. These operating techniques gave Sandvac a decided advantage over its competitors.

In 1980 Sandvac production managers and engineers began to leave the company; first one, then another, then yet another. The first told Sandvac's CEO, Roland Vesige, that he was tired of the Middle West (in this case Illinois), and was looking for a position on the West Coast. Sandvac wished him well. Six months later Vesige encountered his former employee at a trade show, where he was representing Sandvac's major competitor, a company based in Ohio.

Alerted by this incident to the possibility of subtle raids by its competitors on its key staff, Vesige looked for a way to respond. First, Sandvac developed two confidentiality agreements. All employees were required to sign a short form; all salaried employees signed a longer agreement. The long form included a commitment by the salaried employees not to compete with Sandvac for two years from the date of signing (a restrictive covenant). The company also executed nondisclosure agreements with its vendors and consultants.

Several months after these agreements had been signed by employees, a larger company only peripherally a competitor of Sandvac hired a production manager from one of Sandvac's plants. Fearing that this defection presaged a move by the other company into Sandvac's core business, Roland Vesige took the unusual step of writing to the division manager in the larger company who was the supervisor of Sandvac's former employee. The letter noted that the larger company had recently hired a Sandvac manager, and cited the terms of the noncompete agreement between Sandvac and its former employee. The letter said only that Sandvac wished the manager's new employer to be aware of the existence of the confidentiality agreement.

Vesige received no reply. But two months later Sandvac employees who had seen the former manager reported that he was very unhappy. Apparently, his new boss had been surprised and a bit intimidated by the letter he had received from Sandvac. In consequence he had transferred the former Sandvac manager to an assignment very different from his expertise. "He's so unhappy with what he's doing," Vesige was told, "that he's thinking of trying to get his old job back at Sandvac."

The third departure did not work out so nicely. A process engineer went to another competitor. Sandvac sent a letter advising of the confidentiality agreement, only to receive a reply saying that Sandvac should not try to intimidate other companies or its former employees.

"Can we enforce the noncompete agreement?" Vesige asked his attorney in a meeting following receipt of the letter.

"Have you specified what trade secrets you have? If not, the employee will simply say he wasn't aware of confidentiality."

"We haven't done that," Vesige replied. "But we will. However, couldn't we sue to keep him to the noncompete agreement?"

"You could try; but a court will not look favorably on your trying to keep the guy from earning a living."

So Sandvac did nothing, but it tightened its security system. Documents were now classified as "highly classified," "secret," or "not secret." A list of competitors was attached to the non-compete agreement; a confidentiality section specified the categories of trade secrets and provided that at termination or resignation all classified and secret documents were to be returned.

Sandvac's market continued to expand and competition intensified. More than ever Sandvac's advantage in the marketplace was derived from its manufacturing know-how. But know-how was very hard to classify and was not always put in writing. The confidentiality agreement seemed of decreasing value. In his mind Vesige relied more and more on the noncompete agreement.

Then Sandvac's executive vice president left to join a competitor. Vesige was stunned, both by the EVP's disloyalty and ingratitude, and by the windfall of technical and operating knowledge his competitor was likely to obtain. Furthermore, the EVP was party to all Sandvac's financial and product strategy for the upcoming five years, including Sandvac's plans for its first major product innovation in years.

Vesige heard of the loss of this key executive the night before the EVP had planned to tell him of it. Racing to company headquarters Vesige had security guards empty the EVP's office of all personal belongings, and place them in a pile on the front lawn. All company related papers remained in the office. When the EVP arrived at the company parking lot the next morning he was met by two security guards who escorted him to his pile of belongings, observed him as he carried several armloads to his car, then told him to drive away or face a trespassing complaint. He was no longer an employee of Sandvac.

At this point Vesige embarked on a survey of how larger firms handled the problem of the loss of key employees. Despite newsmagazine reports, he could find only a few companies which used a formal employment contract with employees.[2] Some of the contracts were indefinite in duration ("evergreen") and required an employee to give six months' notice of intent to leave. If the notice were given, the company would have the time to deny confidential information to the person leaving; whatever the person took would be outdated.

One large oil company required all managers to sign letters of resignation which could be accepted by the company at any time it chose. Other contracts were for six months at a time, continually reexecuted, and provided job security for the employee during that period. If he or she were discharged or laid off, the company paid the salary for the remaining months in the contract.

Some contracts provided for no competition by the employee for up to three years, but nonetheless obligated the company to only a few months' severance pay if the employee were let go. These provisions seemed more common abroad than in the United States. "No surprise," thought Vesige, who believed them to be unenforceable in most U.S. courts.

Vesige was surprised to find that some of the better high technology companies made no attempt to use noncompete agreements. Some which had used them in the past had abandoned them decades ago. In general, the legal problems of enforcing noncompete agreements in the United States seemed insurmountable. So much so that key companies did not even attempt to legally restrict

---

[2] See, for example, Keith McManus, "Who Owns Your Brains," *Forbes*, 6 June 1983, 168–179.

salespersons from going to a competitor and then attempting to sell the clients they had serviced for their former company. The legal impediments were two: first, the lack of willingness of many courts to interfere with free competition. Noncompete agreements seemed designed to interfere with freedom of the marketplace. Second, the willingness of courts to hear favorably the complaints of employees that a former employer was attempting to prevent their making a living in the trade they knew best.

Finally, an overwhelming concern was that restrictive covenants seemed to have a significant depressing impact on employees' morale. Vesige had noticed how engineers and managers hesitated to sign Sandvac's restrictive covenants. "Does this mean that I can't get a job elsewhere if you fire me?" he was asked. "This seems awfully strict," another complained. Yet another asked if his own lawyer should review it before he signed it. Clearly people were apprehensive about the document, and distrusted the company for insisting on it.

If a noncompete agreement was destructive of morale and could not be enforced in most situations, of what value was it, Vesige wondered. He decided to give it up. In its place, he convened a meeting twice a year with his key managers and engineers where he explained to them the importance of working as a team. "Sandvac is the means by which we earn a living, provide for our families, and obtain stature in our professional lives in the community. We are a team and Sandvac's success provides these things for all of us. If one of us leaves and goes to a competitor, he does a lot of harm to each of us; to us as individuals. I can't legally keep you from going—it doesn't work, as you know from our failures to get after the people who have left us in the past. And I don't know that I'd rely on the law anymore even if it worked. We have to rely on each other—that none of us will sell his or her teammates out."

CONFIDENTIALITY AGREEMENTS

While restrictive covenants seemed fruitless, confidentiality agreements did not. Sandvac carefully defined its "intellectual property'' and prepared agreements for its executives which included commitments not to divulge Sandvac's confidential material to outsiders, either during or after employment at Sandvac. Also in the agreement was an assignment to Sandvac of each employee's entire right or interest in any idea, invention, or design whether of an article, process, or procedure, whether patentable or not, which related to Sandvac's business and resulted to any degree from work done for or at Sandvac.

With restrictive covenants eliminated and confidentiality agreements buttressed, Vesige was pleased with Sandvac's legal position with respect to knowledgeable employees. Larger companies had been successful, he knew, in protecting their intellectual property by filing complaints when they suspected that defecting employees had passed on confidential information to competitors. The complaints rarely were litigated; far more commonly, private settlements were reached out of court. A big company with substantial legal resources and a good case was often able to intimidate its competitors into settling complaints. He wondered if a small company could be as successful.

In the end, having employees who felt closely involved with the company and accepted a moral obligation to it was a far better defense than the law against the loss of confidential information to competitors. Vesige committed himself to a series of meetings with his key employees to help them understand the competitive significance of their knowledge; only when they became conscious of this, would he ask them to sign Sandvac's confidentiality agreements.

SUMMARY

Holding key people is important not only because of their continuing contribution to the company, but also because of the advantage they might offer your competitors if they leave. Efforts to hold good people include good communications, compensation, commitment, and employment security. But these do not always work. Managers need to anticipate the possibility of the loss of key people and to provide sufficient safeguards to the company to protect confidential information. This can be done without inviting litigation and without invading the rights of current employees.

Attention also must be paid to members of the organization who once were, but are no longer, key performers although they may be in key positions. How can their careers be managed and their ability to contribute be accurately assessed?

10

Avoiding Deadwood

In the 1950s Rod Serling made his first film: an hour-long drama about an aging executive who had ceased to be effective in his job, and who was under pressure from his boss to resign.[1] It is not a comfortable film for managers to watch. Many can see people they know in their own companies in a similar situation; perhaps they can visualize themselves there as well not so many years from now.

Because the film is little seen today, it is useful to give a brief account of the story. Andy Sloan had been in his position at corporate headquarters for twenty years. In the beginning he worked for the company's founder. Years later a new chief executive officer took over, a man with great ambitions for the company. Over the next several years the new CEO built the company by aggressive marketing and acquisitions. He was a man tight with a dollar and hard on subordinates. He saw business as fiercely competitive, and tried to keep himself as firm and determined in his personal relationships as he thought was required in the harsh business climate. The more the company prospered, the more the CEO became convinced of his own rightness. And the more he resented what he saw as Sloan's failure to contribute.

[1] "*Patterns*" shown on the Goodyear Television Playhouse.

Soon Ramsey, the CEO, began to take his displeasure out on Sloan in the semipublic atmosphere of the company's management boardroom. At one point Ramsey exclaimed to Sloan after hearing a report, "You haven't had a new idea in years!" Sloan blushed. "That's not fair," he started to protest, then sank dejectedly into his seat.

Sloan had been promised an enlarged office in the executive suite of his company's headquarters. Instead, the additional space was allocated to a younger executive, newly hired as an assistant to the CEO. The new executive's responsibilities seemed surprisingly like his own. To everyone else in the company's top echelon it was clear that Sloan's successor was already on board.

Ramsey stepped up the pressure. The new executive was invited into the corporation's executive committee meetings. His viewpoints were routinely praised by Ramsey; Sloan's contributions, which grew fewer in number, were held up to ridicule.

Talking to a friend one day Sloan admitted that he now kept a bottle of liquor in his office, and often drank too much. He spoke of his wife, who complained that he had given his life to the company in preference to the family, and of his children who justified their father's continued absences by his position of importance in the company. "Your father built that company," his wife often told their sons.

But Sloan was not sure how much longer he could hold on. The humiliation was eating away at him; at his self-respect and his health.

"They keep chipping away at your pride," he confided, "your security, until at last you can't take it any more—and you resign."

"Why don't you just resign?" his friend asked. "Why do you stay here and take this?"

"The bigger the job," Sloan confided dejectedly, "the more you try to hold on to it."

In the movie Sloan took it as long as he could, and then suffered a fatal heart attack. The new executive, his replacement, protested Sloan's treatment to the CEO after his death. When offered Sloan's position, he accepted it, promising himself that he would never accept the humiliation Ramsey had given Sloan.

A NONPERFORMING EXECUTIVE

Managers can ponder much in this episode, both about themselves and about others. Could Andy Sloan have done the job Ramsey wanted? This is a fundamental question. Some managers who have discussed this film believe that the Ramsey–Sloan conflict illustrates a problem of communication: that Ramsey was not making clear to Sloan what he expected from someone in that position. Had Sloan understood, then he would have performed.

Perhaps. In many situations this is an accurate picture of the circumstance; this is the solution many management books offer for dealing with a nonperforming subordinate. In essence, the argument is that when a manager has a nonperforming employee, the manager should look inward first rather than at the employee. Have the tasks and expectations of performance been made clear to the employee? Does the employee have both the resources and the authority necessary to accomplish what is expected? Only after the manager is sure that all managerial responsibilities in the situation have been met should the subordinate's ability or commitment be scrutinized.

This is excellent advice for managers, but leaves unanswered what to do in those instances where it does not work; where the tasks, expectations, resources, and authority are each clear and adequate, and yet performance is inadequate. Managers should not delude themselves. Some people do not perform adequately at any time, and perhaps all people perform inadequately some of the time. There are many reasons; most of them are good in the sense that they are understandable. The job requires expertise that the incumbent lacks. The "Peter Principle" is the label commonly applied to persons promoted to levels in an organization at which they no longer have the skills to be effective. Jobs change as circumstances change. Technology grows more complicated, laws more restrictive, competitors more aggressive; scale expands, and the Andy Sloans fail to keep up.

Further, people burn out doing the same tasks year after year. Plugging away at the same problem gives a person a degree of expertise and professionalism, but it may also cause a rigidity of thinking, a blindness to new approaches, and a boredom that inhibits further contributions. Even though he or she is not effective now, a person who is burnt-out may be effective in a different assignment or after a rest.

Had Ramsey set clear performance goals for him, Sloan might have measured up, and he might not have. But there would have been no communications gap. And in the minds of many managers Ramsey would then have had what he lacked in the film: a legitimate, moral basis from which to fire Sloan. Had Ramsey set appropriate goals for Sloan, who then failed to meet them, and yet refused to resign, then Ramsey could have been justified in firing him. Yet Ramsey could have fired Sloan at any time, right or wrong, but did not. Why didn't Ramsey fire Sloan?

FIRING IS OFTEN UNWISE

"Why doesn't Ramsey just fire you?" Sloan's friend asks him in the film.

"At our level, people don't get fired," Sloan replied grimly. He was under no illusion; he knew Ramsey would not fire him, and that the initiative, whether to stay or resign, was his.

But why? People who have not managed a great deal usually resort very quickly to the supposed power of managers to fire unsatisfactory employees. When sales fall off in a division, fire the sales managers. When an acquisition goes sour, fire the person who supported it. When a secretary messes up a key memo fire the secretary. When Sloan doesn't do his job and refuses to resign, fire him.

Yet it is very hard to fire people; sometimes it is impossible, and often unwise. This can be true at any and all levels in an organization. Where employees are represented by a union, the manager must document inadequate performance and repeated warnings. Lacking this an arbitrator may reinstate the discharged employee.

If the manager in a nonunion company is seeking to avoid unionization (which applies to most American companies), such documentation may be just as necessary as if it is a union situation. The discharged employee may be a member of a protected group—a minority, woman, older employee, handicapped, or even a white male. Then the manager must document the employee's alleged inadequate performance so that no claim of prejudice or discrimination by the discharged employee can be sustained in court.

Today managers are as apt to file suit against a company for unfounded discharge, often alleging age discrimination, as are blue-collar or clerical workers. Regardless of the potential legal pitfalls—and they were far fewer in the 1950s when Ramsey felt he could not fire Sloan—discharge is to be avoided for other reasons. In the collegial atmosphere of people who must work closely together, firing is a jarring note. While the manager may know the discharge is justified other employees may not be aware of the circumstances. They are likely to ascribe different motives, "Sloan made a mistake on the Acme acquisition," they may say, "and that's why Ramsey fired him."

Managers are expected to take risks. If Ramsey will fire Sloan for a mistake, then he might fire another executive for one. "Better clear everything with Ramsey first," others might conclude. When this reaction occurs, the firing manager gets rid of one individual who is a problem at the cost of ruining the organization, causing other team members to quit acting as responsible contributors. Furthermore, a team usually works well because its members feel accepted and secure. They invest their energy and commitment as a result of that feeling. When a member is fired, others look to their own outside options. "It could happen to me," they fear.

This is not to say that good managers should not and do not discharge people. They do. Union contracts permit discharge for many reasons; company rules require it for certain behavior. A question which some top managers pose in assessing the suitability of up-and-comers for high management positions is, "Whom have you fired lately, and why?" Top managers expect the answer to be "Yes, I've fired some people, and here are the reasons why."

So a manager must discharge people, but it happens rarely and more often for some overt and generally indefensible act, such as embezzlement, rather than for lack of performance. The organization and the society in which the manager functions make firing an unusual and infrequent option.

OPENNESS VERSUS MANIPULATION

Unpleasant as he may seem, Ramsey's behavior requires consideration. What options did he have? He felt that he could not fire Sloan; yet Sloan was not performing. Ramsey knew he had in hand a replacement who could do better. And, if the replacement was like many up-and-coming managers, he or she was impatient to get Sloan—that old fogy—out of the way so that the next generation could show its mettle.

Whether or not Ramsey had adequately communicated his expectations about performance to Sloan, Ramsey had no doubt that Sloan knew he was dissatisfied with his performance. What then were Ramsey's options? His choice was to pressure Sloan overtly to resign. But he could have been more subtle. Perhaps the course of subtlety, or manipulation, which we will examine next, is even more reprehensible than the one which he chose. Cruel though Ramsey was, he was at least direct. In the actual course of events, Ramsey did not manipulate Sloan. He pressured him. For an example of manipulation in terminating an employee, we turn to a different incident.

John Turvey was vice president for manufacturing at a large diversified firm. His staff position at the corporate level had no operating responsibility. Over several years in his position he had accumulated respect and liking from his colleagues in both the line divisions and other corporate staff functions. The company for which Turvey worked began to have financial difficulties, at the heart of which were high costs in its manufacturing operations. The company's CEO became convinced that a more up-to-date and effective person was required to prod and assist the manufacturing executives in certain key divisions. But Turvey was too much a fixture in the company to be discharged.

The CEO called in the executives in charge of two large divisions with substantial manufacturing capacity. "Ask Turvey to get involved in your operations," he told them. "Bring him into the decisions on new technology. Ask him for programs to improve worker productivity. Pressure him for plans by which to get give backs from the unions." While each of these areas involved legitimate needs of the divisions, each division had capabilities in-house, and Turvey had not been asked to be involved before. The CEO suspected that Turvey would not think himself able to do much to help the divisions.

Several weeks later Turvey took the CEO aside at a company dinner and wondered aloud if the company could afford to let him retire early. "I'd need a substantial package," Turvey suggested.

The CEO assured him. "John, you're very important to this company. You know how we're struggling with getting our manufacturing costs down. I don't want to let you go."

The next morning the CEO called both division heads and told them to keep the pressure on John Turvey. Two more weeks had passed when Turvey next asked to see the CEO. Turvey started by mentioning that Bert and Sam (the division chiefs) were asking for lots of help. "I'm kind of swamped."

"Well, give them lots of help," the CEO encouraged him. "They need it."

"Shouldn't they have more capability in their own shops?" Turvey asked.

"No, John," the CEO answered. "You're our key guy on manufacturing. That's what you're here for. They ought to come to you."

Turvey left, visibly downhearted. More time passed, till yet another encounter took place between Turvey and the CEO. "How are you doing, John?" the CEO asked.

"Well, I'm having trouble keeping up. The divisions want me to do a lot of things I haven't done for a while. Maybe I should consider getting out. Remember we once talked about a better retirement package?"

"John, I'm not going to make it any easier for you to leave," the CEO said. "You're one of the best guys we have. If you want to leave, you've every right to—but I don't want you or anyone else thinking I'm pushing you out. I want you to stay."

"I know," Turvey answered, "and I appreciate it. But I think that I want to go. I can't do what the division guys are asking me to do."

Next morning the CEO called his two division chiefs. "Lay off John Turvey," he told them.

"But," one responded, "what if he changes his mind?"

"He won't," the CEO responded. "He's a straight guy, and he's ready to get out."

AVOIDING A BITTER END

Was the CEO a straight guy? That he was manipulating Turvey was certain. Would it have been better to be direct with him? Without the pressure from division executives, Turvey would not have wanted to leave. Yet their requests, though contrived, revealed to Turvey and confirmed to the CEO that Turvey could no longer do what business needs now required.

Again, a fairer, more direct, and more honorable method could probably have been found by which Turvey did not leave the company. An alternative assignment, perhaps a task force, could have used Turvey's talents while permitting a new person to take his current assignment.

So, in the end, in the sagas of Andy Sloan and John Turvey there is a problem with the CEOs and the retiring executives. Probably neither CEO was straightforward enough about what was expected. Surely both CEOs could have found alternative places for the displaced executives in their organizations where each could have made a contribution and felt renewed. Though the CEOs could not fire these executives, they could certainly transfer them, or insist that each accept an assignment to a different job or to a different task.

Much of the problem of managing people no longer fully effective in their jobs lies with the ineffective individuals. Why would

Sloan not resign? What caused him to hold on until the bitter end?

The pyramid of positions in an organization gets very narrow as it nears its apex. Of the many people who enter a company full of ambition and promise, very few will make it to the top. Most careers reach a plateau sooner or later. At some point, probably unknowingly, each person will reach the position which will, in time, turn out to have been the highest level of responsibility. And then, after a few more years, each person will begin to seem to be less effective in the job than previously.

For most it will not be that the manager is less capable in any absolute sense; comparatively, however, that person will be declining. The boss will want to see what a new viewpoint, new talents, and energy can bring to the position. It is a bit of the "What have you done for us lately?" syndrome, and unfortunately it comes at a time when what the executive wants to receive is gratitude for previous contributions. Gratitude there should be, but gratitude is not the basis on which an effective organization should make assignments.

Consider two managers who diverge in their contribution to the company. Joseph is a top performer; Samuels far less so. In the long term Samuels's satisfaction in his job will probably not long match Joseph's. People who make a real commitment to an organization draw much of their satisfaction from how effective they are in contributing.

Much of Andy Sloan's unhappiness in his job was due to his harsh treatment by Ramsey, but some of it undoubtedly was occasioned by Sloan's dawning recognition that he was no longer contributing what he had in the past, and what the organization now required. "Bring me proposals," Ramsey once shouted at him in a meeting, "not just carping."

The worst thing that can happen to a person in the business world is not ingratitude, which almost all experience, nor even to be caught in a political struggle (also common), but rather to become trapped in a position in which one becomes ineffective. Then a person struggles to hold on, knowing all the while that it is probably futile, and deriving little or no satisfaction from the job.

This is what happened to Andy Sloan. It will happen, in time, to almost all. But it is not inevitable, because long before the Ramseys of the world begin to force a person out, that person can assess his or her own situation and take steps to avoid the pain and embarrassment.

If a person recognizes that in time a decline in effectiveness will occur, then the person can watch for the signs that this is beginning to occur. Does the formal record show less effectiveness? Has the organization that person manages ceased to be as profitable? Do subordinates or colleagues appear less admiring, less respectful? Does the manager feel bored? It is not necessary to take an emotional pulse every day; but it is appropriate to do so periodically.

The point is to initiate a change while one still has influence and respect. Asking for a new assignment is not going to offend a superior who can always refuse. It makes a far smoother transition possible for the individual involved, however, even when the reassignment is to a parallel or lesser position. Then everyone knows that the person is no longer climbing the promotion ladder. Would it be better to suffer Andy Sloan's fate?

The executive vice president at the corporate headquarters of a large international metals company reached his fiftieth birthday. Carefully assessing his prospects, he decided that he was unlikely to gain the CEO position although he was personally convinced of his suitability for the post. It was unfortunate, he thought, and perhaps unfair, but the top job was almost certainly not going to be his.

Still, he was not old, not ready to retire (whether off or on the job). So he asked the CEO for an assignment to the operating level. Six weeks later the executive left his corporate level job, flew to Europe and a week thereafter assumed control of his company's operations in Europe. Far from corporate headquarters, as his own boss on the European scene and with the intense activity that operational jobs provide, he felt renewed by the challenge.

Why did his superiors at the corporate level not take the initiative in suggesting that he go to European operations? Partly because the reassignment might appear to be a demotion and they feared he would resent it. By proposing the change he rescued his career from a plateau and helped make it respectable in that company to move laterally or even down the organization's ladder in search of a place to contribute effectively.

The vice president of a large pharmaceutical company commented, "We have many scientists whose knowledge has become outdated. What are we going to do with these people? We've been trying to do some retraining, but the field is changing so rapidly that we can't keep up. We prefer to recruit from the colleges and let the outdated people go."

Most companies, despite good intentions, end up thinking this way. It is simply too complicated and potentially costly to try to manage the careers of scientists, engineers, and even managers whose skills are becoming obsolete.

This places considerable pressure on the individuals involved to plan their own futures by either attempting to keep up with changing technologies and skills, or attempting to find new assignments. Even if the new assignment is below the individual's current pay and classification level, it may still be the wisest move. Sometimes it is necessary to take a step backward in order to get the opportunity to move ahead again.

A multinational computer company's foreign affiliate could not get its U.S. divisions to send them effective managers. Executives plateaued in the United States were not retrained or given alternative assignments; instead they were shipped off to Europe. Repeated efforts by the top management in Europe finally identified a means to stop the practice. Each U.S. manager proposing a person for a two- or three-year assignment in Europe had to develop a "reentry" plan for the person proposed. The plan had to specify a job in America to which the executive would return after his or her foreign assignment.

This requirement reduced by half the number of persons recommended for foreign assignment. American managers had been sending people to Europe they did not want back. With the new requirement, assignments to Europe were made for managers who would benefit from the experience for their future assignments in the United States.

PEOPLE NEED NOT BE DEADWOOD

Individuals who are deadwood in their current positions may often be revitalized by a change of assignment, whether initiated by the company or by themselves. So much evidence in the experience of managers supports this conclusion that the real deadwood in companies may not be in individuals, where it is usually expected, but in units of the organization.

When a company builds a new facility, its officers think of the activity as an investment in a building and in equipment. Further, they know that the new facility will not last forever, so they make provision on the financial statements to replace the building and equipment at some time in the future. Specifically, the company takes a deduction against its earnings each year so that over a number of years a fund is set aside from earnings to replace the facility. Recognizing the need for companies to replace their plants and equipment over time through depreciation or a sinking fund, tax laws permit deduction of depreciation from a company's before tax earnings.

Buildings and equipment, however, are not the only aspects of a company's productive resources that wear out over time. After a new facility is built it is staffed with managers, supervisors, technicians, and employees. People learn how to operate the facility and establish ways of dealing with each other. After a few years the relationships become routinized.

Good managers keep physical equipment in good running order by a program of maintenance. They do the same for an organization by careful attention to the human relationships. Personal contacts are kept current; supervisors and employees get occasional reassignments and opportunities to develop themselves. Individuals are kept from plateauing by a combination of retraining and challenges.

Maintenance, however, does not keep plant and equipment from slowly becoming outdated. New technology is built into new machines. Old machine tools may be kept operating, but cannot usually be refitted for the advances made by digital controls. Old plants are designed to fit a certain layout of production, and cannot ordinarily be renovated to fit newer concepts; just as the old multistory building manufacturing complex cannot be upgraded into the large, one-story single building so much favored today. Maintenance keeps both plant and equipment in working order, but does not ordinarily modernize them—a new investment is needed.

Similarly, maintenance of the human organization does not ordinarily update it. Maintenance fills gaps in the ranks with new hires, transfers, or promotions; it keeps the lubricant of communications flowing so that activity does not grind to a halt. But the established ways of doing things are not altered. The human organization was fitted to the technology it first encountered. If both equipment and people are maintained, the two continue to work well, though they will nonetheless slowly become outdated. If the company updates technology by a major new investment but fails to update the human organization, it may encounter a mismatch and lose much of the blessing of the new technology.

Companies routinely set aside funds to replace the plant and equipment as they become obsolete. But companies make no such provision for the renewal of their organizations. This is a serious oversight, for a human organization can only be renovated with expenditures of funds on training, reassignments, job redesign, and substantial commitments of managerial time and effort. All of this is costly just as a new investment in the plant and equipment is costly.

Even though present-day accounting practice does not recognize the costs of renovating or replacing a human organization, experienced managers recognize the costs of changing the work habits of experienced employees to make the organization competitive. In some companies the problem is not limited to a few facilities, but may involve the key elements of the entire organization.

A new CEO recently took over one of the nation's largest financial service companies. The organization she inherited has its central office in a skyscraper in a large East Coast city. Even though some 25 organizational layers existed in the building, management had little idea about what employees thought or how they interacted at work. "Our biggest problem is that we have thousands of very fine people," the CEO commented, "who are working like hell and getting nothing done."

Nothing done! For years the company has sold and administered one of the nation's largest volumes of insurance. Unfortunately, as government decontrol hit financial services, a myriad of new products has been offered by competitors. But this company has not kept up. Its efforts to persuade political authorities to continue the regulations which protect its central business from competitors are failing. Its people are not yet developing products and sales efforts for the new environment. So thousands plug away as they always have at administering products which are increasingly outdated, while top management tries desperately to discover how to turn the organization around.

To get the attention of their people the company has begun to subcontract minor services. If employees begin to see some of the work they do going to others, perhaps they will be more accepting of new products and cost-cutting measures. But even should employees accept the need for changes, the company faces massive retraining and reorganizing costs.

ORGANIZATIONS AS DEADWOOD

In a sense, there is much deadwood in American companies. This deadwood seems to be made up of employees who are no longer effective at their jobs; but this is only the tip of the iceberg.

Far more important is the large number of organizations within our companies which are themselves outmoded; their methods of operation and interrelationships no longer fit the competitive challenge.

Managers often mistakenly presume that the problem in an ineffective plant or office is ineffective individuals, when it is the organization itself which is outdated. Usually people who appear to be deadwood can be revitalized with new challenges. The more difficult and costly matter, by far, is to revitalize an organization.

SUMMARY

Traditional management practice endorses the concept of dead-wood—people within the organization who are no longer capable or willing to contribute. In either case, before writing people off the company should take a good look within itself to see if there are structures or attitudes that encourage or even create deadwood. The values of the new managers make them more willing to assume responsibility for noncontributing members. The problem cannot always be solved, but it is well worth trying to save the company's investment in its human resources where at all possible. Getting rid of people believed to be burned-out does not necessarily get rid of the problems. In some cases the employee may have a better idea than the manager about how to begin to make a contribution again—perhaps a very different kind than the current job assignment allows.

11

Letting The Work Force Do More

As Rich Howards, the plant manager at Acme Motors' Danville plant, totaled up the year end figures he was startled. He knew that turnover among the plant's supervisory personnel had been high—but nearly 50 percent? He was even more shocked when he looked at the figures for newly hired or promoted supervisors. *Most* of them had left—either voluntarily or because they had been asked to leave.

In a quandary, Howards leaned back in his chair. What was going on? Sure, the job of manufacturing supervisor was a tough one. Supervisors were responsible for managing the production process including scheduling, equipment maintenance, ordering and inspecting parts, identifying and solving production problems, and maintaining quality and performance goals. The people side of the job was as large if not larger. Each supervisor was responsible for nearly 50 people on the production line, including responsibility for dealing with union officials, handling grievances, managing tardiness and absenteeism, establishing work standards and disciplining employees. The turnover data confirmed his growing suspicion that somehow things at the supervisor level were badly out of control.

"Workers today want eight hours' pay for eight hours of self-satisfying, well supervised work. Supervisors can't give it to them," Howards had told the vice president of his division. "So we have low morale, low productivity, and high costs.

"The first-level supervision bears the brunt of it. We put pressure on them from the top, and the workers put pressure on from below. They can't take the heat, so they get out.

"Recently we instituted a month-long training program for new supervisors. We knew from attitude surveys that there was a morale problem in the plant among supervisors, especially dissatisfaction in the areas of career development, communication, and supervisory and management practices. We tried to tell them how to do their job better. We thought that would lessen the dissatisfaction, because if they were better prepared for their jobs, they'd have fewer problems. It did help a little, but not enough.

"The underlying problems that the supervisors must deal with are unchanged. The workers are still dissatisfied, probably because they want a greater role in our decision making. What we've done for years is provide better and better pay, as if we could buy satisfaction without changing any of the underlying factors.

"It's like safety. Years ago we used to give people who worked in especially hazardous jobs higher pay than others received. We still had accidents, of course. Finally, we decided to spend money making the jobs safer instead of paying people to do unsafe jobs. It has worked out better that way.

"But we still pay people to accept a work system they don't like; that they resent. They take the money, but performance doesn't improve. I don't know where to start changing things. I can't change the jobs without changing the plant layout. I can't let people participate in planning production without trying to get our managers to be more tolerant of workers' ideas, even if some aren't very good. And I can't get the supervisors to act differently while the workers in the union are always sniping at them. Everything is interrelated and difficult to change. At times I feel I'm attempting to arrange a beach of sand with a teaspoon. Just when I think I've made some progress, a storm blows in to rearrange my work. The problems among our supervisors are pervasive. I'm getting discouraged. I'm at a loss about how to begin to turn the situation around. On the worst days, I wonder if it can be turned around at all, ever.

"Maybe," he concluded, "we've got it backwards. We have been setting the plants up for efficiency first of all—but we get the workers and supervisors at each other's throats as a result. It undermines our efficiency and drives up costs. Maybe we ought to organize the work first of all to fit the people, and then see if we couldn't get efficiency as a result."

A NONTRADITIONAL PLANT

At the same time that Howards was feeling trapped in a production system that seemingly could not be changed, his predecessor, Jim Finley, now plant manager at one of Acme's major customers, was trying to familiarize himself with his new company and his new position. His general state, however, could best be described as "in shock." Finley knew that he was considered a capable manager with an excellent track record. His selection to manage the company's new plant was a testimony to the company's high regard for his talents. Yet, at that moment he was not at all sure that he had made the right decision when he decided to accept the company's offer. After being at the plant for two weeks now, he could not shake the feeling that he had been transported to a foreign land, far from the usual signs, language, and rituals that comfort and give guidance to life within a plant. More troubling, he was only now learning the alternative set of assumptions they were operating under. Often things didn't compute right, which was unusual for him. His instinctive reactions to situations that came up in the plant seemed strangely awry.

First, this plant had far fewer managers and supervisors than other plants where he had worked. The first few days Finley was at the plant, he spent most of the day wondering where everyone was. Further, managers acted not from their desks but from the shop floor where they seemed to meet spontaneously with groups of people to talk over problems and solutions. As a matter of fact, they did not seem to be managing at all, but rather to be part of the environment around them. There were moments when Finley thought the whole organization had been turned upside down. The managers were serving as assistants and coaches to production workers rather than the other way around.

Finley was not alone in his feeling that this plant was different from plants he had been part of before. On Finley's first day Anderson, a production worker, had spent part of a day taking the new manager around the plant and describing some of the culture shock he had experienced when he first came a year before. "When I came to work here I was used to physical labor, but not mental labor; we've got both to do here."

This comment compounded rather than clarified Finley's confusion. Of course, he had heard of the new work system before he took over the plant but the reality of it was much different than his abstract, intellectual conception.

On their walk around the plant Anderson continued, "My job at the old plant was just to run the machine; now I've got to do that and make sure the machine and the whole process keep running. I'm always learning a new part of the processes here so now after a year I know just about the whole assembly line. At first I didn't like it much. Some other people got so scared about all there was to do that they left. There's a lot of stress. Sometimes too much."

Finley thought he was beginning to get enough clarity to pull him out of his disorientation. "Too much heat from supervisors?" he ventured.

"No, not supervisors, peers," Anderson responded quickly. "We work in teams and if one of us isn't carrying his weight, he'll get more grief from the rest of the team than he'd ever get from a supervisor. I know, I've felt it when I was having a bad day. Everyone has them. You have to contribute around here or things just don't work out with the team."

Several months later Finley was at a work station in the plant when a woman in a light tan suit and coordinated tie approached him. She introduced herself, "I'm Vivian Wendel from Servomatic Systems. I'm here to look into installation of the equipment we delivered last week and I want to know how it fits into the production flow. Who am I to talk to? Where is the supervisor for that area?"

"We don't have one," Finley responded quietly.

"What do you mean you don't have one?" Wendel pressed.

"Just what I said."

"Then is there a general production superintendent or manager I can see?"

"None of those either. I've got three assistant managers, but they're not up to date on the process in that area."

"Well, who knows about it?"

"The team leader or one of the team members."

"You mean the workers?"

"Yes."

"But I need someone I can rely on."

"You can rely on them."

"But they can't speak for the company."

"Yes, they can," Finley responded. "If what you need is more than one of them can do, he'll bring in someone else, including me if necessary."

Seeing that Wendel was still hesitating, Finley turned to a nearby team member. "Take Ms. Wendel over to the line and put her in touch with the team in the area where we want her equipment, okay?"

A few hours later Finley saw Wendel again. "Did you get the information?" Finley asked.

"Yes," Wendel replied, "but I'm not accustomed to dealing with blue-collar workers."

"Don't they know their stuff?"

"Yes, but still I'm uncomfortable," Wendel persisted. "How did each one learn so much about the whole process in the section?"

"They rotate through jobs on their teams."

"Doesn't that make it hard to pay them? I mean, doesn't their pay keep changing as they go from job to job and then back to the first one?"

"No, we pay them for the number of jobs or skills they've mastered, not for what they're doing at any given point."

"How long does it take to master a skill?"

"Six months to a year, on the job mostly."

"When you've mastered all the skills . . . ," Wendel began.

"You get the same rate everyone else gets who has mastered them all," Finley interjected, finishing Wendel's sentence.

"Then what do people do?"

"That's a problem," Finley admitted. "I haven't been here long, but already I can see that individuals get used to learning new tasks and growing personally. We're going to have to think of some way to give them additional opportunities as they start to plateau out in the production teams.

"When I came here my predecessor told me this was his biggest long-range problem," Finley continued. "He told me about an oil refinery in England which started this kind of system 14 years ago. It has lots of people at the top of the pay scale, and its competitors keep hiring people away for management positions in their traditional facilities."

"Why did they leave?" Wendel asked.

"Partly because they've reached the top of the pay scale, but more basically because they've been encouraged to be ambitious and learn more, and can't find any more opportunity within the organization."

Finley noticed a cynical grin darting across Wendel's face. Too many executives are always too anxious to find something wrong with the new system, he thought. Any problem is enough for them to write it off as impractical.

"But look how far we've come," Finley said in response to Wendel's silent cynicism. "When I was at Acme's Danville plant, I spent lots of time trying to figure out how to motivate people—

to get them to show attitudes and behavior that would make the company a success and I never got close to doing it.

"Here, my problem is how can I keep up with the work force. They're high achievers with high expectations. Now, I'm not trying to push them ahead, or to lure them forward with some bait. Instead, I'm trying to keep ahead of them. It's a real problem, but I'd rather have this one than the one I had at Danville.

"How big is your plant?" Wendel asked.

"We've got 1,700 employees," Finley answered.

"How many layers of management?"

"Three. What do the plants you usually deal with have?" Finley asked, knowing the answer.

"Five, six, or even seven," Wendel responded. She paused, "Is the plant cost effective?"

"Just between us, it's about 15 to 20 percent better than our traditional plants."

"But you've got to have considerable overhead, at least on the people side," Wendel protested. "Everyone has been trained to do several things."

"Yes," Finley agreed. "But we have lots of flexibility and adaptability in return. People work smart here; and, of course, we have very few managers or white-collar specialists, like scheduling, inventory, or materials specialists. The team members do all that."

"Do you have a lot of turnover?"

"Why do you ask?"

"I'd expect people to come and then leave when they see how much work it is—how different it is."

"We have some turnover, though less than most plants. But we screen people carefully. We interview applicants, then show them a videotape with current team members talking about the plant. The tape makes several key points: First, that people here have to work with their heads and take work home if necessary. There's stress in that. Second, that people have to participate in the teams, go to meetings and be able to communicate with each other and the group. Third, that people rotate among jobs. You can't just find something you like and hold onto it by seniority or whatever. There is no job ownership. Fourth, that they have to accept criticism from fellow team members. No one likes to be criticized, and some people will want revenge on those who criticize them. That just doesn't go here. You've got to take and give constructive criticism.

"Finally, they have to learn lots of different jobs and then teach other people to do them. It's like going back to school. We tell them, 'If you're the kind of person who likes to put screw A in hole B, you won't like it here. This wouldn't be a good place for you to work.'

"The tape doesn't play this place up," Finley concluded. "If anything, we are critical of it. We make it a challenge to a job applicant. Lots of people see the tape and then select themselves out. The ones who accept a job have an idea of what they're getting into. So we don't have much turnover."

"Do you like it here?" Wendel asked.

"It's not been an easy adjustment for me," Finley replied candidly. "It's stressful, but a funny kind of stress. I'm used to pushing myself and other people very hard. Here I have to pull back. I have to let other people do things. I can assist; I can try to develop the environment a little; but I have to discipline myself not to do things.

"I've had to change my whole style of management. When I was running Acme's plant at Danville, I used to sit in my office in a suit, pretending that everything was as I had ordered it— that everyone was afraid of me.

"Now a team member—who at Acme would be a blue-collar worker—walks through layers of management right into my office to say she needs help on this or that. It doesn't make sense to wait for them to come in, so now I spend time out in the plant, walking around.

"You know, we get a big gain here in rework. It was rework that ate us up at Acme. Forty percent of our expected profit got lost doing things again that had been poorly done the first time.

All I would do at Acme was to speed up the production—to push people harder. I couldn't get them to pay attention to quality or to be careful. Here I don't have that problem. We have very little rework, and so I have a better bottom line.

"I don't envy my successor at Acme the problems I left him," Finley commented reflectively. "Do you know him, Rich Howards?"

"No," Wendel answered.

"Team members are more involved with a whole range of activities here than they have been at the other plants I've been at. Here, meetings between managers and team members usually end with the team making a statement about what the next step would be rather than the manager drawing conclusions from the exchange and issuing an order."

"I don't think I would like it," Wendel suggested.

"Lots of managers don't," Finley agreed. "I have had more trouble with managers who don't fit in here than with people we bring in off the street into the teams."

"Why?"

"I think it's an issue of personal power," Finley offered. "If you grow up in the old system, you look up the line and say, 'Someday I'm going to be the one giving the orders, making everyone jump.' Then you get your chance, and you really use it. You do everything. Tell everybody else what to do. But if you were here, you'd have to pull back. No more big boss. The personal power seems gone. Sometimes I think I work for the teams, not them for me. They tell me what they want from suppliers, or from corporate, and it's my job to try to get it. That's stress.

"Still," he added, "when you really think about it, there's not much loss of power and control for a manager in a plant like this one. There's no loss of power because you have the ideas of the entire work force to draw on, not just those of a small management group. There's really more power to share.

"There's also more managerial control, in a sense, because of the way responsibilities are delegated. Feedback systems tell me what is going on; and peer pressure causes people to get the work done. There's actually more control here than in a traditional plant—but it's achieved and exercised differently.

"I used to spend time on people problems at Acme," he continued, "always trying to get people to observe rules. Here, rather than the letter of the law, I spend time on solving problems with lots of flexibility. Managers have greater power here. I can act without fear of setting a precedent that a union will use against me. The flexibility is an important additional degree of freedom.

"What a manager really wants is for employees to do two things: first, to understand the objective of their work; and second, to understand how it will be measured. Then the employee can organize and do the work, and see that it is high quality.

"The manager is then free to work on problems and remove obstacles to getting the work done. I've learned that managers who have worked in nontraditional environments," Finley added, "find it hard to go back. I think I'd be like that. I ran into a guy from a large oil company last weekend at a management conference. He was young, like me, and enjoyed solving problems—really working with people to do a hard job well.

"He'd been at a synthetic oil plant in western Canada, owned by a group of oil companies. They'd set it up in the mid-1970s like my plant here—with little supervision and everybody doing whatever was needed to make the plant go. He said it was a great place to work—everybody had a can-do attitude.

"The higher-ups in the oil companies got worried about how their investment was being used. So they put in lots of supervisors. Soon productivity collapsed. Before, if a guy on a bulldozer had trouble, he'd hitch a ride on a pickup truck, go to the plant, get some tools, go back to the bulldozer, and fix it. Now he sits there idly on the machine waiting for someone to miss him, look for him, and then send others out to fix the machine.

"The guy told me that kind of thing drove him crazy, so he got transferred out. I think if I had to go back to a plant like that, I couldn't stand it either.

"There's one last thing," Finley concluded. "I've talked to a lot of people about the direction that organizations are going in the future, because I don't want to be left out. I wondered if they are going to become more or less formal in the future. This is a less formal organization, and I think it will be the wave of the future for two key reasons: First, this is what people want—an opportunity to use their heads, to participate, to make individual contributions. They don't want to be bossed around and they work better without it.

"Second, we don't have to be as formal because the computer is making it possible to distribute information much more widely. Information doesn't have to go up and back down the hierarchy any more. A team member doesn't have to go to purchasing to check on our effort to get a new machine. He just goes to a terminal and it tells him the status of the order. And if he has a problem with that, he just sends a computer message direct to the rank and file guy in purchasing to speed it up or whatever. No more need to make inquiries of his supervisor, who then goes to a supervisor in purchasing, back down to the rank and file in purchasing, then back up to the supervisor and over to production again. We save lots of costs in cutting out all that movement up and down the organization."

Jim Finley was not alone in the adjustment he was having to make. He had many counterparts—managers trying to adjust to new style responsibilities, finding it alternatively stressful and rewarding.

A COMPETITIVE ADVANTAGE

Today, virtually every major American industrial corporation has at least one or two plants in some respects like the one Finley is managing; experimental, yes, but well beyond start-up. Some plants like Finley's already have logged more than seven years of operation. Hardly a flash in the pan. But there is some reluctance to publicize these efforts. In most companies the nontraditional plants remain controversial in management ranks. There seems to be an audience within each company's executive group watching for signs of failure.

Those who are optimistic also have a reason for silence. For many companies nontraditional plants are an important gamble in their efforts to gain an advantage on competitors. If costs can be lowered and quality enhanced, they will make a significant gain in the marketplace. Why tip off competitors to a device which might work?

Until recently secrecy about management techniques has not been a characteristic of most American industrial companies. Secrecy about costs, customer relations, and technology and business plans—yes. But work force management skills have not been viewed as an element of competitive strategy until recently. Today a kind of corporate curtain has been drawn over the topic— obscuring from the public the extent of experimentation and success.

Behind the curtain, the variety of efforts is very broad. Some do not go as far as Jim Finley's plant, but are significant nonetheless. At Champion International Corporation, a major paper manufacturer, managers and employees are encouraged to volunteer for problem-solving teams. The activity is truly voluntary, because where it is forced to occur in a context of strained relations between management and union, it can make things worse.

The company's staff people go first to plant management. If they are interested in participating, the union is contacted next. Then employees are given an opportunity to volunteer. Some do. The idea is not only to get employees' suggestions, but also and more importantly to identify and try to solve problems. Problems can be in production, or they can be in working conditions— whatever the group sees as difficulties or opportunities and wants to work on. It is, however, ideas that help solve problems. "An employee who submits an improvement idea is truly a business partner of the company," that company's CEO has become fond of saying.

In order to get things done, the voluntary groups need resources. Furthermore, rank and file employees and lower level managers are unfamiliar and unsympathetic with a large company's time-consuming capital budgeting and investment approval processes. In order to streamline financial procedures and foster employee involvement, the company's board has established a fund administered at the discretion of the vice president of manufacturing. After the board approves expenditures not knowing exactly how they will be spent, the manufacturing vice president acts quickly on proposals he believes have merit.

The company carefully audits its expenditures on the teams' projects and the cost savings that result. In a five-year period ending early in the 1980s, the company's audited savings rose from less than $1 million per year to over $20 million. Its capital spending in the final year was some $1.5 million for team projects, with an average investment of about $20,000 per project.

The company grants only recognition awards, no bonuses for suggestions or for cost savings. It does pay overtime to employees for participation in the teams, when overtime occurs. The reward for participation is primarily in the process of involvement and the success of the groups' ideas. In recent years the company has established similar voluntary problem solving teams in its accounting department for clerical groups.[1]

Other companies have gone further than Jim Finley's plant. General Motors Corporation has a plant now operating with no first- or second-level supervision. Employee teams perform all the functions commonly associated with direct supervision in a traditional plant.

Dana Corporation has a 3-year-old midwestern plant with 200 employees and 3 managers. The employees supervise themselves. "How's it doing?" a Dana manager was asked. "Very well. So well that we are trying to remove a layer of management out of many of our other facilities."

---

[1] Roger Tewksbury, "Employee Involvement—The Champion Experience," *Proceedings*, American Paper Institute, 18th Annual President's Forum, November 3–5, 1983 (New York: API, 1984), pp. 52–57.

A large lumber producer is attempting to convert its facilities to a system in which workers do more and management adopts a different style. When asked why, the company's executive vice president replied, "We have billions of dollars worth of timberland. Yet each employee costs us more than a million dollars over his career. So we have even more billions invested in people. The 10 percent of our people who are managers don't have enough brains to outweigh all the others. We've got to utilize all our assets —not only timberland but people."

One of the most extensive, longest running, and effective efforts to let the work force do more is taking place at Procter & Gamble. In the mid-1960s the company began to build new plants with the type of work system Jim Finley experienced. And in the early 1980s, after a long period of frustration, dramatic progress has occurred in installing nontraditional systems in some of the company's older plants.

The company has coined a phrase for the new psychological contract it has tried to establish: "The Adult Business Deal." This relationship among people at all levels of the organization is characterized by trust, respect, commitment, and security. Without public pronouncements, the company is attempting to provide employment security to employees throughout the corporation. Unlike efforts in many other companies, Procter & Gamble's efforts, like General Motors', involve union plants as well as non-union.

Renamed a technician in the new arrangement, the traditional blue-collar worker is intended to be well informed, broadly trained, and business oriented. The typical technician spends a half hour each work day discussing production problems and budget forecasts with coworkers and managers. The interface between managers and technicians is intentionally blurred, in order to place no upper limits on the ability of people to take on greater responsibility in their jobs. People qualify for higher rates of pay based on what they know, what they can demonstrate they can do, and how well they work in teams. To support the system, expenditures of training dollars are double what they are in the company's traditional plants.[2]

Managers like Jim Finley are aware that there is much misunderstanding of nontraditional work systems. He recalled a conversation with an executive about participation. "Do those who favor participation seriously suggest that a European form of participation, with formal worker representation on boards of directors and work councils, be adopted here? Is this the next wave?"

"No," he assured his executive friend, "what we are really talking about is not best described as participation in decision making, but as delegation. It is not having a committee meet to make a decision and in the process dilute management's authority and responsibility, but instead, allowing people to take on more activity and scope in their jobs." Finley continued, "When I think about it, the times I've been most successful as a manager are those when I've told people the general outline of what needed to be done and let them proceed from there to get it done, with my involvement being to coordinate and keep things on track, not to tell them how to do it in detail.

"What this is about," Finley tried to explain, "is simply letting people in our work force use more of their talents. When you've seen it in action, you realize that there is considerable ability, intelligence, and capability in all levels of the work force. My task as a manager is to capitalize on these talents for the interest of all the constituencies of our company: employees, shareholders, customers, and suppliers.

"We are attempting to harness the talent by letting people do more—call it delegation or participation—and by changing the quality of our human relationships. It works, but it's difficult to get started. Lots of managers say they can't do it because it would take too long. So they just take whatever past practice or the

[2] From a discussion with David S. Swanson, Executive Vice President, Procter & Gamble, Boston, May 10, 1984.

external environment gives them. Often, what they get is a mess, like at Acme's Danville plant where I used to be.

"But if you think of what you put into starting a new system of delegation and better relationships as an investment, then you'll recognize that it will have returns as time goes by. In this company we think that the effort starts slow, then grows like a weed. Of our 100 or so plants, the corporate executive vice president says one-quarter have the new system onboard, one-quarter are asking about it, one-quarter are wondering about it, and one-quarter are doing nothing at all. What we get for the investment is a change to an inherently more productive organization."

EXPERIMENTAL WORK SYSTEMS

Early misfires persuaded many people that there was nothing worth pursuing in experiments to let workers do more. Certainly a first acquaintance with experimental efforts often did not suggest that they constituted a possible major modification of American employment practices. Quite the contrary. As the years have passed, however, the experiments have continued and a great deal has been learned. Today the experimental work systems promise an opportunity to reform and improve practices in our country.

What do these experiments consist of? They are complex and can only be briefly outlined here. It is simplest to contrast two alternative models. The first model involves current practice. Generally in our country, employees perform jobs which are narrowly defined in content; employees stay in these jobs and specialize in them, unless promoted or transferred. Pay is according to the specific job, and sometimes according to individual performance. The employee works under close supervision and employee performance is evaluated by direct supervisors. Persons are assigned overtime or are transferred temporarily under elaborate rules. Over many years the employee tends to continue in the same job, so that the employee's career, in retrospect, is one of rather extreme specialization. (As a practical matter, ordinarily there is no concept of the development of an employee's career in American business except in the managerial ranks.) An employee who has specialized in a narrowly defined set of tasks and was hired to perform at a specific geographic location is at the mercy of changes in technology or the marketplace which might make this particular job redundant at that location. Under a union contract, seniority may protect the employee from a layoff, but only by subjecting less senior employees to very substantial employment insecurity. Recent research has shown that most American nonunion firms also stress length of service with the company in conducting layoffs.

The experimental model departs in almost every detail from the one just cited. Because of these many differences in detail, it adds up to something that as a whole is markedly different from the more prevalent model. In the experimental model, jobs are broadly defined, teams of employees are assigned to perform a group of jobs, and employees are rotated through the various jobs. In effect, the team is given a business to conduct. The team is responsible for inventory, materials scheduling, personnel scheduling, production goals, cost targets, and product quality. Employees are paid according to the number of tasks which they have mastered. Ordinarily employees are assigned a particular task for six months or more, so that there is a built-in length of service element in the pay system. There is little direct supervision. Employees are supervised and evaluated by the team. An employee responds to the requests of peers rather than the orders of a supervisor. Possibly a peer's request is more compelling than a supervisor's orders would be. In place of rules about overtime and transfers there are a few general practices (such as six-month job rotation periods) and informal arrangements stressing shared burdens among the team members. An employee's career begins in one skill and continues as the employee masters the assorted skills required in the teams. Because the breadth of tasks is wide, an employee with an aptitude for technical or administrative advancement is able to demonstrate it. Furthermore, the company considers that it employs a broad-gauged person with various capacities, rather than a machine-like, specialized, and limited-usage input to the production process. Finally, because of broad skills and flexibility which the team approach brings to production—often including better productivity than under the other system—employees' jobs may be somewhat more secure (see Table 11.1).

These experimental systems in the United States have been developed largely in the nonunion environment and in the context of new production facilities. Several major companies, however, are now attempting to introduce them into unionized facilities, both newly constructed and old. It is interesting that the introduction of the experimental models into existing union facilities requires less change in the formal rules of the work place than would be expected. Team concepts do not conflict with the work rules as much as they simply make the rules obsolete. The sharing

Table 11.1
Traditional and Nontraditional Work Systems

Traditional	Nontraditional
Narrowly defined jobs	Broadly defined jobs
Specialization in a single job	Rotation among jobs
Pay by job	Pay by skills (or jobs) mastered
Business information kept primarily to managers	Considerable business information furnished to employees
Work performed under close supervision	Little direct supervision
Supervisor pressure to perform	Peer pressure to perform
Little training	Continual training
Work as individuals under supervision	Work in teams

of responsibilities within the teams makes rules about temporary job assignments and overtime unnecessary to a large degree. Pay scales that reflect skill levels rather than job assignments also tend to make unnecessary rules about how an employee on temporary assignment is to be paid. Thus, the experimental work systems do not untie the knot of existing rules; instead, they cut it.

New systems make their greatest demands on both management and employees in the area of trust. The great flexibility in the experimental systems requires considerable trust between management and labor to make them work successfully. Employees must not be concerned that management will utilize flexibility to exploit workers. And, managers must not be concerned that employees will use flexibility to impose inefficient practices on the company. The new systems do not build trust between labor and management; they depend upon its prior existence. They do not produce mutual confidence; they consume it, at least initially. Over time, of course, the successful operation of the new systems does tend to generate confidence between management and labor.

Understanding these new work systems is much facilitated if two common errors are avoided: First, although they draw some impetus from the need to counter the Japanese challenge in the marketplace, these systems are not adaptations from Japanese models. The new American systems emphasize teamwork, it is true, but not at the expense of the individual. Instead, they are firmly rooted in basic characteristics of the individual American psyche, particularly that of the baby boom generation: the desire to make one's own contribution, to do one's own thing, to develop one's own capacities by work and education, to be recognized for one's own contribution, and to be part of a successful team. This is unlike the Japanese concept of self and society. Because the new work systems are grounded in the American individualist psychology and not in an attempt to import a Japanese psychology, they may well fare far better in our business world than many expect.

The Japanese are able to blend managerial authority with good human relationships. Americans are not very good at this. The new work systems do not try very hard to make Americans better at it; instead, they dramatically reduce the significance and role of authority. Supervisors largely disappear from the plants. The work team manages itself. "This," say Japanese managers who have heard the new systems described, "goes very much further than we do in our plants."

Second, the new work systems are not primarily concerned with changes in the relationship between managers and the work force. These are not a touch and feel experiment between supervisors and employees. Most Americans are justifiably cynical about these, given our history and culture. Although the relationship aspect has received much publicity, it reflects a misunderstanding. The new systems will not change the supervisor–employee relationship; instead, they break it by abolishing the supervisor. The new plants have no first-line supervisors in the traditional sense. Employees do not work under direction, close oversight, or disciplinary scrutiny. Instead, employees largely manage themselves, and are managed by the team to which they belong; that is, by their peers. The few managers in the new plants perform coordination or communications functions near the work force, without providing direction, oversight, or discipline. Without traditional first-line supervision, there is no particular importance attached to the quality of relationships between the work force and first-line supervision.

The important relationships are those between employees who must treat each other with respect; learn to communicate, criticize, and teach each other; and also individually learn and grow. These are the dynamic processes that make the new systems work. When the work force essentially performs supervisory functions itself, the supervisor–employee interface loses its significance. This result forces unions to redefine their roles. If a union has thought of itself primarily as a device to protect employees from supervisors, it has little use in the new system. When thought of as they were originally conceived in the United States in the early nineteenth century, unions have a significant role as self-help and personal improvement organizations for employees.

The important issue in the new systems is not whether there can be a better relationship between employees and supervisors but whether a plant can be successfully operated in the long-term in this nonhierarchical fashion. Maybe it is an alternative, but only time will prove it so.

The life of an employee is different under the new system. Rather than carrying out orders in a somewhat mindless and repetitive fashion, leaving all problems at the work place each evening, the employee assumes more far-reaching obligations. The stress of meeting production targets now falls directly on the team members. Employees must learn to accept criticism from other members of the team, and to react in a constructive fashion. Employees continue to learn on the job as new skills are mastered and new processes, technology, and products are introduced. In effect, employees assume what are now managerial functions and they experience the stress which accompanies administrative jobs. When the employee takes the job home at night, family relationships may be disrupted unless the employee is able to cope successfully with stress. The new systems require a much higher degree of commitment to the work place from the employee than do the old systems. Their advantage in productivity arises from this higher commitment and the flexibility in production which accompanies high commitment.

THE MOST HAZARDOUS MOMENT

"Our future head of manufacturing will probably come out of one of these far-advanced plants," said the CEO of a large auto equipment company, "not because he or she has been a supporter of this idea, but because he or she has used these techniques, among others, to be our best performing manager. I don't know that this will happen, but I've seen such outstanding results from these new techniques that I'm reasonably sure it will."

Because of their belief that the new systems will prove themselves in the marketplace, executives like this CEO devote considerable attention to spreading the concept among managers in their own organizations. For years a small number of people in business and in the universities supported the new concept in the belief that change was necessary. They achieved only little progress, partially because other people did not understand why change was desired. "You're just trying to tamper with what has been our heritage," they seemed to say.

When finally able to show recent business results from the new systems, proponents at one large company found their task far easier. The new plants—greenfield sites—include some substantial successes; they are marvelously efficient plants to managers and favorable environments to workers. So rather than talk about the possibilities, proponents are now able to send interested but skeptical people to experience the new environments. "Stay," workers are told. "See that it is not just another scheme to get more out of people for less dollars." "Stay," managers are told. "See if the new systems are not more flexible, less costly, and more livable for you as well as for the workers."

"We had strategies for all elements of our business," said the vice president of a large financial services company. "But we kept them locked up in corporate headquarters. Now we let the information out. No longer do we meet resistance to our need to be doing things differently because of new competition. Instead, we can't keep up with the pace as our lower-level managers try to keep ahead of the competition. 'Wait for us,' our top management seems to be saying. 'We're your leaders.' "

How about managers so immersed in the older system that the newer one cannot gain a beachhead? One large company operates its divisions on a traditional chain of command basis. Each division has a group of basic functions including advertising, sales, manufacturing, research, finance, and personnel; each operates in hierarchical fashion. Each division has cost cutting teams also, which are purely participatory and have no line of command. Each group has some rotating members and trains those who volunteer to be on the team. The teams operate without hierarchy, with managers and subordinates as equal members. In these teams it is the quality of an idea that counts, not its source. Because of the existence of these teams, the company's managers experience two different managerial styles: one traditional, the other more participatory. In the teams managers learn about the newer style and develop empathy for the new work systems.

This structure which places planning in teams and operations in a hierarchical system is reminiscent of commando teams in the Second World War. These small organizations, which required the utmost discipline in battle, also relied on the experience and ideas of each member in the planning that preceded an operation.

In a new system, managers have to be thinking all the time about how their actions affect the overall process. Human commitment is slow to be built, quick to be destroyed. Consistency builds trust, and consistency is created by self-aware managers. There must be continual reiterations about why this or that is being done. Moments of business emergency or crisis are the most hazardous. Will a manager who has responsibility for a participative system revert to directives, deadlines, and authority when the pressure mounts? If so, actions will speak louder than words and undercut the new system.

THE MOST AMBITIOUS EFFORT YET

The most comprehensive and self-conscious effort to fit a business to the capabilities and attitudes of today's work force is being made at People Express Airlines, Inc. This is the first company to try to adapt to today's work force by a radical departure from the traditional concept of a company. The attempt has many intriguing features and has been accompanied by dramatic initial success. In consequence, People Express is the most interesting company in America today.

Don Burr is the company's founder and chief executive officer as well as the mastermind behind the People Express approach.

"We start with certain human values about how we want the company to be run; then we develop a business strategy and link the two up in a powerful way," Burr has commented. Because People Express was a start-up company, Burr was able to think through the link between the business and its people far more fully than if he had been in an ongoing organization. Unfortunately most start-ups fail to take the opportunity that newness offers. Burr seized the opportunity and made it a major element of his business's success.

Most managers begin their thinking with a business purpose and then ask themselves what people the organization will need. At a very early stage, Burr asked this question the other way around. What kind of organization and business can be fitted to the capabilities of the people potentially available to the company?

In many well-managed companies, top managers do ask the question this way for certain key individuals. "What can we do to get Joan Rollins to come work for us?" they ask. Discussions with Rollins will sometimes fit the organization and its business objectives to her in return for her joining the managerial team. What Burr added to this was his vision of the potential contribution of many individuals much further down in the organization; people who could build a business that would permit them to make the greatest contribution.

Burr combined an opportunity in the airline business with the availability of talented young people and built a company that has sparked a revolution in the airline business. Burr recognized that there are many people in our country yearning for an opportunity to contribute to a company in whose success they can share.

The airline business did not look ripe for new entrants in the late 1970s. Instead, it gave the appearance of maturity, but that was a false appearance. In 1980 the Civil Aeronautics Board (CAB) deregulated the industry, permitting new carriers to enter the business. Among the first out of the starting blocks was People Express. Two years later, founder, president, and CEO Don Burr ended his company's quarterly financial meetings with these words: "We're now the biggest air carrier in terms of departure at any New York airport. We expect to see a good profit this year . . . we have a concept that works and is unique."[3]

In the audience sat many of People Express' stockholder managers, there to hear about and celebrate the success of their young company. In large part, this success was due to the innovative way Burr and his associates attracted employees and gave them each a stake in the business and an opportunity to contribute.

It helped that Burr knew the airline industry from several years at Texas International Airlines, and that he and his top management team had a marketing concept for the new company. Marketing was to be based on a combination of very low fares and convenient flight schedules. This combination would permit People to broaden its customer base to persons who would ordinarily not have flown, but used other forms of transportation. People Express initiated the competition which Greyhound Corporation found so difficult to respond to, leading to Greyhound's 1983 strike and concessionary labor agreement.

People Express was also fortunate in being able to raise capital very early on at low cost by tapping the equity market. In its application to the CAB for start-up authorization, People indicated its intention of raising $4–5 million, buying or leasing one to three planes, and hiring 200 people or so. Because Burr had contacts on Wall Street, who were able to see the company's potential, People was able to sell 3 million shares to the public for some $24 million. With so much cash raised, and no interest to pay (since financing was via equity and no debt), People purchased an entire fleet of 17 Boeing 737s from Lufthansa Airlines and was instantly in business on a fairly large scale.

In later months as the company expanded rapidly, it found that its own purchase of 737s had caused other companies to value the plane and had caused prices to rise. So People Express bought 727s, only to see others turn to 727s, and prices rise.

[3] Lucien Rhodes, "That Daring Young Man and His Flying Machines," Inc., January 1984, 42–52. Also, Barbara Palmer, "Flying on Empty at People Express," Institutional Investors (December 1983): 79–82.

Finally, People Express turned to 747s and, to utilize them, opened routes to Europe.

Marketing and finance gave People Express an opportunity in the deregulated airline business. The advantage People gained over its longer established competitors had more to do with its employee practices than with any other single factor. For example, although the marketing strategy was very important, its key component—low prices—could only be achieved if costs also were kept low. To achieve this, personnel costs, an airline's second biggest expense following fuel, had to be kept low. Fuel costs could be minimized, but other carriers were adept at this also. Minimizing personnel costs took greater ingenuity.

People's approach to the people side of its business broke the maturity pattern in airlines and opened the business to a host of new competitors. Many imitated in their own fashion the model People Express had created. Lowering labor costs dramatically People combined lower out-of-pocket pay with better human performance.

To minimize human overhead, People kept its initial organization to only three formal levels of authority: the President/CEO and six managing officers; eight general managers; and finally, a large group of full-time employees variously designated as flight managers (pilots), maintenance managers, and customer service managers. The last group was the largest; it was trained to perform all passenger-related tasks, including security clearance, boarding, flight attendance, ticketing, and food service.

Staff positions such as executive assistants or secretaries were noticeably absent. Managers did their own typing, answered their own phones, and generally kept bureaucratic paper shuffling to a minimum. All full-time employees carried the title of manager. And all were required to buy stock in the company at a discounted price. Managers did not supervise in the traditional sense; instead they worked together. The more senior among them provided direction, motivation, teaching, and coordinating, but not close oversight of others. These methods gave People an advantage in terms of human overhead costs against its established rivals.

People Express also gained a cost advantage from the performance of its personnel. Generally young and ambitious persons, People's managers put in long hours and hard work. The airline was continually understaffed as it outgrew its personnel complement day by day. Burr wanted to run a lean organization, believing that people could work far harder than they were usually challenged to do.

Finally, People's compensation costs were low compared to its rivals. Often People paid one-half or less for corresponding occupations. Pilots, for example, received around $30,000 per year including salary and profit-sharing, when Eastern Airlines pilots might make about $100,000. People's pilots worked longer hours as well. But a surplus of pilots caused fully qualified pilots to go to work for People as flight managers. One People Express pilot commented: "Most pilots know very little about what's going on in their company. In a People Express flight manager's position, the knowledge people gain in this ratty old building [People's headquarters in Newark] is incredible. It's a phenomenal opportunity. It's very stimulating and exciting. I never thought I would have this much fun."

Customer service managers received far less than pilots, and less than their counterparts at the established carriers. But for many it was an opportunity to advance themselves. "I was a special education teacher making $12,000 a year, receiving little recognition, getting tired, and looking for something else," reported a customer service manager. "I started here at $17,000, already have received $600 in profit sharing, and will soon own about 800 shares of stock worth $10 on the open market." Lower pay, higher effort, and little overhead combined to give People far lower labor costs than other carriers, and permitted People to pursue successfully its strategy stressing low fares to travelers.

It was not an all-purpose airline. Amenities were few; baggage checking and food during flights carried extra charges. Business travelers were sometimes not fond of People; but a broad cross section of the population was delighted at low fares, cared little for amenities, and accepted charges for incidental services. The airline grew and grew.

Within three years of its inception, People had sparked a revolution in the industry. Other carriers began to search for ways to cut costs; in some instances, strikes resulted. In others, very imaginative deals were worked out between unions or unorganized employees and their companies—all aimed at staying competitive with People Express and its imitators. Established companies that had seen their businesses as mature had let new competitors enter and open the industry to new ideas. Now they desperately tried to keep a foothold where they had long reigned supreme.

To the established carriers and their employees, People Express seemed to be profiting from unfair ways of doing business. Especially galling was the low pay of People personnel. However, People's success was not due solely to lower pay; but also to greater human effort and low overhead, coupled with effective marketing and finance strategies. In these ordinary business areas the imaginative managers and committed employees at People Express gained an advantage on their competitors. These were not elements of unfair competition and they were the most important things. Without its philosophy of management, People's organizational policies would not have generated the employee commitment which gives its high productivity.

True to the close intertwining of business and people strategies, People Express provides up to six weeks of technical and attitudinal training before it makes a final decision about whether to hire an applicant. Why is this necessary when People Express is a new company and can organize itself as it wishes to?

"Because there is really no clean slate at People Express," answers Lori DuBose, one of the company's founders and officers. "People bring their attitudes with them from the general business world and their behavior from what they learned in other settings. They are brought in to learn the principles we have established at People Express, but some can't make the transition."

The problem of the residue of traditional attitudes extends not only to people newly hired into the People Express organization, but to the original 16 officers of the company. They had a concept worked out with Don Burr for the company's business and people strategy, but did not know how to transmit it. The company began operation with 200 employees. Three years later, it had some 5,000 and was continuing to grow rapidly.

How were the principles to be communicated from the officers to the rapidly growing work force? Speeches and exhortations from the top down did not work well. The officers could reach only a small group directly, and the upward pressure of the outside influences brought by new hires countered the impact that People Express officers had on supervisors in the middle of the organization.

In Burr's view, the principal problem centered around the sharing of power, and this problem he identified with the company's officers as well as its middle-level managers—that is, with everyone, including himself, in the company. Due to outside social norms and to business pressures, people in charge tend to take over, to insist on their way, to abandon participatory management. The sharing of power is forgotten.

So difficult has it been to preserve and extend the People Express principles in the face of outside values and rapid growth, that Burr says the alleged freedom of a new company to do things its own way is much overrated. "The older carriers," forced by People Express into a turnaround mode, Burr comments, "need not envy People Express very much." The rapidly growing start-up airline has different problems from the turnaround trunk carrier, but they are serious problems, nonetheless. As always in today's competitive environment, commercial success will go to those managers best able to resolve the unique problems which their chosen strategy and position cause them to confront.

People Express has no manager/employee distinction, but it does have persons who hold power, and those who do not. Trying to minimize the distinction between the two and to provide an opportunity for nonpower holders to make as full a contribution to the company as they can, Burr is insistent on minimizing perquisites. As at Midwest Insurance Company, issues like reserved parking places for executives arise to bedevil the chairman's vision. The issue is symbolic and critical. "It's real important for me not to have executive parking places and other perks," Burr commented, "but I'm afraid I've got 15 key officers at People Express who don't think this way."

How, then, does Burr hope to handle the issue? "You can't take a power-hungry person and change him or her," he answers. "Instead, you've got to turn around how that basic aggressive drive is used." The inherent difficulty of the problem with which Burr is struggling is the reason he is reluctant to say his own difficulties are fewer than those at the older carriers.

Yet, for People Express to prosper, the issue must be resolved. At People Express, the business and people strategies are intertwined. The business will not succeed if the people strategy fails. Falling productivity and commitment combined with rising labor costs will undermine the company's low-price marketing strategy. The company Burr launched on the force of a unique work force strategy is also hostage to it.

At many companies, some of which have made long-standing efforts to develop nontraditional working relationships, an instrumentalist view of the new systems is dominant. "We do these new things because it is a means to an end," said the executive vice president of such a company.

"Yes," added a high executive from another larger company, also deeply involved in experiments in nontraditional systems. "I will agree, if you add that the means are also important."

But Burr at People Express does not accept either of these propositions. The new systems are not simply a means to the end of a more profitable business, nor even an important and independently valuable means. The new systems are not instruments of profit making at all, but rather values to which People Express should be committed regardless of the outcome on the business. The means are an independent commitment, he insists, regardless of the ends.

People Express does intend to make profits, of course. A private business in our country must be profitable to remain in business.

But profits are expected to be the result of the new work systems; a by-product so to speak—like financial success is a by-product of a distinguished author's success in writing. Profitability is not the target itself. The difference between Burr's position and that of the other executives is subtle, but the intensity with which each position is asserted is evidence of the importance attached to the subtlety.

For the executives who see the new systems as instrumentalities, any other view is both Pollyannaish and unlikely to win top management support for the new systems in their companies. "If our top people have to accept these systems as values in their own right, they'll never do it," said one. "For example, treating subordinates decently does not travel to the executive suites in our headquarters complex. There it is boss and flunky just as it has always been. They'll never change; but they don't have to change for big changes to be accomplished in the plants and other offices. So long as they think the new systems generate better productivity and profitability, they'll welcome them—regardless of what they think of the new ways themselves."

Burr and those of like mind disagree vehemently. "We are committed to the new ways of dealing with people, regardless of what happens to our business," they insist. "Any other view is just more of the old management manipulation and exploitation—just a new form of it. The rank and file will figure that out, and they'll quit taking it seriously. They'll say it's only a new way to get the bodies to work three times as hard."

To those supporting the new ways, public expression of the instrumentalist view by other executives is the largest single danger facing what People Express is trying to do. If some top executives continually describe the new systems as primarily designed to enhance profitability, and imply a commitment no deeper than the next quarter's results, then the American work force and public will soon write off the new systems as manipulative, and management's commitment as shallow and expedient. The work force will cease to accept the new efforts at face value, and the opportunity to run a business on a different human basis will be lost. This is the outcome which Burr fears. "People won't trust us if business executives say the new systems are only a means to an end."

To avoid People Express's own work force coming to this cynical conclusion, everyone at People Express is immediately brought into the people strategy. From the first day's orientation classes, some of which Burr personally conducts, new hires are taught that the company's competitive business strategy is the creative involvement of people—optimizing the rule of the individual.

The biggest management problem at People Express is how to get the roots down; how to help people in the company develop a real understanding of what the human strategy requires. "Perhaps 3 percent of our people have a 100 percent understanding," Burr comments; "10 percent have a three-quarter understanding; 30 percent have a one-half understanding; and 55 percent have a one-quarter understanding. The roots of the people strategy go down only about a foot in the organization. They ought to go down 10 feet."

The influence of the outer world remains strong, even at People Express. In 1984 as the economy continued to recover from recession and airline travel expanded rapidly, People Express began to experience resignations. Particularly among flight managers (pilots at other airlines), nostalgia for the past—for little flight time, high pay, no crossover duties—caused people to leave. The majority who remained at People Express believed the defectors were pursuing a will-o'-the-wisp, the old days of the regulated industry with its protections from the challenge of the marketplace. There was greater job security, they felt, at a competitive organization like People Express than in the trunk carriers, although an uptick in the economy had permitted the other carriers to resume hiring for a while. Concessions, two-tier hiring systems, and other devices imposed at other carriers to try to respond to the competitive challenge posed by People Express and its rapidly growing group of emulators meant that the old days would never really return. People Express has shown what ambitious young people can do when given the opportunity through a complete revolution of the traditional work system. Its influence has not swept away the traditional systems of other carriers, but has caused many of them to be modified beyond the recognition of those who long for the old days.

Through innovative personnel practices, coupled with an effective marketing and finance strategy, People Express has seized the opportunity created by airline deregulation and has pushed the airline business out of its maturity phase into one of dematurity. In so doing, it has propelled itself into very rapid growth. Can the company continue its growth? Will its resources, people, and administrative systems give way under the relentless pressure? Certainly competitors and many other managers who observe the company think so. People Express is not popular among managers for its unusual people policies. "Far too revolutionary; too threatening to the established ways," many say. There is grudging respect for People Express's remarkable business success, but rapid growth is perceived to be the company's Achilles' heel.

"People won't be able to continue to work so hard," some argue. "The stress will break them down." "They'll lose that personal touch," others insist. "They'll get bureaucratized and become rigid, unresponsive, and costly like the rest of us." "Wait till all that growth stretches their finances," the more sophisticated said, "and the stock market lets the equity price take a drop. Then you'll see People Express employees lose their motivation, when the stock they own loses value."

The implication in all this was that if People Express wishes to be successful in the long term, it must slow its growth and reorder its organization and work practices. But it does not have this option. Rapid growth is forced on it by the need to acquire and utilize airport space before its competitors can acquire the space themselves and shut People Express out of landing slots. People Express had headed up the competition in the airline industry; now it is as much driven by the pressures of competition as any of the other firms in the industry. People Express has started the ball rolling and now cannot control its velocity. Whatever the future holds, success or failure, People Express must rely on its unique combination of nontraditional work systems and business strategy. It will be successful if its innovative systems fulfill the promise Don Burr has seen for it; if it does not, People will not succeed.

LIMITATIONS ON HIGH COMMITMENT

Are these new systems for all times and conditions? Are there significant limitations? Many managers insist there are. The new work systems in general, and People Express in particular, are the subject of much discussion in American management. Is People Express giving its people too much leeway, too much freedom? Even though people work hard at People Express, is the work ethic being undermined by the absence of the close direction, supervision, and discipline? Among the other criticisms are the following:

1. Small organizations can surely be participative, but not larger ones.
2. New plants may be fertile ground for new concepts, but not older, established facilities.
3. Participatory plans cannot survive a layoff, thus they will not take root in cyclical businesses.
4. Most managers will not relinquish power, so that participatory schemes are inherently limited.
5. If a company is able to carefully select employees, it will probably locate a group who will enjoy the new systems, but most of the work force lacks the interest and initiative to be involved.

A kernel of truth lurks in each of these observations. Participation is easier in small units than large; new plants have been the most successful places for experimentation; in some instances layoffs have undermined the trust between employees and managers necessary to a participative system; the greatest resistance to new

systems is encountered in mid-level managers; and many successful experiments have been predicated on careful selectivity
in hiring.

As the earlier examples in this chapter show, there are responses
to each of the criticisms. Larger companies are able to involve
people in their work at the facility and division level, that is, in
the smaller groups. Some companies have begun to have successes
in established environments. Despite serious layoffs in the early
1980s due to a major business decline, efforts to develop and
nurture nontraditional work systems have survived. First- and
middle-level managers are slowly gaining experience with the
new systems, and some are becoming proponents. In numerous
instances once management has indicated its seriousness by actions
as well as words, the work force has expressed interest in the
new systems.

Today, in the search for enhanced competitiveness, the work
force is being allowed to learn more and to do more, and management is stepping back. Not yet the norm, new systems are
nevertheless healthy infants no longer restricted to rare and unusual
circumstances. At many top companies new work systems are
on the way to becoming effective for a variety of companies.

In traditional circumstances, the blue-collar or lower-classi-
fication clerical worker is expected to put in a work day under
close supervision in return for a fair pay scale and decent working
conditions. The employee is not expected to give attention to the
work outside of standard hours, and is expected only to devote
a certain minimum level of commitment to work.

Professional and technical employees, in contrast, expect more
and have more expected of them. In addition to fair pay and
decent working conditions, professional and technical employees
expect challenging work, high quality supervision, and state-of-
the-art technology with which to work. In return they are expected
to be not only reliable in attendance, but also creative and imaginative enough to solve problems which arise on the job. They
must keep their skills up to date and perform at a high level of
competence (see Table 11.2).

Table 11.2

Mutual Expectations Between Employees and Companies

Traditional Expectations for Blue-Collar and Clerical Employees		Expectations for Professional and Technical Employees	
Employees' Obligations	Company's Obligations	Employees' Obligations	Company's Obligations
Show up for work	Provide fair pay and benefits	Be available for work	Provide fair pay and benefits
Perform tasks as directed under close supervision	Provide decent working conditions	Solve problems	Provide up-to-date tools and technology
Do a fair day's work	Provide safe working conditions	Keep skills and knowledge up to date	Offer challenges at work
		Contribute to company's future products, processes, services in creative way	Provide opportunity for a career, often including personal development
		Be flexible and adaptable	Provide education and training opportunities

Top performing managers, searching for new competitiveness, are today extending the company's arrangements with its technical and professional people to production and clerical employees as well. The result is a substantial improvement in the company's effectiveness; and a valued opportunity for greater respect and contribution by the rank and file.

SUMMARY

An important element of performance by very good managers is the ability to encourage people at all levels in the organization to contribute aggressively to the company's success. Traditionally in the United States, jobs have been refined to such narrow limits that the range of opportunity for people to contribute has decreased. To take advantage of untapped human potential, some companies are now experimenting with expanding opportunities for employees to contribute in their current jobs. This new style of management is necessary for competitiveness and requires new skills of managers. Even if managers and employees are prepared to do more to help the company be competitive, will the unions permit it?

12

Identifying True Purpose: Unions And Management

The 1980s have been a remarkable period in labor–management relations in the United States. With no clear pattern in negotiations, established relationships have come unstuck. There are new departures and new opportunities. Today, the opportunities for companies in dealing with unions and workers are limited only by the vision and wisdom with which they pursue their objectives.

American labor has lowered its sights in collective bargaining. In addition to very low pay increases, for the first time since the Great Depression no union-initiated generalized wage push is evident in the American economy. In the last few years, nonunion companies have been much more generous with their employees than unionized companies where collective bargaining has provided for employees.

Why has all this happened? In part it is a result of the deep recession in 1981–1982. Companies faced difficult times; and having observed the much publicized bankruptcies and substantial layoffs, workers came to understand that. Moreover, even after the economic recovery was far advanced there were long lines of people seeking jobs regardless of whether there was a strike on or not, or whether employers even indicated that they were hiring. High unemployment rates put a lot of pressure on the unions.

But the recession is only part of the story. The other part is an enormous jump in the competition which unionized companies face in the marketplace. Both foreign companies and nonunion American firms are providing stiff competition for many unionized companies in this country, and lower labor costs are usually a key competitive disadvantage for the unionized firms.

Faced with falling market share and declining employment, both unions and unionized companies are attempting to find ways to respond to their competition. Part of this difficult problem arises from fundamental aspects of the union–management relationship in this country. This chapter explores the competitive consequences of problems that lie at the heart of union–management relations in our country. The following chapter describes the efforts of companies and unions to forge a new relationship.

A CONTEST BETWEEN MANAGEMENT AND LABOR

Ted Lewis, a union steward at Western Chemical Company, knew what was coming when Fedder, a grade three pipe fitter, approached him looking angry and upset. Lewis knew the company had posted openings for three grade two pipe fitter jobs within the last several weeks. He learned through the plant grapevine that Fedder had bid for one of these jobs and had been turned down in favor of an employee with less seniority at Western.

Lewis's instincts were correct. Fedder was practically in a rage as he told Lewis about his failure to be awarded the promotion. He was upset about the company's assessment of his qualifications, but what really infuriated him, as he shouted at Lewis, was "I've been working for Western for 26 years and what do I get back? The chance to be passed over for some younger guys who were in grade school when I started at the company? Whatever happened to seniority, doesn't that count for anything anymore?"

Lewis tried to calm Fedder, and took his statement of the facts surrounding the denial of promotion. He promised Fedder he would present it to the grievance committee as soon as possible. Within the week, Lewis called his committee together to go over Fedder's grievance, to outline options, and decide on a course of action. Lewis and the other members of the committee knew well what position the company would argue. The "case," as it was already being referred to by committee members, would rest on the section of the collective bargaining agreement between the union and Western that provided: "Promotions and transfers shall be made on the basis of relative ability, training, safety, knowledge, efficiency, and physical fitness, provided that when the above qualifications are equal, plant-wide seniority shall be the determining factor." While there was no question that Fedder was the most senior of the job bidders, there was substantial question about whether he was the most qualified.

The grievance committee came up with three possible courses of action: They could vigorously pursue Fedder's grievance and argue that the promotion should be made on the basis of his seniority and marshal whatever facts they could to shore up their acknowledged weak argument that Fedder's qualifications for the job were equal to those of the pipe fitters who were promoted. A second alternative was to try to convince Fedder to drop the grievance, essentially arguing the company's case to him that his qualifications for the job were not equal. This tack put the union on the horns of a dilemma. Was their job to represent Fedder before the company or to attempt to evaluate and decide the merits of the case themselves? Several members of the grievance committee felt uncomfortable making the decision. One proposed a third alternative—pursue the grievance through the first of the three steps of the grievance procedure, but submit it to a vote of the first- and second-class pipe fitters before taking it to arbitration. The members of the grievance committee concurred.

The options defined and narrowed in this way, Lewis prepared the grievance statement and started it on its way through the process by giving it to the maintenance department supervisor. As the grievance moved through the first steps of the grievance procedure, union and management solidified their arguments and positions. Given the adversarial process that grievances had assumed in the past, the union automatically began countering the company's argument that Fedder lacked the qualifications. This was not an easy task. Although Fedder had worked for five years as a grade two pipe fitter when he was first hired at Western, he had to take a lower paying job and rank as a result of a reduction in Western's work force. Reassigned nine years later to a grade two pipe fitter position, he was removed after two years when management claimed that he was not demonstrating the necessary qualifications on the job. Six years later, he was reassigned to the grade two position where he stayed for another 11 years until another reduction in work force made him a grade three pipe fitter which he was at the time of the grievance.

This checkered history in regard to the grade two position was compounded by Fedder's fellow workers' assessment of his suitability for promotion. Many thought Fedder was a goldbrick whose work was performed mostly by others. This was the feeling among management too. How could Fedder's fellow employees fail to know it, management wondered? So as the union prepared to defend Fedder's work history, management began to amass information not only on Fedder's shortcomings, but on the successful job bidder's qualifications.

Technically, the question to be resolved by the grievance committee became an issue that is frequently the grist for the grievance mill. As one of the most commonly arbitrated questions, it touched an important nerve for both management and labor. Where does the right of management to promote the most qualified of its work force end, and the right of the individual employee to promotion based on seniority begin? The issue seemed to cut to the heart of both management's and the union's authority.

In the early days of unions in this country, a complaint like Fedder's might have led to Lewis taking the foreman aside, talking the situation over, and trying to settle it right there and then on the shop floor. Since those early and less litigious days, an elaborate and legalistic motif has developed around the grievance machinery. Contracts have grown longer, past practice has been rigidified into rules, and unions and management have looked to lawyers to play increasingly prominent roles in dealings with each other.

The question of how Fedder was treated also raised the specter of possibly unfair treatment for all employees. To many people, the right to "present one's case" protects the rights of all through an individual case. The existence of a forum for the expression of grievances and the right to a hearing are important to an employee's feelings of receiving a fair hearing. Yet both the union and management have legitimate interests in the economic efficiency of the business; this point should not be lost in the effort to provide fair representation and due process for the individual grievant.

What are the goals traditionally pursued by a union in the handling of a grievance such as Fedder's? The union seeks for its position to prevail. If it cannot win a clear victory, the union wants to show its members that it was doing its job by representing Fedder. These two objectives are in addition to protecting Fedder's rights under the contract through the grievance procedure.

And management? There is no more fundamental function for management than the setting of goals for the enterprise. Success in the marketplace as measured by growth and profitability are long-term goals. Efficient operations and a productive work force contribute mightily to growth and profitability. Once goals are identified, managers have the responsibility of explaining them to others and applying them in specific circumstances.

What goals does management set when it enters grievance discussions with a union? Its objectives traditionally mirror those of the union in an attempt to maintain its ground. Management's position is necessarily a reactive one because the union, not management, has access to the grievance procedure. So management's objectives become to protect its prerogatives and discretion from union encroachment and to prevent or minimize its losses— either financial or in prestige—to the union.

In Fedder's case union and management vigorously pursued these traditional goals, the one arguing that seniority should govern the decision over who was to be promoted to the grade two pipe fitter position; the other arguing that management's rights entitled it to select the most qualified employee which Fedder was not.

In the outcome, the company and union prepared for arbitration. Management evaluated their chances of winning an arbitration on Fedder's case as only 50–50 and prepared to concede the promotion to the union. Management did not know, however, that the union had previously decided to submit the question of whether to arbitrate the case to its membership, a common but not universal practice. During the discussion at the meeting, several pipe fitters commented along these lines: "Fedder is a nice guy and everything, but he just doesn't pull his weight. If he is promoted, we'll end up doing his work for him. It wouldn't be fair to the rest of us, although maybe he deserves it just because he's been around so long." After a heated debate, the union leadership's proposal that the grievance be arbitrated was defeated, and the union dropped it. The other pipe fitters didn't want Fedder as a grade two. Management had been right, though the union would not formally admit it earlier in the grievance process.

The company was pleased with the outcome, but confused about what it signified. In three meetings, the union leadership had advanced Fedder's grievance, refusing to acknowledge the merits of management's judgment of the grievant's work skills and habits, despite the opinions of several pipe fitter union members that the company's position was valid. Who did the union represent: the individual (Fedder), or the group (pipe fitters)? And why was the grievance process unable to get at the merit of the company's position, as the pipe fitters themselves saw it? Were individual rights being given too much weight by the union in comparison with the company's need for efficiency and cost control? Or, since the union had in the end dropped the matter, should the company be satisfied that the process as a whole was working properly? Fedder still felt he had suffered an injustice and the company was left with no way to improve Fedder's unsatisfactory performance.

SHARED INTERESTS

The interests of Fedder, the union, and the company might have been furthered if they had agreed to search together for a formulation of the underlying problem and a solution. For example, collapsing the three pipe fitter job classifications into one or two rather than the current three would have provided greater flexibility in assignments to management, while paying everyone at a grade two rate and grandfathering grade one positions at their current rate to protect employees' earnings. As a quid pro quo for this greater management flexibility, the union might have been willing to embrace extension of a system of training and probation to all employees at Western, including senior employees like Fedder, not just new hires.

As grievances are currently handled in many American companies, it is unlikely that these possibilities would have been discussed. If they had been, they probably would have been a sideline to the main attraction: the attempt of each side to prevail over the other.

Without the union, a well-managed company would have tried to handle Fedder's grievance with an eye toward improving its relations with the work force as a whole. Arbitrary treatment of Fedder would have been avoided, so that other employees were not given cause to be concerned about management's possible attitude toward them.

On its side, without management the union would have been concerned to see that the company was allowed reasonable flexibility in its choice of persons to promote—so long as the promotion was based on merit, not on favoritism. Otherwise, the company cannot be successful and the union members' jobs may be imperiled.

So, in the long term, management has an interest in the fair treatment of employees and the union has an interest in the efficient operation of the plant. But in Fedder's case, what happened to these overlapping areas of concern? Union and management lost sight of them.

Imagine for a moment that the union and the company were each pursuing their basic objectives within the grievance process, not their secondary objectives vis-à-vis each other. Defining their roles differently and more broadly, each would seek to reach consensus on a way to address Fedder's sense of injustice at having been passed over for promotion, while preserving the need for efficiency in production. The company would have sought to improve relationships with all the employees, not just specifically Fedder. And both parties would have kept as an explicit part of their agenda preserving jobs and paychecks via a successful company. Each grievance would provide an opportunity to enhance employees' morale and the economic viability of the firm. Grievances, then, could be viewed by management not as an attack on management's rights and prerogatives, but rather as a means of learning about the production process and an opportunity to improve efficiency while addressing individual problems. The fact that a union exists would not distract management from its interests in treating the work force fairly. Long-term objectives would not be lost sight of in trying to win a contest with the union.

Too often what our adversary system of labor relations tends to do is to divide responsibilities artificially between management and union. Management attempts to take sole responsibility for efficiency, leaving to the union all concern for fair treatment of individuals, while the union devotes virtually exclusive concern to fairness, leaving to management any interest in efficient production. When management and unions pursue a single objective against the other, each may be faulted for having lost sight of mutual concerns.

Under certain circumstances a system of divided responsibilities and resolution by negotiation or economic conflict can result in a reasonable balance between fairness and efficiency. In many of our industries such conditions existed for several decades after World War II. The adversarial system, with labor pursuing fairness and management pursuing efficiency, yielded a rough balance that was viable in the marketplace.

Today the system has become self-defeating in many instances. Too often the press of new competition tips the balance of power in favor of management or union. When the press of competition is so great that a company cannot take a strike, the union may have gained the preponderance of power. Then the union may press for and obtain its concept of fairness to the exclusion of efficient operation—thereby undermining the company's long-term survival and its members' jobs.

When the press of competition drives a company into closing plants and selling divisions, only to redeploy its capital into nonunion plants and businesses, then the company may gain a preponderance of power. Then fairness may be forgotten as the company presses the union for efficiency and low cost in its remaining unionized operations. In the long run, the company then experiences employee unrest and lack of commitment.

In today's circumstances, a balance between equity and efficiency can be obtained only if both labor and management are prepared to embrace both objectives, each looking for the right balance. Rather than trying to wring as many concessions from management as possible, labor must be concerned with finding a balance which also promotes efficient operation. Rather than trying to wring as many concessions to efficiency as possible from the union, management must attempt to find a proper balance with fairness. A contest between labor and management is not likely to yield that balance when new competition tilts the power far to one side or the other. Instead, a joint attempt by both sides to work out the balance is more likely to succeed.

For management and labor the issue is often seen as a choice between cooperation and conflict. This may be misleading. There is room for disagreement by management and labor over how to go about obtaining the balance between fairness and efficiency. In the interest of preserving the business, neither side can wish to resort to economic force to resolve a disagreement; both sides must agree on three goals: first, a joint effort to balance the two objectives of fairness and efficiency with both sides making an honest effort to advance both objectives. Second, a renunciation, as much as possible, of pressure tactics which hurt the business and help its competitors. Third, a commitment to agree upon a course of action.

While these three objectives may seem naive in the rough and tumble of customary labor–management relations in this country, they have in fact been followed for years by some branches of American industry.

In the electrical construction industry, for example, committees with equal representation by management and labor meet to resolve labor–management disputes in which no third party is involved. Labor commits itself not to strike and management not to lock out while the committees meet. In effect, labor and management agree to agree, then find a way to do it. This is an American version of Japanese labor relations. Keeping the industry strike-free helps preserve companies and jobs from losses to their competitors. The fact that the electric construction industry has used this system for over 50 years suggests that it can be done here when management and labor are wise enough to try it.

The effort to find a different relationship is now being explored by management and labor in many different circumstances in our country. The remainder of this chapter looks at two of the more unusual of those circumstances: an employee run company, and an American subsidiary of a Japanese company. To highlight the effort to change the labor relations environment without introducing variations due to different industries, the examples have been chosen from a single industry, automobiles.

WHEN EMPLOYEES OWN THE COMPANY

What happens when employees, faced with a plant closure and the loss of their jobs, decide to buy the company, become owners, and thus presumably become tied more directly to the economic viability of the firm? Do different industrial relations systems necessarily emerge when employees gain an ownership stake? And, most important to our consideration here, what is the effect on management?

One cold January day in 1981, the employees of a General Motors Corporation roller bearing plant in New Jersey arrived to find the local management leafleting the plant. The reason for this apparent reversal of roles was that a core management group had become convinced that with a strong employee ownership effort among employees the other parts of a buy-out deal could be put together and a viable firm created. Management's interest in the buy-out was neither merely ideological nor altruistic. General Motors had frozen management transfers within the company. Closing of the facility would mean job losses for the managers as surely as for other employees. The employees accepted management's initiative and pursued employee ownership of the plant.[1]

Although there had been a minor explosion in employee buy-out plans through employee stock ownership plans (ESOPs) brought on by the hard times of the recent recession, the General Motors buy-out was different in some critical ways. It was the largest transaction financed through an ESOP; it provided for the distribution of stock equally among all employees; and made provision for voting rights with the stock ownership after ten years, when the covenants were satisfied.

The challenge of garnering support from employees and managers, and then negotiating financial and labor arrangements with the banks was just the beginning of a long process of change for the relationship between management and labor at what was to become Hyatt–Clark Industries. The United Auto Workers (UAW) local involved was known to be militant; it was viewed as a maverick by then international president, Doug Fraser. But the attitudes and capabilities of management to make the system work were more pivotal to the success of the employee-owned company. Initially opposed to the buy-out, one union official later converted and stressed the critical role management would play:

"People should concentrate on departure from the normal worker–management type system. They should work toward breaking down and changing that system when they have the

[1] See WGBH-TV, "Buy-Out," Enterprise Series, Boston, 1982.

power to do so which is in the critical stages of negotiations. What that would mean would be two things: Either the thing would be a success with a new kind of management, or it wouldn't go through at all. And either of those things is better than having to go through it with the old style of management."

The change in the legal structure of the company was an outward sign that changes in relationships were needed. One of these changes was to improve the union–management relationship. The union had been unwilling to make concessions that would have kept the plant going as part of General Motors and lost the lifeblood of support from the parent company. Would it be willing to make concessions now?

The central question the union and management had to grapple with was whether they were still adversaries or now owners. Throughout the negotiations among union, management, banks, and General Motors, this was a question that would not declare itself. The old resentments and attitudes did not vanish. Problems came up over whether supervisors and employees should be subject to the same discipline and how the lines of authority should work. That is, who should have a role in hiring the new plant manager (if indeed a plant manager was needed at all under employee ownership) and how should wage and salary reviews be distributed between managers and other employees? Should it be by percentage of salary or an across-the-board figure unrelated to the higher salaries of managers? How was compensation to be administered for the president and other key officers of the company? If bonuses and increases were withheld to make the compensation at least internally consistent in principle, how was the newly formed company to retain top management? How could the new venture succeed without a committed management team?

Some issues such as plant layout, capitalization, and hiring the plant manager were eventually worked out. In an effort to create an ongoing forum for the discussion of knottier problems and to prepare employees to assume full ownership in 10 years, Doug Howell, the new president hired by Hyatt–Clark Industries, instituted a variety of training programs and participatory management processes. Key among these, in Howell's view, was a series of roundtable discussions with groups of 10 hourly employees held four times a week. Howell felt "The roundtable discussions helped me to get a sense of the pulse of the company. They were my window into the work life and concerns of the company's future owners." An employee summarized the process: "There was evidence that the roundtables were getting results in a broader sense as well. A kind of peer pressure was emerging which promised greater cooperation. People did not hesitate to complain about workers, hourly or salaried, who did not carry their fair share of the load." One employee commented: "Some clown out there tells me I'm not going to make it, and I'll put my shoulder to the wheel and double the effort just to prove you wrong." And another explained: "Everything is much better now. Before it took you forever to get a pack of pencils. All that red tape and everything. Now people say, 'Sure, when do you want it?' And, if they can't get it for you right away, they tell you where you are on the list and get it to you as soon as they can."

The future of the Hyatt–Clark employee-owned plant remains uncertain. Will management be able to establish a commonality of interest with the shareholder work force so that productivity enables Hyatt–Clark Industries to succeed as a supplier in the same competitive environment where it failed as part of General Motors?

WHEN THE JAPANESE OWN AN AMERICAN PLANT

Employee-owned companies are one place in which the older modes of labor–management relations are crumbling. Foreign companies which now operate in the United States are another. Will these foreign companies be successful at eliciting better quality and quantity from American workers than their U.S. counterparts?

One of the most interesting and fruitful ways of beginning to answer this question is to observe Japanese plants operating with an American work force. Among the largest is Nissan Motor Corporation's plant in Smyrna, Tennessee. There, a new way of working is evolving under the company's American president. Local interest in the new plant was remarkable. Nissan received 80,000 applications for 2,600 production jobs when it opened. The opportunity to participate in a high commitment work system driven by changes in management style proved to have broad appeal. Through a team structure "production technicians" (one of only four job classifications at the plant) are responsible for both assembly and inspection.

Now, in a very interesting extension, General Motors and Toyota Motor Corporation have undertaken a joint venture, New United Motor Manufacturing, Inc., at a former General Motors facility in Fremont, California. The UAW and General Motors-Toyota have had a heated controversy over whether the new facility will be union or nonunion. As the following excerpt from the March 30, 1984, letter sent to workers on the recall list suggests, the management of the new venture is aiming for a new era in labor–management relations, whatever its union status:

"As a new and independent company, our policies and labor relations will differ from those that existed when General Motors owned the Fremont facility. None of the former agreements with GM apply to us. If you are selected for employment, you will be considered as a newly hired employee of our company. We want to build an innovative labor relations atmosphere built on mutual trust and cooperation. We seek high morale and motivation among all employees. We consider each employee to be a valuable resource. The full involvement of all employees in the workplace is essential to our mutual success. Our production system relies heavily on the team concept. Each employee will be assigned to a team, will perform all work tasks of that team, and may work within other teams and departments to maximize quality and productivity.

"Our company will use an innovative production system based upon Toyota's production methods. Our goal is to build the highest quality cars in the world, at the lowest possible cost to the American consumer, while providing fair wages and benefits.

"We recognize that high caliber people are necessary to successfully meet the challenge of this competitive industry. We will *pay you a competitive wage. In return*, we expect excellent attendance, high productivity, and the best quality work from you. Too many auto plants have become noncompetitive because of high absenteeism, low productivity, and poor quality. We cannot repeat past mistakes. Each team member (salary and hourly) must cooperate to make this plant a competitive and productive facility. It is only through these joint efforts that we, as a team, will be able to secure your future."

According to the same letter, applicants to the new plant will be selected after four days of "interviews, job simulations, and detailed discussions about our philosophy and objectives," followed by a 90-day probationary period. New hires will be selected for one of three broad job classifications (far fewer than when General Motors owned the facility): Division I (production), Division II (skilled trades), and team leaders. It is the explicit expectation that team members from both divisions will perform all other assignments in the group as well as his or her own.

New United Motor Manufacturing, Inc. may well succeed in growing an alternative work system on American soil. It may address the need for American companies to begin to demonstrate the successful blending of quality and efficiency that will put American management back into the competition.

What is striking about Hyatt–Clark Industries and the Nissan plant at Smyrna is that they illustrate the willingness and ability of American workers to be competitive in the international marketplace. A change in management and labor relations helped to bring out the latent potential of the work force. The workers at Hyatt made a commitment to the new company that they were not prepared to make to General Motors. The workers at Smyrna have responded to Japanese ownership more productively than most American workers respond in American-owned plants.

Many books point to Japanese managerial practices as a key element in getting work force support. But more than managerial practices is involved. The long history of conflictual labor relations between many American companies and their work forces predisposes management and labor to poor working relationships. It is a part of our culture; not a necessary part, but a pervasive one. Most managers who have never dealt with a union will, if thrown into negotiations, immediately adopt a confrontational stance and seek to best the union in a contest. Rank and file employees elected to union office for the first time ordinarily adopt a posture of demands and threats of work stoppages if demands are not met by management.

This national tendency to confrontation over secondary goals, in particular the effort to best the other side, is excused in the United States as part of our culture—as if a culture could not be modified. A real divergence exists between the interests of management and labor, some say, so there must be overt conflict.

There is also a real unity of some interests—so must there not also be overt cooperation? The American worker is fiercely independent, unwilling to accept management direction without question, it is said, so that confrontations are inevitable. There is some truth in this. But the American worker is also capable, hard working if given the opportunity, and hopeful of being recognized for contributing. Therefore, if management is reasonably sensitive and responsive, confrontations need be few.

A major indictment of much of American management is its inability to work out a more constructive relationship with unions and the work force. The opportunity has never been greater. And it is a striking indictment of much union leadership that it watches as jobs are lost yet finds no alternative strategy to benefit union members than that of confrontation. Today's economic environment offers an opportunity to managers and union officials to escape this indictment. The pressures to be competitive in order to survive permit, even require, both sides to identify their most fundamental objectives and to pursue them directly in relationship with the other side.

SUMMARY

Managers in unionized companies will encounter special obstacles to greater competitiveness. The old ways of doing things—often conflict ridden and legalistic—have led to labor and management patterns of behavior which often obscure the true purpose of their relationship. Even with this history of conflict a manager today has no excuse for not attempting to work with union officials both to enhance the competitiveness of the company and to provide fair treatment for the employees.

Experiments with employee ownership and by foreign companies with facilities in the United States suggest that there is much room for broadening the cooperative aspects of labor–management relations. The next chapter will describe the efforts of some managers to provide direction to the union, and of some unions to provide direction to management, in order to become more competitive.

13

Unions And Competitiveness Thinking

Nearly one in five American employees belongs to a labor union; in the industrial sector the proportion is closer to two in five. These people and the companies that employ them are an important part of the American economy. Yet it seems that unionized companies are often the most vulnerable to competitive pressures. Can unionized companies survive in today's marketplace without government protection? Managers in some companies are trying to find a way to do so, sometimes with the active assistance of union leaders.

The union steward at a large northeastern auto assembly plant commented: "Things are different around here today. In the past I came in on Monday morning and the first thing I did was to ask for a list of disciplinary actions that the company had taken over the weekend. Who had been suspended for fighting? Who'd been suspended for drinking or insubordination? Who'd been docked a half-day's pay for being late or absent?

"When I had the list, I'd look it over, then go out on the plant floor. I'd spend the day looking for company violations of the contract to file grievances about. Where was some guy assigned to work outside his classification? Where was a foreman doing bargaining unit work? Where was the area cluttered and unsafe? When I got enough grievances I'd be able to trade them off in grievance meetings with the company against the disciplinary actions that had been taken over the weekend. That way I'd keep people from being suspended or having their pay docked.

"But I don't do that anymore. When I come in on Monday morning I still ask for a list of disciplinary actions taken by the company on the weekend. But when I've got the list, I don't go dig up company violations anymore. Instead I call the company's representative and I say, 'I've got a list of disciplinary actions from the weekend. Let's get together and see what we can do to work these problems out.' "[1]

This change in approach on the union's side is a major shift in the spirit and manner in which industrial relations are practiced at the plant. It is based on a new philosophy—one that takes the competitive stance of the company into account. In recent years managers have been working hard to develop a common understanding of competitive problems with labor; they hope that from this will evolve an opportunity to successfully confront competitive challenges. In some instances unions and management have engaged in bitter strikes; in others a cooperative effort has developed without a confrontation. In still others the union has taken the initiative itself. This chapter is about these different approaches to the problem of building a labor–management consensus about competitiveness.

CHANGING ATTITUDES THROUGH CONFLICT

It used to be said that union and management are adversarial when bargaining over the terms of a collective bargaining agreement, but they become cooperators during the life of the agreement to make it work. Yet, for many years the areas of cooperation

[1] From a discussion with James MacDonald, President, General Motors Corporation, at Boston, April, 1981.

narrowed as contracts became more and more detailed. What started at General Motors Corporation as a 1-page agreement in the 1930s had become a 300-page national agreement with a 200-page local supplement by the 1980s. The contract rules became the relationship and for both management and labor negotiating as adversaries during the life of the agreement frequently became the modus operandi. As a direct result, opportunities for cooperation were lost.

Under the impact of increased competition, with jobs being lost, change is beginning to occur. The process of change can be long and difficult and there is no guarantee of success. Because of this, managers have to work hard at turning poor union relations around.

The negotiations at Townsend Chemical Company illustrate the intersection of old ways of practicing labor relations with a new need to face and meet competitive pressures. During both the 1978 and 1981 negotiations management's principal aim was to win concessions from the union. They believed these give backs were necessary for the survival of the firm and union members' jobs and paychecks. Although progress was made, the cost to both management and labor was great.

In early May 1978 Robert Hart, vice president for manufacturing at Townsend, began contract negotiations with Local 904 of the Chemical Employees International Union. His goal for the new contract was to make substantial changes in the work rules and job classifications. As he explained: "Most of the work rules had once been simply common practices that management had agreed in bargaining to follow as if they were part of the contract. A lot of them had evolved out of the production process and plant layout that is unique in chemical manufacturing . . . with separate buildings, over the years, informal work groups developed . . . strict bidding procedures controlling moves between the sections were gradually bargained into the contract.

"All of this grew up rather haphazardly at the beginning. We had to get things done so someone figured out a way to do it. Putting them into the contract tended to make them seem like they were engraved in stone when really they just started out as one way to do things. Maybe they weren't the best ways to begin with or maybe things have just changed around those ways of doing things so that they no longer make any sense. Whatever happened, because of these rather spontaneously developed practices that are now written rules, you can hardly make a move around here without checking the contract first.

"Frankly, I don't even know what some of these rules mean or how to administer them. And I bet if you asked some of the union people, they wouldn't really know either.

"We spend a lot of time trying to figure out the meaning of complicated language and intricate procedures just so we can say we are doing it by the contract. There must be a better way for us and for the union."

When contract negotiations began, Hart set about to win back some of the flexibility that the company had negotiated away. Hart took 128 work rule changes to the bargaining table and insisted that they be resolved before wage and benefit issues would be discussed by the company—a hard bargaining stance designed to let the union know the company was serious. At the same time, the company prepared for a possible strike by making large shipments and building high inventories.

It took two rounds of bargaining—in 1978 and 1981—for the company to make major gains toward winning the flexibility it needed to compete. The need for two rounds of negotiations shows that bargaining to achieve competitiveness is sometimes a long process, not achieved overnight or over a year or two. These negotiations also put enormous pressure on the relationships among managers, labor representatives, and the rank and file until the new way of doing things is accepted as necessary for the long-run viability of the firm. In the process human relationships may be strengthened or permanently damaged. Of course, managers play a determining role in guiding the course of these events.

In 1978 bargaining at Townsend over the proposed work rule changes continued up to the contract deadline. Key language changes would have allowed the company greater flexibility in temporary work assignments and overtime distribution procedures. These language changes were eventually won in exchange for the largest wage and benefit settlement ever offered at the Townsend company. The company viewed the settlement, although costly, as a necessary investment in its future ability to manage profitably. The company obtained a new agreement which was a complete agreement. This meant that all past practices not in the new contract were no longer binding on the company. Although the direct cost of labor was higher, the constraints of the past were considerably loosened.

Gains from the work rule changes won in 1978–1979 began to founder on the shoals of implementation. The large pay settlement, fresh in the employees' minds and pockets, had helped to win initial acceptance for the new contract. In further attempts to escape increasing competitive disadvantages, Townsend reduced its payroll by 20 percent in 1980, including an 18 percent cut in salaried staff. Combined with an increase in overtime and subcontracting, the layoffs were seen as an indication that management was not really trying to retain jobs for employees.

By 1981 the rule changes were beginning to affect the most skilled employees, who began to resist. From Hart's point of view the cost of buying back the work rules had already begun to pay off: profits were beginning to increase, productivity was on the rise, and employee attitudes seemed to have improved. Total employment had been reduced and by 1981, with the increased productivity, overtime was down sharply in comparison to previous years. As the 1981 contract talks approached, Hart began to sense a growing resistance to further rule changes in the contract.

He saw an increasing number of grievances as an outward manifestation of resistant attitudes. Everett Brown, Townsend's president, saw these developments as critical. He was trying to reduce the number of written rules. In place of rules he wanted to create a relationship with employees that was less reliant on written agreements and more committed to ongoing problem solving. As Hart explained: "I'd like to just be able to come up the best solution that the employees and I can provide at the moment. Why can't we just do things in an efficient manner rather than the convoluted and sometimes outlandish way we've had to in the past because of the contract—or someone's understanding of the contract—the two not being always the same?

"Some of these rules are so complicated that I don't see how they can be of any use to the guy on the floor who just wants to know where his job stands if there are layoffs or what to do if his supervisor asks him to work overtime.

"It doesn't do him any good to have to get an official informal ruling, sort of like an attorney general's opinion, before he can figure out what to do. The time, the energy it takes is unreasonable."

The company's major objectives in the 1981 contract negotiations were to continue along the path begun in the 1979 contract talks: to press for increasing flexibility to compete through further changes in the work rules and job classifications. An important ingredient in this new formula for competitiveness would be its ability to build some trust among employees who would have to be convinced that the competitive threat was real if they were to ratify new changes in the contract.

Changes in managerial personnel since the time of the last contract seemed provocative to employees, especially to the most senior employees who were just beginning to be affected by the rule changes. The presence of new managers confused employees. They were uncertain if they were making rule concessions to a known management that needed the changes to compete or to strangers who may not have understood the situation well enough to know if the changes were required and what sacrifice was entailed for some of the employees.

Jackson, a production worker at Townsend for 20 years, questioned a member of the union's bargaining committee: "Just who am I making these sacrifices for? Is another new manager going to come in with some new ideas on how I should keep my job—and demand even more? . . . Will managers be around to remember that I made a sacrifice? Will it make a difference?"

Protection extended through work rules in the contract was precious to employees like Jackson, who commented: "I wouldn't know where I was working from day to day. They would make me feel like a skilled craftsman one day and a janitor the next. I feel like they want to take my seniority away."

When the negotiations opened in June, Hart and Brown again took a number of rule changes to the table—this time 119—and insisted that the work rule changes be discussed before pay issues. Specifically, Hart and Brown needed to win increased control over work flow, greater flexibility in assignment and transfer of employees, a streamlined grievance procedure, and general modifications of the contract to make it applicable to a work force reduced from 400–500 to 159 employees in 1981. Most of the remaining employees were in their 40s and 50s and had 20 years of seniority. In exchange for the rule changes, management again offered a large financial settlement.

This time the membership balked. Shortly after the negotiations began the company implemented a plan to further reduce the work force and laid off more employees. Tension mounted and on July 27 the union voted to strike rather than to accept the proposed additional rule changes and economic package proposed by the company. The strike wore on for months with no apparent movement by either side. At one point the union suggested that the dispute be submitted to arbitration. Management rejected the proposal as Hart explained: "We don't want someone who doesn't know our business coming in and making decisions about what we can and cannot do."

As the strike continued management decided to implement a decision made earlier in the year to acquire a second packaging and distribution site in the south. The decision was announced at the end of October. To drive the point home to striking employees, a large "For Sale" sign was put up at the warehouse within a mile of the main entrance to the plant.

In late September the union's national president intervened in the deadlocked situation and proposed to the company through a third party that a private top level meeting be convened. Following the meeting the union's regional director took over as chief spokesman from the local leadership in the negotiations. With this change in players, negotiations were moved off dead center. Within a week the union had agreed to accept the company's last offer and the strike ended. On November 4, 129 union employees returned to work at Townsend.

Initially there was bitterness among the employees as a result of losing the strike. Similarly, supervisors resented the long hours the strike had imposed on them. To his credit, company president Brown did not try to take advantage of the union; instead he set about to improve communications and relations with the returning workers. As part of this effort, the company decided to settle rather than litigate the unfair labor practice charge that the union had filed over the company's decision to subcontract out some of its bargaining unit work. Brown also initiated a series of face-to-face meetings with the hourly workers in an effort to demonstrate that he was both accessible to them and concerned about labor–management relations in the plant.

These efforts bore fruit; Brown commented, "Productivity is up, grievances are down, people are performing in the new broadened job classifications, and are sometimes willing to go even beyond what was negotiated."

OLD WAYS IN THE NEW ENVIRONMENT

The events at Townsend Chemical Company are a typical microcosm of old style collective bargaining in which the union viewed with skepticism management's claimed need for greater flexibility to maintain or restore competitiveness. Even where the competitive threat is clear to employees, the benefits and guarantees they enjoy are difficult to give up when their sacrifice is viewed as enhancing corporate profits. At Townsend, the union was fortunate to maintain a presence in the plant at all. Other companies might have moved swiftly to oust the shrinking, somewhat divided, and certainly strike-weary bargaining unit. In the case of Townsend, management's purpose was not to rid the company of the union.

Most of all, the process of winning greater management flexibility at Townsend was an expensive proposition for all the people involved. All invested a great amount of time that could have been devoted to other things during the long negotiations and strike. The union was nearly destroyed and was left much smaller and weaker.

The Townsend experience and others like it raise critical questions that unions will have to resolve as the competitive pressures of deregulation and foreign rivals continue to require higher productivity and lower costs for firms that expect to survive. Do unions have to defend contract provisions no matter what their current impact is on present production requirements? Must they defend individual rights under the contract or past practice without regard to the impact of the grievance on the business as a whole or on other members' jobs? Is there a way for them to work with the company to save jobs while simultaneously carrying out their mission of representing the membership? Do unions have to stand or fall?

At Townsend Chemical Company events took labor to the brink of disaster before it could agree to settle a strike and change its relationship with management. Not all unions need to be brought to the precipice in order to respond to the competitive market. Packard Electric, a GM division, provides an example of a union that was able to anticipate events and to respond to them. Although the eventual outcome has not yet lived up to the promise of a new day in industrial relations, it shows potential. Perhaps management was initially a bit more skilled in handling the situation at Packard, so that a confrontation with the union was avoided. The clearest difference between the two situations is seen in union leadership's conception of its role and responsibility to the rank and file. At Townsend union leadership saw itself solely as guardians of the status quo. At Packard union leadership saw itself as creators of a different environment to help preserve members' jobs. At Townsend management had to fight out a long strike to change union leadership's vision of its role. At Packard management was able to achieve the same end by persuasion. At both companies, however, management accepted the role of actively influencing the union's concept of how best to protect employees' interests.

PLANNING TO COMPETE

As Bert Olsen, Packard's general manager, rose to deliver a speech to employees in 1973, he knew that he was ushering in a new era at the plant. He also knew that the group gathered before him would not be glad to hear what he had to say. "There will be no more bricks and mortar added to this facility until things are turned around," he began.

Although Olsen knew that all the employees were probably aware of the problems in the plant that had led management to this conclusion, he took the opportunity to summarize them:

"As you all know, since 1961 we've had a boom in business here. Because of the rapid growth in sales we've been able to expand existing facilities, add new ones, and increase the number of employees we have been able to provide for. But over that same period of time things got a bit too loose around here. You all know what I mean—higher labor costs, low morale, shoddy work, declining productivity, and too much absenteeism. Relations with the union have deteriorated to the point where management feels like it's an armed encampment some days. All of this has to get turned around and fast. And here is how it's going to get turned around. Although even now we need additional space and facilities which would lead to new hires, we are not going to commit one more dollar to expanding this facility until we get some real cooperation from you in getting our products out the door quicker, with less foul ups and poor work along the way. Simply put, you guys have got to start producing."

Subsequent to the "no more bricks and mortar" speech in 1973, Packard Electric came under increasing pressures from competitors and declining auto sales. Packard's wire assembly operation, where most of Packard's employees worked, was particularly vulnerable to competitive threats. The operation was labor intensive, employed low skill workers, and robotics was limited in applicability. In addition, most of the changes in new car models' wiring required reworking of production processes every year. The components operation at Packard was less vulnerable. Components tend to have consistent designs. They are also more easily kept cost competitive because the process is considerably automated, capital intensive, and high-volume.

Between 1973 and 1977 Packard executives studied and began to implement other strategies to help keep them competitive. In 1977 the election of new union leadership suggested for the first time that the union might play a constructive role in helping the company meet competitive challenges from home and abroad. After campaigning on a platform supporting the preservation of jobs through cooperation with management, Mike Bindas was elected the shop chairman, and Morris Muntz the new local president. Shortly after their election a series of weekly communication meetings with management was initiated, a program of jointly sponsored activities developed, and a management task force to improve productivity established.

These initial efforts at better communication led to the establishment of a jobs committee in May 1978 and a series of off-site meetings out of which grew a joint labor–management quality of work life committee. The initial ground rules for the committee required that discussions about quality of work life in the plant would be off the record, that no job loss would result as a direct consequence of projects undertaken by the committee, and that bargaining would be left to the bargainers. The broad mandate of the jobs committee was to "develop an ongoing union–management approach that will maintain job security and identify opportunities for hiring at the Warren operations." It was also to concern itself with employee involvement in business operations.

Composed of eight members from upper management and eight union officials the jobs committee made quick progress. Their philosophy was formulated:

"We believe every business has a responsibility to its customers, its employees, and the community in which it exists, and shall strive to satisfy the needs and security of each.

"We share in the belief that a successful business provides and maintains an environment for change and is built on a foundation of trust, where every person is treated with respect and offered an opportunity to participate. We are totally committed to the patience, dedication, and cooperation necessary to build this foundation.

"We also believe that this can be accomplished through a functioning partnership built on the wisdom, the knowledge and the understanding of the employees, the union, and management."

The jobs committee initiated the development of four additional plants to be known as the Warren branch operations. The new operations were based on a new product line. The committee planned to make the new operations competitive by combining assembly classifications to reduce job fragmentation and rotating on-line and off-line jobs to build teamwork and broaden skills. On February 20, 1979, the jobs committee announced that 115 additional employees would be hired.

By June 1981 the jobs committee could show remarkable achievements. Based on the principle that expansion should be in the area where the company could successfully compete, 379 new employees had been added to the work force, 850,000 square feet of additional floor space had been added, and a total of $100 million invested.

Despite these impressive achievements all was not bright and rosy at the plant. A jobs committee plan to locate a future molding operation facility in North Carolina aroused opposition from some managers and employees. Larger concern about the loyalty of the union officials on the committee also surfaced: "The task force will sell us down the river." "More work? I want more money." "The union is taking management's side. They don't care about us."

Ultimate acceptance of some of the jobs committee's recommendations and plans would, of course, rest on acceptance by the members through the ratification process.

Despite these labor–management efforts through the jobs committee, by 1981 it was clear that Packard would not remain competitive. If current methods of remaining cost effective were followed, only 64 percent of Packard's operations would be competitive in 1986. Again, labor and management were able to formulate a strategy for dealing with the company's long-range competitiveness problem. This formulation, called the Plan to Compete, had four main components: Labor intensive final assembly operations would be moved to low wage rate locations; personnel would be decreased through early retirement, voluntary termination of employment, and part-time employment; work that had been out-sourced to Mexico would be brought back and automated to make the operations cost effective. The plan also called for an overall strategy of maintaining GM's business; increasing sales outside of GM; developing new products, and reducing material costs, inventory, and operating expenses. The last and most controversial part of the plan was designed to keep assembly work. It called for the establishment of a two-tiered wage structure where only new hires paid $6.00 an hour would perform assembly work in Warren. This was called the Final Assembly Option (FAO).

The jobs committee recognized that in the current environment, further reductions in GM wage rates, in effect at Warren through an International Union of Electrical, Radio, and Machine Workers (IUE) contract, would be necessary. They selected a subcommittee to suggest possible approaches to the negotiators. On May 3 negotiations were opened for the new local agreement in Warren. Negotiations at the national level between the IUE and GM had been completed and called for an industrywide freeze on cost of living adjustments and other concessions. On June 24, 1982, the IUE local ratified a new contract embodying all of the principal components of the Plan to Compete except for the FAO. Ratification of that part of the contract was postponed until the entire work force returned from layoff.

Attempts to win acceptance of the FAO from the membership foundered. Members rejected the creation of a two-tiered wage structure in 1983, despite the employment security guarantees offered in exchange. They went on to vote out of office the shop chairman who had recommended acceptance of the plan. Along with him, the entire bargaining committee, except for one member, was also removed from office.

The trust built through the quality of work life committee and expressed through the Plan to Compete was not enough to carry the new approach through the bargaining process and eventual rank-and-file ratification. Implementation of the plan was ultimately dependent on the ability of management and labor officials to convince the rank and file of the plan's efficiency. In this case, they were not successful. Members opposed to the FAO argued that behind the plan was an attempt to break the union by substantially lowering the pay of new hires. Members failed to recognize or believe the direct relationship between the concessions and the economic viability of the Warren division, using instead the perspective of GM in its entirety and seeing the plan as a boon to GM's profit margins.

Although the FAO was rejected, the efforts at Packard had moved the company to a more competitive position while enhancing the job security of the work force. What was important was not only the progress made but also the capacity of the union and management to set up a structure to address the problems and to use the collective bargaining process to present choices to the membership that might have further protected jobs. The fact that the membership was not willing in 1983 to go the whole distance did not doom future efforts to failure. In this new world filled with domestic and foreign competition, the membership was understandably reluctant to sacrifice until they were convinced it was necessary and would do some good. Over time the competitiveness thinking developed in a few unions at the leadership level percolated down to the rank and file who are, after all, most directly affected.

WHEN THE UNION LEADS

Hard bargaining by a company to try to establish competitiveness is not necessarily inimical to collective bargaining. On the contrary, accounts of concession bargaining show that unionized facilities can respond to economic distress and that difficult adjustments can be made by the union involved. Work rules can be cut, efficiency and cost competitiveness recaptured, and jobs saved. Under the current system, however, an extraordinary amount of pain is inflicted along the way for both sides.

There is another way. In certain industries and in some companies the parties are going back to the bargaining table, this time not to argue over the division of the shrinking economic pie. This time they are more like architects working together to design a new structure more suited to and resilient in present and future economic environments. It will not replace the old structure but rather arch over it and provide a framework for the old institutions to begin to better serve new requirements. Some call this new approach competitiveness thinking.

Unions are just now beginning to use competitiveness thinking. Among the leaders is the International Union of Bricklayers and Allied Craftsmen (BAC) under the able leadership of John T. Joyce. The union has established a committee on the future that has assessed and analyzed the labor and product market of its industry and established programs to increase the union employers' share of work.

This task is likely to require a new view of the purpose and role of the international union. From the point of view of managers who are trying to become competitive, this alteration in the union's view must be encouraged. To be able to do so effectively, a manager must understand the union's perspectives, both old and new.

The traditional attitude of unions, such as the BAC which represents employees in an entire industry, paid little attention to individual firms. Whether a particular company succeeded or failed seemed of no importance because no jobs were at risk for the union. This is because the union had the entire industry organized. If a particular company lost a project or went out of business, another union company could be expected to pick up the business and along with it the jobs. Since the union represented employees at all companies, the union would represent these new people also. Perhaps they would be the same laid off individuals. Thus, in terms of the key objective of jobs, it did not matter to the union which company failed or succeeded.

In the automotive industry, for example, the United Auto Workers (UAW) used to represent virtually all employees of the American automobile companies. The UAW had complete control of the industry, so that when Studebaker, for example, was threatened with going out of business, the union helped the company's employees through the terminations. The union did not consider that its own existence was threatened or that the job security of a large proportion of its members might be imperiled.

Today, however, the UAW does not have the same control of the industry. It does not yet represent employees of the Japanese companies now operating auto manufacturing plants in this country; these Americans employed by Japanese companies are nonunion. Thus, should an American company lose its share of automobile sales, most likely a foreign company would gain the sales. Years ago if market share were lost by GM, then Ford or Chrysler would have been likely to gain that share and UAW members at Ford and Chrysler would benefit. Today should GM lose market share, it would more likely be gained by a Japanese firm, whose employees in Japan and America are not UAW members.

In consequence, the UAW must be concerned today when an American company's market share declines to a degree not conceived in the past. It must be willing to support the efforts made by individual companies to be competitive, otherwise the UAW's long-run future is in doubt. In a different industry, with little foreign competition, the BAC finds itself in a situation surprisingly similar to that of the UAW. Today's labor leaders know that by clinging to old ways they provide themselves and their members not a seaworthy ship for the future but a leaky and overcrowded life raft unlikely to make it through the present storm.

Today unions have less control over most industries. Increasingly whenever a union employer loses work, the company that picks up the work is nonunion. This dramatic threat to the future employment security of unionized workers is changing the relationship between employers and the union and bringing the union much closer to the competitive marketplace. This closeness has already begun to cause labor and management to ask a whole new set of questions about their relationship. Answering the questions is the tougher part of the job, but union and management have begun.

The pressure to operate nonunion is not based solely on labor cost factors, although they do play a role. If it were solely a matter of cost, then a union might secure its future and that of its members by generous wage concessions and special local deals to hold on to the work until the market improved. But this alone will not be successful. The competitive pressure also comes from a web of traditional practices and attendant rigidities, and from technical changes in the industry.

What are the unions thinking about? Attention to maintaining their present enrollment and recruiting new members is, of course, essential to the process. Beyond this they are looking at their industries as a whole and trying to design programs that respond to questions not traditionally addressed by unions in this country. How can the volume of sales as an industry be expanded? Can the distinctions which consumers see between union and nonunion tradespeople be sharpened to the union members' advantage? How can their product's share of the broad market, in communications or construction, for example, be expanded? Broadly, what role can the union play, not in advancing the interests of its members against employers, but in advancing the unionized sector of the industry? This is the essential element of competitiveness thinking, or trying to make the industry in which the union's members work more competitive and successful.

The strategy for implementing competitiveness has to be carefully thought through and designed to respond to the particular dynamics of each industry and area. Some tactics, however, may be common to most industries. These include contract flexibility, the willingness to experiment with innovations, and forging new alliances with management and consumers.

Above all, competitiveness thinking requires a commitment at all levels of the union to the survival and performance of the individual firm within the industry. The union employer and the union have never had a greater commonality of interest. The employer needs a competitive edge to acquire work volume and the union needs that edge for the employer, too.

This need of the union requires it to look at a broader role than it has exercised in the past. Traditionally the union has negotiated collective bargaining agreements and pursued the grievances of employees. These remain important functions. If collective bargaining and grievance handling are pursued as traditionally conceived, however, they become self-defeating in our competitive world.

Traditionally, the collective bargaining process progresses in two ways from the union side: First, it enlarges the scope of management activities which are subject to rules established by the agreement. Thus, agreements which began as one-page documents between management and labor have come to be hundreds of pages in length.

For years law professors and other commentators on labor relations hailed the process of negotiating more and more detailed contracts as the development of "common law of the shop." They referred to the grievance procedure in which increasingly complex labor contracts were interpreted and applied as "industrial jurisprudence." They hailed the substitution of a "rule of law" for open conflict between management and labor, in their view the only other alternative.

But the commentators failed to realize that the shop floor law they hailed was creating a work place full of shop floor lawyers: supervisors, workers, and union stewards who forgot that to be competitive the people in the business enterprise have to work together to resolve problems, remain flexible, and be efficient. Industrial jurisprudence was intended to throw out the unfair treatment of employees, but too often the baby—the economically viable enterprise—went out with the bath water.

Did the employees, the union members benefit? Yes, to a degree. Compensation and benefits rose; working pace and effort slowed. Then the layoffs began. The building trades have an expression for this: "What good is it to be the highest paid worker in town, if you're unemployed?" The employee also benefited from the grievance procedure—until too complex agreements and too formal procedures began to entangle legitimate grievances in a web of red tape.

As competition eroded the position of unionized firms, and union members by the tens of thousands lost their jobs, the unions continued business as usual. There were two exceptions: Local union officers in communities where layoffs were especially drastic began to accept concession contracts, like those at Townsend Chemical. And national union leaders watching their membership rolls decline began to ask if there were not some way to stem the tide.

As one of the first steps in its revitalization, the BAC commissioned polls of its members. The BAC, like virtually all other unions, has good downward communication to its members, but weak upward communications. Rarely do as many as 10 percent of its rank and file attend local membership meetings. Strike votes or contract ratification bring far more out into an emotional atmosphere to make a short-term decision. "Who is in touch with the members?" has become a question of serious concern to national unions over recent decades.

Politicians have faced the same problem—how to stay in touch with voters when political meetings are generally poorly attended by average voters. Mailings, newspapers, radio, and television permit politicians to carry a message to the voters—but what do the voters want to hear?

The politicians' answer has been to place increasing reliance on public opinion polls. What is public opinion today in the United States? Effectively it is what the polls say it is. Ask a politician what is public opinion in his or her district and more often than not a recent poll will be cited.

Could labor leaders take a leaf from the politicians' book? Doing so, the BAC commissioned a series of national polls of their membership, conducted by LDG Associates, a Gardner, Massachusetts, opinion polling firm. Included in an early survey was a series of questions about how rank and file members perceived their employers. Did the employer care about quality on the job? Was the work place safe? Did the supervisor consider the worker's opinion about the job? Was the worker's contribution recognized? For comparison to the responses of the rank and file, the same set of questions was given to the union officials who were asked what they thought the members would reply.

The results of the rank and file poll showed a membership substantially more favorably inclined to the supervisor than the union's leadership thought it would be. While areas of distrust were revealed, on most issues majorities of 80 percent and more described the employer as concerned about the quality of production, the safety of the worker, and the worker's opinions; and willing to recognize the craftsperson's contribution. If these were the conditions in the field, then the union's traditional concerns — advancing the rules in the agreement and pursuing grievances — seemed less important; not unimportant, but less important.

The union already knew that focusing on negotiations and grievances was not keeping its membership from eroding. It was beginning to understand why. Complex agreements limited efficiency; concentration on grievances serviced only a minority of the members. The desire of the rank and file to cooperate with employers to create more employment was being ignored. All surveys showed unemployment as the greatest concern of the rank and file.

The union then undertook a research effort to discover the source of the decline in its membership. Was it nonunion competition? The answer was yes, to some degree; but just as important was the decline in union masonry construction caused by aggressive competition from substitute materials—wood, metal, and glass—whose firms were outselling masonry companies in the marketplace.

More farsighted than most unions, the BAC had a few years earlier established a series of institutes with their employers to jointly improve the masonry industry. A jointly directed institute conducted research and development efforts in masonry technology, advertising, and other promotion programs. Materials manufacturers were drawn into committees with the union and contractors to consider the problems of the industry as a whole.

What could the union do to help make the masonry industry more competitive against substitutes? A number of possibilities emerged: The union was able to develop an enhanced training effort for members, help provide funds for industry research and development, promote quality construction among its members, and reduce costs by altering provisions of labor contracts where necessary. Most importantly, by internal communications the union began to persuade its local union officers that they must accept responsibility for helping to reverse the decline of the union by playing a more imaginative role in promoting the business success of unionized masonry construction.

Disagreements between management and labor continued to occur; however, the union could no longer afford to limit its attention to the area of disagreements. Instead a substantial new arena of cooperative effort had to be developed, and a united front shown to customers of the industry: one stressing quality and cost effectiveness in construction.

What label would the union attach to this new broader conception of its role? "Enhanced collective bargaining" suggested some; "competitiveness thinking" suggested others. The important thing was not the label, of course, but the reality.

CONTRACTS FOR COMPETITIVENESS

Encouraging signs at the national level indicate that collective bargaining can effectively address the problems posed to both labor and management by foreign competition. The 1984 agreement between the UAW and GM is a landmark contract in this regard. Rather than seeking wage increases as the major goal of the talks, the union focused on employment security. Union leaders explicitly recognized the long-term financial health of the company; this approach is likely to exert a substantial influence on other agreements in industries facing increased domestic or foreign competition.

It was acknowledged by GM that a partnership with the union is a necessary ingredient of its business strategy. The company granted what may turn out to be large employee pay increases through profit sharing while enhancing its competitive position by not awarding outright wage increases. Another essential ingredient for competitiveness was the union's flexibility in negotiating terms with the company, liberating rather than hamstringing the company in its struggle to produce a quality product at a competitive price.

One of the most significant elements of the agreement concerns the union's evolving view of what contributes to job security. Traditionally, unions seek job security by imposing regulations on management's right to do such things as subcontract work or close plants. The problem is that such restrictions can cripple a company's ability to compete.

General Motors and the union showed considerable sophistication by adopting a different path to job security. To preserve jobs, the UAW adopted three main strategies: One was to give GM greater flexibility in its labor costs by giving most pay increases as bonuses tied to profits, not as wage increases. This will help GM meet Japanese price competition.

The Japanese auto industry has used bonuses to keep its own "fixed" labor costs low. By adapting this practice to American conditions, GM is likely to sell more vehicles. The UAW is likely to be better able to maintain employment, even though, if competition drives profits down, pay increases via the bonuses will be lower. This creates a direct tradeoff between wage levels and employment levels in which the UAW for the first time opts convincingly for preserving jobs, not gaining higher pay levels.

The second part of the job security strategy is to work with the company to expand GM's business. The UAW sought and received from the company written commitments about future small car production in the United States. The company also cited past and prospective investment commitments intended to keep the company competitive. The UAW saw its best chance for job security in the company's being a strong and effective force in the marketplace. It chose to work with the company rather than to add to the obstacles GM faces.

A difficulty in developing an extended concept of collective bargaining has been to identify the role of the trade union leader when the union has as great a need to cooperate with management as to challenge it. The UAW–GM contract is full of opportunities for cooperation via various joint labor–management committees. In one particularly intriguing example, the agreement established a New Business Venture Development Group to promote prospective nontraditional businesses in order to provide job opportunities for UAW members. Union representatives on this group will have a remarkable opportunity to sharpen their business understanding and to influence the corporation's long-term direction, representing a noticeable leap by unions into entrepreneurship.

Finally, the company and the union established a $1 billion fund to assist workers in retraining, relocating, and readjusting to the changes and possible dislocations created by adapting to the competitive marketplace. The agreement of the company and the union to shoulder this responsibility goes a long way toward removing it from the backs of taxpayers.

Under this agreement, the concept of earning pay increases has largely replaced that of pay increases as a matter of entitlement. The pact imposes only limited additional costs if GM finds itself in a difficult position in the marketplace but rewards employees handsomely if the company prospers.

Similarly, the agreement attempts to respond to competitive pressures in the labor market by widening differentials between skilled and unskilled employees, thereby inducing less skilled employees to upgrade their capabilities, and permitting the company to compete with other companies for skilled people.

Management and labor have committed themselves to a partnership dependent on good will to make it successful. By putting so many new elements together, and linking them by a joint commitment to be successful in the marketplace, the UAW and GM have a fair claim to be credited with a revolution in American industrial relations.

THE SECOND BOTTOM LINE

In both union and nonunion work places successfully managing America's companies in an increasingly competitive environment will depend on the goodwill and cooperation of the work force and their flexibility in adapting to the new environment of 1980s competitiveness. In many cases, elaborate sets of work rules negotiated over the past decade in union plants must be broadened or eliminated in order to win this flexibility. There are signs that this can be done without destroying the relationship with the work force. There are signs it can be done while simultaneously enhancing labor–management relationships. In the previous illustration where this has been accomplished, management has played an active and initiating role in influencing the processes of collective bargaining. Rather than sitting back and letting the union come to them with demands, managers have begun to make demands where the competitiveness of the firm is at stake. This new approach, however painful to both parties in the short run, is distinctly positive in the long run.

The collective bargaining process has shown signs of resiliency in responding to the new demands that are being placed on it to win or maintain competitiveness. So far reactions from the union side have been understandably mixed. How have the unions and their members responded to efforts to adopt strategies to keep companies competitive, plants open, and people employed? Often with suspicion. First, unions have tried to ignore management initiated efforts. Then, unions have attempted to obstruct efforts, fearing a chance for management to communicate directly with employees on matters usually involving the union. Finally, in some instances the union's role has evolved toward a degree of participation in the efforts, as it has become clear that management's interest is not flagging, that the programs will not disappear, and that some employees welcome the opportunity to do more.

American managers are accustomed to a competitive marketplace. Endorsement of the values of cooperation often leaves them uncomfortable. This is appropriate, because American society has flourished in part due to competition among business enterprises. There are those who fear increased cooperation between management and labor will undermine our competitive marketplace. There is, however, no absolute choice to be made between competition and cooperation. Cooperation among people is necessary for any organization to function effectively. When management and union are at each other's throats at the work place, nothing gets done. Our economic system has a proper place for both cooperation and competition. A high degree of cooperation is required within firms in the broader marketplace. On one hand, as in sports, internal cooperation among team members is necessary to the effectiveness of the team. On the other hand, competition between management and labor can prevent a firm from competing successfully in the outside market. So cooperation and competition are not alternatives but rather complement each other in the economic process. Well-functioning business enterprises in which management and labor work together contribute to the vigor of competition between firms in the external marketplace.

Where there is too much internal conflict, the energies of managers and workers are diverted from satisfying the goals of each to the contest between them. Mistrust turns every aspect of industrial life into an occasion for a possible battle between management and labor. Trust permits the energies of people to be devoted to something other than adversary conflict. The high level of mistrust between managers and union officials in many American plants is one reason why managers prefer to have nonunion operations: it frees the attention of supervisors for matters other than conflict with unions. American unions are too good at their adversarial role. When they meet management head-to-head in our industrial work places, the unions often prevail. As a result, management tries to avoid the contest by being nonunion.

This is an aspect of American industrial relations that the British understand and other European and Japanese managers often fail to comprehend. In contrast to American managers who seem to be obsessed with being nonunion, their own experience in Europe and Japan suggests that union relations can be managed successfully just like other aspects of business. By and large European and Japanese managers do not confront the presence of strong and militant unions on the shop floor as American managers do. Instead the pressure of militant European and Japanese unions is felt primarily in the outside political environment, or at the industrywide level in collective bargaining. The combination of militant trade unionism with a strong base on the shop floor is unique to the Anglo–Saxon countries.

American managers do not wish to preserve this hostile environment. An opportunity exists to improve the employee relations environment using emerging attitudes and structures that complement and expand rather than compete with existing bargaining structures. If these new structures are successful, the unionized sector of our economy will have the opportunity to regain both competitiveness and increased employment security. Of course this will be of benefit not only to the companies, but also to the managers and other employees whose jobs depend on the success of current efforts.

Traditionally industrial relations concerns have been only loosely linked to the overall business strategy of the firm. The bottom line surely encompasses the firm's labor costs as a factor. But often the quality and nature of management's relationship to its work force got lost in the competition for management's attention.

This is beginning to change. In some companies, this process of evolution has already started. Philip Caldwell, when chairman at Ford, emphasized the crucial role labor relations play in his company's business strategy by referring to industrial relations as the "second bottom line." For the second bottom line to be positive, managers must actively try to understand, influence, and manage not only the outcomes of bargaining, as they have done previously, but also the processes and tenor of the interactions that ultimately influence what kind of bargain can be struck. Managers must see the work from the rank and file worker's point of view. It is no longer enough to view the union as an institution interested only in getting more rules and money than the last contract provided. It is also less reasonable now to view the union as an institution essentially outside the structure of the business with no interest in the economic realities of the firm. Management now has an opportunity to demand better performance in the handling of industrial relations not only by themselves, but by their counterparts on the union side. Based on a knowledge of the union's concerns and internal dynamics, management can begin to propose new solutions to old problems and to try to elicit the same from the unions. Rather than expecting that the union does not want to know or cannot understand the effects of new foreign and domestic competition, effective managements are beginning to assume the opposite and operate from that new vantage point.

In the same way that the innovative managers described in Chapter 11 are letting the work force do more by providing information and discretion, other managers with a vision of the future are providing more information about the business and encouraging the union to take a role in its success in the marketplace. This is far easier for today's managers than it was for their predecessors. Today's managers are less comfortable with conflict, more willing to communicate with others, and more willing to let others carry their share of the responsibility for an organization's success or failure. Applied to labor relations, these are great strengths.

SUMMARY

Competition and economic adversity have created an opportunity not seen for 60 years for management to forge new relationships with unions. Unionized companies are finding they cannot survive without union understanding and support. Reciprocally, unions are recognizing that they cannot survive when the company is in danger of collapse from foreign or new domestic competition. Extreme conditions have brought a changed role for both management and labor. Some unions are beginning to devote attention and resources to new approaches toward future relationships with management. It is crucial for managers to recognize the significance of these initiatives from the unions and to respond constructively to them.

The new generation is bringing its less conflict-ridden and more competitively oriented values to leadership positions in companies. How can a manager ensure that these values are transmitted to others in the organization?

14

Teaching A Work Ethic

When a person applies for a job at Acme Motor's nontraditional manufacturing plant described in Chapter 11, he or she is shown a videotape. On the tape current employees at the plant describe what it is like to work there. "It's no bed of roses working here," one says. Another offers, "You can make a good dollar here, but you have to earn it." Subtitles on the tape divide the employees' comments into sections. The first has to do with stress. "There's a lot of it, a lot of headwork," an older employee comments. "You have to take your work home to think about it."

VALUE IMPRINTING

Other employees describe problems in adjusting to what is expected of them by the other members of their production teams. One retreated into tranquilizers; another into alcohol. Both had problems at home. "But it isn't us," one says on the tape, "it's the pressure at work." Still, both have learned to deal with the stress, to think about work without being unduly pressured by it. "Things are great now at home," an employee says. "We've learned to deal with the problems."

Another subtitle is communications. "It's very important here," says an employee. "I went through the training in communications that's provided here at the plant. It was important for me because I was one who was apt to respond without really listening to what the other person had said. And that can really get you in a lot of trouble."

Another employee added, "We had some people come on. They never talked in meetings. They just didn't work out. We're based on a concept—participation. You've got to participate."

A third subtitle is learning and teaching. "You have to learn the whole assembly line," says an employee. "It's almost like going back to school. Some people have a problem. They're not used to learning. Here you have to keep learning all the time."

Another person recounted her personal experience with job rotation. "I finally got to enjoy what I was doing. I had about six months while I loved it. Then I had to give it up. I hated that. But I got the experience of training a new person to do my job. There's good and bad about that. But there's no job ownership here—it's share and share alike."

The final subtitle is advice. A young man in a knitted cap with a beard edging his jawline says succinctly, "I tell my friends, if you're the kind of person who likes to spend the day fitting screw A into hole B, then you'd never fit in here. You wouldn't like it at all. There'd be trouble from beginning to end." With these words the videotape ends.

Hardly a rosy picture of the plant. Is the company trying to turn away job seekers? The answer is yes, and no. It is trying to turn away a certain group of people—but it is also trying to attract a different group. Despite interviews and testing, the company is not certain it can identify those people who possess the human qualities it wants: acceptance of a challenge, acceptance of mental as well as physical labor, adaptability, desire for teamwork, and participative skills. So it has applicants view the videotape and hopes that those who find the description of the plant challenging will accept job offers, while others will go elsewhere. It is a negative sales technique: the applicant is encouraged to go elsewhere if the plant is not attractive to him or her.

In using the tape the company is also attempting to structure the expectations of its applicants. The danger in a plant which differs so dramatically from the norm—a plant where teamwork replaces a supervisor's direction, and where employees are expected to think and participate in production meetings—is that new employees will not fit in. If they bring expectations about behavior established elsewhere they may become dismayed about their new jobs and disrupt the existing organization in the plant. To avoid rapid turnover and to orient new hirees, the company uses the videotape to tell them what the plant will be like, and how they will be expected to behave.

Finally, via the videotape the company begins, even before an applicant is hired, to teach the values upon which the plant's work organization is based. Mutual effort, participation, learning, and teaching are not just techniques at the plant. They are positive values to be bought into by new employees and to be reinforced by periodic training.

When new employees are hired at J.M. Smucker Company their supervisors spend several days at an orientation session with them reinforcing the introduction which the employees get to the values and attitudes the company wants them to have.

When Nissan Motor Corporation committed itself to building a large manufacturing facility in Smyrna, Tennessee, in the early 1980s, it sent its first large group of American workers to Japan for training at its home plants. The training combined production skills, attitudes, and behavior. In Tennessee applicants were rigorously screened for suitability to the company's work ethic. Some went through several interviews and preemployment training before being offered a job.

At other Japanese facilities in the United States about 40 percent of the initial training of employees is devoted to work attitudes and values, and about 60 percent to technical information and skills. The Japanese are very conscious of the importance of attitude building; the translation of their term for it is "value imprinting."

These approaches to selecting and orienting new employees contrast markedly with those followed in most American companies. Traditionally American companies hire for a specific job, seeking specific work-related skills or ability. Training has been brief and entirely skill-related. In many instances training consists of no more than an hour's instruction at the job site by a supervisor or fellow employee. The basic philosophy seems to be, "We can train them in a week or less for a specific job, and let them go when business turns down or the job disappears." At the American and Japanese companies previously cited, months are spent in interviewing and selection, and more months in training—both about the job and about attitudes and behavior. The philosophy seems to be, "These are important people, whom we may well keep for a long time."

By and large American companies have been more concerned about introducing new managers to the mores of the company. But even there, less imagination has been devoted to this than one might expect. In many American companies it is still a fact that if one asks a group of managers what are the important values in the company and what are their own responsibilities in this regard, one is met by blank expressions or cynical observations. In many companies today's young managers, who are strongly value-driven in their own lives (although their own values are often different from those of the preceding generation), seem to be looking for just this sort of leadership from top management, and seem very dissatisfied that they do not receive it.

In some of our country's best performing companies discussions about mores and behavior are no longer neglected. At General Electric Company, managers concerned with executive development noted that what the company wants is commitment to its mission and values from its executives. Commitment is what a person puts into something. When thinking about values and mores most people conceive of something that is taught, being received passively by those to whom it is directed. Recognizing the inconsistency, GE added to their managerial training several days of out-of-doors projects and exercises intended to build teamwork, personal loyalty, and respect through involvement. Formal lessons come later.

This approach is similar in spirit to Nissan's sending American employees to Japan to see Nissan's values in action, and only later telling employees about values formally. It is also similar to Smucker's demonstration of how important it thinks the company's values are by having supervisors spend time with new employees. At GE, Nissan, and Smucker, to name but a few, actions speak as well as words.

Selection and training are beginning to be recognized as significant contributors to the performance of people in business; as such they are getting renewed attention. At a major rubber manufacturer, testing at assessment centers is now being used to select supervisors for new plants, often from people outside the industry. The results have been effective. The same tests revealed that some 25 percent of the supervisors in existing facilities should not be supervisors.

The rubber company's plants often operate on rotating shifts, a particularly difficult schedule for many people. In the past, applicants have accepted jobs without realizing what rotating shifts can mean, making turnover rapid and dissatisfaction continuous. To minimize turnover and to obtain a work force with greater job commitment, the company established an extensive orientation program prior to hiring. Applicants for employment are asked to bring in their families to discuss how a rotating shift operates. Then they are asked to go home and think about the job offer before accepting it. This procedure helps to avoid a spouse coming in a week after a person is hired and complaining, "I didn't know he/she would be away at night or on weekends."

Associated with greater selectivity in the hiring process at this company has been a dramatic enhancement of training. This has been accomplished largely through improving the quality of training personnel. The company's high flyers now pass through stints in training, and its influence in the company has risen greatly. At the company's new plants all three heads of training are now on their way to being plant managers. Selectivity in hiring and a new emphasis on the quality of training—both developments reflect the company's increasing awareness that the commitment and performance of rank-and-file employees are important to the company's business success.

At People Express Airlines, Inc. the training and management development group has special clout in the organization. The group's job is developing management skills and transferring the company's vision of itself as described in Chapter 11 to new employees. The training group has been composed of managers rotating through. Managers at People Express may apply for assignment to the group, but have to be selected. The primary criteria for selection to an assignment in the group is how well ↖ the applicant understands and can articulate the People Express vision. The choice of this criterion as the primary one reflects the company's top management view that technical competence can more easily be learned by new employees than can the company's vision and mores.

Recently a major magazine changed its selection process for advertising representatives. According to a key executive, the old hiring process was a series of luncheons at a private club. "If you survived the martinis and the meatballs, you got hired," he said.

In contrast, today five people do all the interviewing. One of those is an outside psychologist who has followed the magazine advertising industry for years. The psychologist is very knowledgeable about what makes a good salesperson.

Applicants are discussed and compared. The psychologist administers a test several hours long to each candidate and reports the results to the hiring group. Of particular significance is whether a person has the quality of persistence. Will he or she keep going back if the sale was not made on the first visit? This is a crucial element of the behavior the company seeks; persistence is also important because the advertising business depends on repeat customers.

At McDonald's Corporation and Holiday Inns, Inc. the corporate training facilities aspire to a university environment. Degrees are given to successful students. To some observers there is something comic about the combination of academic pretension and the reality of grilling hamburgers or keeping house for a living. Yet, by reaching for a professional attitude in their site managers both companies are able to get a uniformly higher standard of quality in the services offered and in the business aspects of their widely scattered establishments. Both companies realized that many people aspire to professional status and will respond with greater effort, improved ethics, and enhanced commitment if treated as professionals. Each company's top managers reinforce and direct these aspirations in people who are often poorly educated in a formal sense. By recognizing the desire of today's generation to advance up the social as well as economic ladder, managers are able to harness that desire and at the same time advance their competitive positions.

The curriculum at these training facilities is both accessible to the participants and advantageous to the companies. There is material about business management and customer orientation, all conceptual yet concrete, lacking the ambiguity of curricula at more academic institutions. There is hands-on experience, in which participants actually do things, not just listen in a classroom. There is an introduction to the expected mores and behavior of people in the company as a whole. Finally, there is the atmosphere of professionalism which enhances the participants' self-image.

At the other end of the spectrum, some companies which rely primarily on highly educated professionals for their business advantage also spend considerable effort in selection and training. "Mr. Watson Sr. used to say," IBM's Chairman John R. Opel told a *Fortune* magazine reporter, " 'You can take my factories, burn up my buildings, but give me my people and I'll build the business right back again!'[1] And he was right. There really isn't much magic . . . it's human qualities that make our company strong.

"We're a positive bunch of people," Opel continued, turning his attention to IBM's selection criteria. "I believe that like begets like. You look for people with the same qualities as other people who are building the company."

---

[1] "Views From the Top," *Fortune*, 9 January 1984, 54.

Initial selection of employees plays a critical role at IBM for several reasons. The company has a lifelong employment policy and places emphasis on promotion from within. Selection standards focus on academic performance and ability to fit into the corporation. The personnel staff at IBM conducts an initial screening, assessing an applicant's general academic credentials and personal characteristics. But IBM does no research, such as credit checks, on applicants; nor does it ask age. The company feels that these things pry into people's privacy without affecting the hiring decision. Standardized intelligence tests are used, however. Hiring decisions are made only after interviews with line managers who focus on an individual's skills and fit to a branch or unit, not to the corporation as a whole.

"We think," said a senior IBM manager, "that as a business we can solve anything with education." The company operates in a way which seems to prove him right. Much of the first 30 days of training for a new IBM manager is in how to manage people—discipline, supervision, development of employees' talents and capabilities, performance appraisal, and compensation. The rest of the training is in finance, manufacturing, and sales, with special divisional level courses on budgets and similar matters. The message is "IBM wants you to manage people successfully." To make the point real and ongoing, the first line on a manager's performance appraisal form asks for an evaluation of the manager's people management performance.

For both new managers and other new hires for the company there are extensive orientation sessions at IBM's corporate facilities where the company's beliefs and standards of behavior are stressed. Managers are expected to exemplify the company's standards and beliefs, including keeping up in a rapidly changing environment. In consequence, all IBM managers attend school every three years, averaging some 40 hours of instruction per year, ordinarily in company training programs. The values of the business are continually reiterated. In sales operations the company's emphasis on individual performance is reinforced through sales schools, awards, and monthly meetings at which individual effort is recognized.

Value-driven organizations, whether manufacturing plants, sales offices, or entire corporations, depend on conformity and peer pressure. "Values are critical here," said one of Jim Finley's fellow managers at Acme. "People have to conform or they have great difficulties . . . those who don't conform to ideals come under a tremendous amount of peer pressure. Our organization works on peer pressure more than on authority and hierarchy. Peer pressure is infinitely more powerful than authority. And peer pressure comes from shared values."

BUILDING A COMPANY'S OWN WORK ETHIC

To harness peer pressure American managers and Japanese managers with American work forces have been turning to overt efforts to inculcate certain work-related values and behavioral mores in employees. These efforts are particularly controversial to persons who encounter them for the first time.

Americans are a mixture of nationalities, races, cultures, attitudes, religions, and values. By the standards of most societies, ours is very heterogeneous. Thus, our companies draw more heterogeneous employee groups than companies in most other countries. Partly as a result of our diversity many Americans are suspicious of sponsored values, whether the sponsor is our government or a corporation. Confronted with corporate efforts to inculcate values, many people, whether managers, professionals, or rank and filers, react negatively. Many Americans identify instinctively with the outsider in any group, perhaps because we are a nation of immigrants—a melting pot. Peer pressure and conformity are viewed with distaste.

Why do some successful companies rely on value imprinting? Is it simply a desire for conformity, or uniformity for its own sake? Does it represent a lack of tolerance for diversity, a preference for a bland sameness? Is an insistence on commonly held values an unfortunate stain on the records of otherwise admirable business enterprises?

The answers to these questions are to be found by looking at the most basic characteristics of human beings in a business environment. Today's competitive economy requires a substantial degree of effort and commitment from people at all levels in an organization. Where commitment is missing, a business can lose its market share to competitors quickly. Hence, managers of successful businesses are continually concerned about the motivation and behavior of people in the work place.

Years ago American managers could afford to be less concerned about these matters. Not that commitment and behavior were less important to business success, they were not; but more people possessed the desired qualities to a greater degree than is common today. Years ago the churches, immigrant groups, and the media promoted attitudes favoring hard work, commitment, risk taking, savings, and deferred gratification. The American work ethic was alive and well. Corporations drew from the society employees already imbued with attitudes favorable to competitive business.

Today this is far less true. A variety of circumstances have effected a change in the attitudes of workers toward their jobs and the work they perform. Observers blame schools, the media, or parents for failing to inculcate values associated with the work ethic. The influence of the church may also have declined. The "me" generation of the 1970s and 1980s epitomizes the values of egocentrism, short-term gratification, and high levels of consumption.

The decline of the American work ethic is especially evident to managers coming to this country from places where the work ethic is alive and well. To Japanese and Korean managers, for example, the work values of rank and file Americans seem short-sighted, greedy, and unproductive. To them, if a company is going to be successful with an American work force, it must spend considerable time and effort developing a more constructive set of work attitudes. This is the reason for Nissan's bearing the expense of sending hundreds of its American employees to experience its Japanese factories and see the example set by the Japanese employees' attitudes. It is also the reason why other

Japanese companies with American plants focus their training efforts on work attitudes.

Most American managers assume too much about today's work force. They presume that employees possess attitudes and behavior sufficiently favorable to the work environment, even though intellectually they know this is no longer the case. They rely on the general society to teach people constructive work attitudes — including teamwork, participation, and commitment—even though there is evidence all around them that the schools, parents, and the media do not do so. They make these presumptions even though they spend a good bit of time bewailing the decline of work-related values. In essence, they have not faced up to what the declining work ethic means to them, and what needs to be done to rectify it.

To a large degree managers have adapted by trying to fit the work environment to the changing mores of people. The workweek has been shortened, informally if not formally, and the work year reduced via holidays and vacations. Standards of performance, particularly the quality of work, have been lowered.

Some of these adjustments have been appropriate. For example, flexible work schedules accommodate working parents and multifamily earners; these actually facilitate the work ethic by permitting people to work who otherwise might be prevented from doing so by other responsibilities. Other adjustments have been disastrous, because they were concessions made to negative work values. These concessions gave away efficiency and quality; they put American companies at an increasing disadvantage in the competitive marketplace.

Yet when many Americans observe the efforts of some companies to teach work-related values to their employees, they recoil in distaste. In so doing they are being inconsistent by favoring both sides of the argument simultaneously. If the work ethic in our country has deteriorated to dangerously low levels, then it is both necessary and appropriate for companies seeking to be competitive to do something about it. Companies trying to improve the work values of their employees should not be condemned.

Increasingly, a company cannot simply accept the work values which today's work force brings from home, school, and television. If it does so, the company is unlikely to do well in the marketplace.

The creation of a company work ethic is not a simple matter. Companies have successfully created a work ethic only after years of experimentation and development. In part this is because a company cannot simply remake an entire generation. There has to be a balance between business values and the human values of the broader society. A company would find it difficult to reinstate the values of the late nineteenth century, for example. So there are important questions about what values should be embraced by the corporation, by whom they should be chosen, and through what process they should be established.

Despite the difficulty and sensitivity required to find a workable balance between corporate work ethics and social values, some corporations are meeting with success in this delicate task. The creation of a work ethic can be accomplished without violating employees' privacy or values. Requiring conformity on job-related matters while allowing and even encouraging diversity on others is legitimate. What is important is a company's ability to be sensitive to the important issue of privacy and to be flexible over time. For example, one large company was involved with the family life of its employees for many years. Spouses were "invited" but in actuality required to attend corporate functions, even of a recreational nature, and to play a visible and supportive role in the life of the company. This may have been reasonable in an era when most employees' spouses were not employed. However, with the tremendous growth in two-career families, a company dinner or picnic requiring the presence of both spouses is a burden that husbands and wives are hesitant to place upon each other when each has a job to attend to. Also, as out of work interests have become more important, employees have resisted fitting their avocational lives into a company pattern. The company has recognized these shifts and has responded by disengaging from so deep an involvement in its employees' nonbusiness lives. It continues, however, to rightfully insist on its values in the work environment.

In order to develop a constructive work ethic, companies need to train not only for a specific job, but for intangibles such as loyalty, teamwork, and dedication. Values of this nature are as crucial to the long-term success of any organization as are work-related skills. People need to know what is expected of them as participants in a work-place society, as well as in narrowly defined tasks. If the expectations of employees are not shaped by the company in a constructive fashion, then it is fruitless for managers to blame employees for behaving as if they lack those intangibles.

Training is the most undervalued thing American companies do. Most companies avoid training if at all possible, preferring to let competitors bear the costs of educating employees, then trying to pirate the better ones away. Even companies that do train employees limit costs by trying to make training narrow and job-specific, often contracting courses out to vendors who, no matter how excellent they are at technical instruction, know little of the company or its values. Therefore they can contribute nothing to the development of work attitudes.

Combining skills training with education about values is a very powerful method of developing a company's work ethic. Training can be provided in productivity, quality, and associated attitudes and behavior. The expectations of people can be shaped; the best American companies spend time, effort, and resources in doing so.

As practiced at the firms which have given it the most careful attention, training combines three elements: development of values, specialization in work, and generalization in knowledge. The employee is expected to participate in training programs which span functional areas. Thereby, employees gain a broad understanding of the context in which their own work takes place. They become not just masters of a task, but problem solvers. They are specialists in work, as well as generalists in knowledge.[2]

Training also is used by some companies as a device to resolve immediate business problems. Concerned about the growth of

[2] Ezra F. Vogel, *Japan as Number One: Lessons for America* (Cambridge: Harvard University Press, 1979): 45–46, 158–183.

nonperforming loans, bankers have turned to psychology courses teaching how to diagnose the personalities of business borrowers. The concept is that if a loan officer can understand the personality of a business executive requesting credit, the officer can better determine not only the executive's credit worthiness, but also how best to pursue the executive if payments lag.[3]

At the other extreme, companies searching for creativity in a fast-moving business climate are attempting to teach executives how to think better. Seminars based on the premise that thinking is a teachable skill now receive attention from many companies.[4]

Thinking may be a skill, but it is attached intimately to a value—that of creativity in dealing with problems. The synergy that makes training so powerful a tool arises out of the synergy between skills and the commitment to do them well in behalf of the company. What is surprising is that so many companies stress the former while neglecting the latter. In contrast, the best managed companies consciously seek both—and seek continually to create a company work ethic. In our country most managers continue to rely on the broader society to furnish values to employees; those companies able to create their own work ethics gain a substantial and long-term advantage in the marketplace. Value imprinting serves these companies as a sustained advantage for value creation in the marketplace.

TAKING PROFITS OUT OF THE CELLAR

Profits play a key role in the free enterprise system. Profits provide a return to equity investors; they also generate funds necessary for investment and growth by the company; finally profits provide a source of compensation for executives and sometimes for rank and file employees through profit-sharing plans. By and large, a private corporation cannot succeed without profitability. Growth

---

[3] Mary Williams, "Loan Seminar Puts Emphasis on Personality," *Wall Street Journal*, 17 November 1983, 1.
[4] Ralph Fletcher, "Thoughts on Thinking," *US Air Magazine* (Spring 1984): 51.

and often survival are contingent on it. An unprofitable company is likely to be beset by closing facilities, layoffs, and/or reorganization.

To managers in many companies profitability is the key target of their efforts. In seeking employee commitment to the firm and its purposes, they are necessarily seeking employee allegiance to the profit motive. It would seem to follow that companies would spend time and effort trying to help employees understand the role and significance of profit in a modern business enterprise; when the company is profitable, the employee stands to benefit through enhanced job security and the opportunities that come with company growth.

These concepts, which are second nature in some of our high technology firms, are surprisingly missing in many of our companies. By and large, companies do not communicate to employees about profits. "We talk about anything but profits," said an executive of one large industrial company. "We talk to employees about jobs, about competition, but never about profits." Surveys taken of several hundred managers for this book indicated that only 3 percent actively discuss profits with employees.

The media frequently refer to the unfavorable choices made by companies faced with deciding between profits on the one hand and human or community values on the other. Companies choose profits over human considerations when they close a plant or lay off workers, it is said. The human advantages of continued employment and reinvestment are overlooked.

Because profits are so misunderstood and so often castigated in the media, to a surprising degree profit has become a dirty word in the United States. Managers shy away from discussing profits with employees because the concept is too emotional, too hot, too misunderstood. Even union leaders who understand the need for companies to be profitable are caught up in the public misunderstanding and attack almost any level of profits as excessive.

People committed to free enterprise must wonder about the long-term prospects of an economic system in which a key objective is misunderstood by so many people. Profits are not a simple concept; nor are the various uses of profits readily comprehensible without education. Lacking education, the public has a negative and exaggerated view of profits; this leaves the concept which motivates free enterprise as the property, so to speak, of the managerial and investor classes only.

There are, of course, real issues about how companies employ profits. What is an appropriate distribution of profits between wage increases, reinvestment, and dividends? Is reinvestment being achieved in favor of ill-considered diversification via acquisitions or mergers?

In well-managed companies managers recognize both the need for employees to understand the role of profits and the importance of their being committed to the company's profitability. Managers also recognize that employees have legitimate concerns about whether profits are being used to strengthen job security or to undermine it.

Communicating to employees about profits and the company's use of profits is an important part of value imprinting. Profitability is not all there is to a successful business enterprise; it is more the measure of success than success itself. Employees must understand profitability and be committed to their company's profitability. Managers who do not communicate with employees about profits contribute both to the undermining of commitment in their own organizations and ultimately to the long-run undermining of the free enterprise system as a whole.

A COMPANY'S PERSONALITY

When a person is being interviewed for a job, he or she will frequently ask questions about what it is like to work at the company. Do managers listen to employees? How will I get work assignments? Do I have input in deciding what assignments I get? What perks do I get with this job? What perks do other employees get? What kind of interdepartmental relationships exist?

Are they formal or informal? In this company are formal processes more important than informal ones, or vice versa? Who evaluates my work? By what standards? Do I get treated individually or as part of a group? How do I get approval and resources for a new project, or for an idea I might have? How does the company treat its customers? Does it want me to be engaged in civic duties? Do people in the company take an interest in my family? Whom does the company look to for leadership? How does a person get promoted? What is valued in this company?

The answers to questions like these reveal what it is like to work at a company. Through their impact on the motivations of people, the answers to these questions create either a climate of high performance or its opposite. The answers to these questions and others like them constitute what may be called the personality of a company. Some companies have strong personalities, meaning that it is relatively simple to answer these questions, and that the same answers are given at every location. Some companies with strong personalities are not particularly good places to work, and may not be places of high performance. At such a company the personality may be that employees are out for themselves, that promotions are obtained by personal loyalties and connections, that there is continual backbiting among employees, and that there are divisive contests between divisions. The personality of such a company is strong and self-defeating.

In contrast, a company may have a strong personality that is a competitive asset. People may be judged individually. Promotions, opportunities, and resources may flow to the best performers. Managers may have an attentive ear to employees' contributions. Key interdepartmental relationships may be informal and friendly. For example, an engineer in one branch may be able to call his or her counterpart in another and exchange views on a common problem without having to go through a supervisor.

Other companies may have incomplete personalities. For example, managers may be able to answer some questions about how their organizations function, but not others. "What gets rewarded here?" "I'm really not sure," is a common reply. "Sometimes I think it's performance, but other times I'm afraid its who you know. I've been concentrating on my own performance, but I'm beginning to wonder if I've made a mistake and ought to shift my tactics," say many concerned employees.

Finally, some companies have almost no personality; each division, each location, each department, and even each manager operates in a unique fashion. Each manager's operation has a unique personality and replicas elsewhere in the company exist only by coincidence. When a person transfers between locations it is like going to another company. And when key managers change, the personality of the organization may undergo an abrupt alteration that leaves everyone in confusion and disarray during a period of adjustment.

The personality of a company (or as some people may prefer to call it—its "culture") is not the same thing as a company philosophy. A philosophy is usually expressed as a relatively short set of overall commitments or objectives. Lots of companies have philosophies, and many sound very much alike. The personalities of companies, however, are rarely alike.

The personality of a company involves the behavior of people in it. In fact, it is behavior which defines a corporate personality. A philosophy becomes part of the company's personality only when the philosophy is strong enough to influence the behavior of people in the company in an important way.

Perhaps the most dramatic example of a corporate philosophy which serves as a key element of a corporate personality was offered by Johnson & Johnson in the course of the Tylenol poisoning crisis. Johnson & Johnson's credo begins with the statement, "Our first responsibility is to the doctors, nurses, and patients, to mothers and all others who use our products and services." When the first reports of deaths associated with Tylenol use in the Chicago area came to corporate headquarters, the company's top management huddled. According to one participant the credo then made itself felt. There was virtually no discussion about whether or not to recall the product, despite the enormous short-term financial loss this would cause the company. "We knew our priorities," he said.

The Johnson & Johnson credo has four paragraphs. The first is quoted above. The second sets forth the company's commitment to its employees; the third to the communities in which it operates; and the fourth to stockholders. In accordance with the credo, the company's managers first protected those who used or might use its products—then turned its attention to rescuing value for its shareholders. The strength of the credo, according to Johnson & Johnson managers, was that they had all accepted it and wasted little time in dispute about whether or not to try to save money by postponing a recall. Because the credo had been bought into by key managers and affected their behavior, it had become part of the company's personality. When the Tylenol crisis was finally resolved, the company recovered quickly and the value of the credo as a guide to smart business decision making was reaffirmed.

Often this is not the case. Many corporations have creeds, philosophies, or credos, but pay them lip service at most. Behavior is based on other values and objectives. The philosophies play no part in the corporate personality.

In today's economy, managers are recognizing that the characteristics of a business affecting people's behavior are important competitive aspects of the business. If the right corporate personality can improve employee performance, then corporate personality is something a manager must be concerned about. And many managers are.

The executive vice president of a candy and specialty products company said, "We have a fun kind of business. The company started in about 1900 and is still run by the same family. The family is integral and important to the business. Our products are fun items. We promote the family business idea with employees and customers. We go down the line with the characteristics of a small company, but we are actually a very large company. People make our company, so management has to be conscious of them. Unfortunately, we seem to have less concern for union people because we figure the union will take care of union people. That's a problem for us. We're greatly concerned about our non-union people—their development, growth, and advancement. But we've got to extend the same concerns to our union people."

At a major producer of engineered metal products the senior vice president for operations commented, "Because we know the efforts of our people count, every quarter our president visits each of our 19 plants to talk with employees. We share one-third of our profits with employees; have annual recognition dinners for employees. After one year with us we refer to an employee as a member, not an employee.

"We think it pays off in the business, although quantification is difficult. We show a steady growth in profitability, and our competition hasn't had the growth record we've had. I am sure there is a relationship, because our track record is good.

"We have a people component in our long-range business plan. It gives us something to shoot at, a reminder that people's performance makes us profitable. It sets the tone for the people we hire. We value the caliber of our people—it's a tradition at our company."

IBM has a widely publicized set of beliefs, as well as a well-defined corporate personality. First espoused by founder Thomas J. Watson, IBM's beliefs focus on personal objectives:

Pursuit of excellence
Respect for the individual
Best customer service
Good corporate citizen

At IBM these beliefs are accepted by the employees and form an important part of the company's personality. IBM's is not a Japaneselike personality, as some writers on business have erroneously stated. This very American personality stresses the individual not the group, and personal not organizational objectives. At the core of IBM's values is the belief that if individuals perform at their best then the company will benefit. IBM does not subordinate the individual to the group, as Japanese concerns often do, nor does IBM call upon the individual to sacrifice personal identity, objectives, or performance for the group.

Companies can be distinguished from one another not only by the personalities they have, or do not have, but also by certain aspects of the company's relation to its own personality. Like individuals, a company may or may not be conscious of its own personality. If conscious of its personality, the company may make it explicit by stating what it is, or may keep it implicit. The company may manage its personality, or may leave it un-managed. Finally, the company may try to have the same personality everywhere, or try for different personalities in various aspects of its business.

Companies that Americans commonly associate with strong corporate personalities—General Electric Company, IBM, and Hewlett–Packard Company—are very active in all aspects of their personalities. Each company is conscious of its personality and wants to reinforce it. IBM makes its personality explicit by reiterating the company's values, Hewlett–Packard by stressing that things are done "The HP Way," and General Electric by extensive management education which reinforces the company's objectives to be number one or two in each of its many businesses. Each company seeks a unitary personality, trying to be the same wherever it operates. Finally, each actively seeks to manage its culture.

More than a decade ago, Hewlett–Packard executives saw that founders Bill Hewlett and David Packard would slowly divorce themselves from the company's operations in the coming years. How were the values and attitudes of the founders, which the company's executives saw as key to the high performance of people in the organization, to be transmitted to new generations of HP employees? Knowing that IBM had earlier confronted a similar problem, HP managers huddled with their IBM counterparts in a meeting. The result was an ongoing program of internal communications featuring stories about the founders and problems met and overcome early in the company's existence.

When a company chooses a personality, this unavoidably involves a balancing of opposites. At Hewlett–Packard, for example, there is value to having things done a certain way, which involves a certain loss of freedom to behave differently. Management by objectives is a professional tool to promote individual performance when done correctly (as it usually is at Hewlett–Packard). Even with management by objectives there is a certain loss of autonomy by the individual. Requiring an employee to get approval for new projects helps the organization with internal communications, and keeps people involved, but it places a certain constraint on entrepreneurship within the company. Finally, seeking consensus among managers on new products often avoids later problems, but also restricts individual initiative. As a top Hewlett–Packard executive noted:

"It often seems that operating the way we do—with a strong corporate personality—doesn't cost us anything. For example, hiring top engineers is easy for us because of the perceived values of our company. But there is a cost.

"We can only select from that portion of humanity who want to live the way we do. There are, as a result, very, very bright people who won't come to HP because they get few prerogatives, there is no management incentive plan for them, and they want not to be participative and collegial, but instead to be autocratic themselves. Losing even a few very, very bright people to competitors in an industry as driven by innovation as our own is a real cost."

Nonetheless, on balance Hewlett–Packard is satisfied with its choice. Its strong personality, carefully articulated and managed, helps the company to attract many outstanding professionals and helps motivate them to high standards of performance.

To many people the concept of a corporate personality or culture seems very abstract—only a new buzz word lacking practical application. This is a mistaken view. The concept of a corporate personality, or corporate character, has a significant place in American law. Courts, regulatory agencies, consumers, and the public routinely assess the character of a company from an incident or group of incidents, and then proceed to evaluate the company's other activities in that light. The human mind, whether a judge's or customer's, always sees an incident in a context, rarely as an isolated event. Hence, incidents in the behavior of a company which its manager may prefer to believe are isolated, nonetheless are taken by others as evidence of whether the company as a whole is a good or poor employer, or a constructive or irresponsible citizen.

A drug company's apparent refusal to remove a defective product from the market, and the company's refusal to accept responsibility for injuries apparently caused by the product, led the courts to a denunciation of its managers and to an adverse judgment about its character. Thereafter, government regulators, alert to the company's poor reputation, began to investigate the company's major product.[5] For an allegedly nebulous concept, corporate character can certainly have direct and substantial business impact—both through the performance of employees and through the attitudes and actions of courts, regulatory agencies, and customers.

Sometimes a whole industry takes on a "personality." The American auto industry, for example, has been buffeted by many shocks—the oil crises, aggressive foreign competition, and the shift in consumer preferences from large to small cars. But exacerbating these external shocks has been an undercurrent of opinion among a substantial portion of the American public that the quality of American cars—particularly their safety features— does not equal that of foreign cars. Auto companies were increasingly perceived as indifferent to the safety of the American driving public. This perception was initially formed in large part by consumer advocates who were highly successful at widely publicizing their studies. But how many people remember that Ralph Nader's Unsafe at Any Speed dealt with the safety of one car—the Corvair? During the decade following the issuance of that report, there were a number of highly publicized recalls. These were not seen as American auto companies showing a very costly commitment to comply with a rapidly changing regulatory environment and increasingly rigorous and complex array of safety standards. Recalls were read by a large part of the American public as evidence of corporate disregard of safety.

The belief that the products of one of our major manufacturing sectors were unsafe and of poor quality led to a definition of its collective personality as "irresponsible," and for a while made the auto companies' attempts to compete with the Japanese all

[5] Subrata N. Chakravarty, "Tunnel Vision," Forbes, 21 May 1984, 214–218.

the more difficult. By herculean efforts auto companies are now overcoming the unflattering perceptions of much of the American public. Yet, the auto companies must grapple to overcome the public perception that a small, gasoline-efficient American-built car still cannot match the quality of a comparable Japanese car. To finally overcome this problem the auto companies have begun to make a special public relations effort to present a united front with the labor force in a "renewed" commitment to quality and safety.

CHANGING CORPORATE PERSONALITIES

Can a person change his or her personality? Psychologists say yes; but it is not an easy task. Can a corporation change its personality? Yes, but it is possibly an even more complicated and difficult task. Yet today many American corporations are attempting to change their personalities.

Nowhere are efforts to change corporate personalities more instructive than those now under way in the banking industry. Beginning in the early 1970s competition heated up first among banks and then with other types of financial service firms. In the fall of 1982, significant steps were taken by the federal government toward deregulation of the industry. In the period from the early 1970s forward many banks recognized that the old ways of work life in banking were going to change.

At a major New York bank, the transition began in the early 1970s with a major reorganization. The important changes were not in the arrangement of reporting responsibilities, but in how managers in the company saw their roles. In the past the business had not been considered risky. The essence of a bank manager's job involved job security and status in the community which came from a combination of working at a large bank and having an impressive title. The actions of a bank officer were largely routine; little risk was involved. Because the range between good and poor performance was not believed to be wide, pay was relatively low.

The magnitude of the personality changes now affecting banks is dramatic as exemplified by today's new perceptions of bank managers. Instead of secure and low-risk, the bank's business is now believed to be both risky and very competitive. In part this is because of significant new elements of the bank's business, including government bond trading, international lending, and trading in international exchange. Today banks recognize that some people—in both the professional and managerial ranks—are able to perform at very much higher levels than others, and that the outstanding performance of the best people is crucial to the bank's success. In consequence, recognition of individual contributions has replaced anonymity in the pack and an orientation toward performance has replaced a generally accepted level of mediocrity. With high risk and the opportunity for outstanding performance has come less emphasis on status and titles, and more on cash. High performers now earn large salaries and bonuses.

To operating managers in the bank, many of whom are new, it appears that they brought the bank's new values in with themselves. In their view, their different attitudes and expectations forced the bank to seize opportunities to move into new financial services offered by a suddenly opening marketplace, as well as to accept greater risks and rapid growth. At last, recognizing the changes under way in the bank, senior management began to alter its own perception of the business and to adopt a new overall strategy. In the view of middle managers, the bank's top officials have been hesitant to acknowledge the changes and they still, in countless ways, hinder them. The new generation of managers, viewing itself as aggressive, risk-oriented, and high performing, sees a major personality change in the bank being pressed upward in the organization against grudging resistance by senior management.

Senior management, not surprisingly, sees the cause and effect relation differently. When acknowledging the transition from low risk, security, and status to high risk, individual performance, and personalized pay, senior management identifies itself as the driving force. By active hiring decisions it brought professionals and managers of the new generation into the bank. This was not an easy task for the new generation looked askance at first at a stodgy establishment bank; and they were highly sought after by brokerage houses and other competitors in the financial services business. In addition to bringing in new people, the bank's senior officers outgrew the narrow concept of banking they had inherited and branched out into related services, offering the new people opportunities to grow. In top management's view, the change in the bank's personality had its origins in the new strategy adopted by the bank's senior officers, a strategy which stressed new kinds of people and new kinds of services for depositors and borrowers. From the new strategy emerged the bank's new personality.

Probably, both the bank's new middle managers and its senior officers are at least partially correct in their analyses of the cause of the changes in the bank's personality. The senior officers made it possible by opening the door to new people and new business initiatives. But the new generation of professionals and managers actually accomplished the changes. Between the two there has been occasional friction, senior management moving more slowly and with less sureness of the correct approach than new managers would like, but moving nonetheless. And both share the certainty that the bank has, in fact, had a significant, widespread and probably irreversible change in its personality—a change that positions the bank far better for today's intensely competitive marketplace than it was positioned earlier. When the marketplace began its rapid turn toward competition in the 1970s the bank seemed to be a slow-moving dinosaur threatened with extinction. In the intervening years, it has adapted itself into a different animal able to run, though still somewhat awkward.

A change of personality is also under way at a major bank on the West Coast, now a competitor of the New York bank just described. But the process was slower to start, has been primarily top down, and has not progressed as far. The West Coast bank's financial results show that it is lagging.

The West Coast bank made few adjustments in the 1970s; not until November 1982 did it acknowledge that a new world of intense competition and rapid change was bursting upon it. People got nervous and concerned in all levels of the organization. The bank's senior officers decided the bank needed a review of its objectives, values, and attitudes. In a period of change they wished to restate, to reiterate, the bank's traditional personality.

To follow their competitors into fast-paced new markets, the bank brought in a few new executives. Watching them, top management saw that much of the bank's traditional personality had to change. So senior management set out aggressively to force the changes to occur. Unlike the New York bank, where senior management hired many new people to set the changes in motion, then gently directed the winds of change to prevent a storm, top management in the West Coast bank initiated and pressed a thoroughgoing change of the bank's personality. They were, after all, a decade behind.

The bank's senior management set out to change the view that legitimacy in the organization came from the manager's title— instead, they sought to substitute the practice that legitimacy came from the manager's contribution to the organization, from his or her skill in getting things done. To reinforce the point, internal correspondence ceased to have any titles on it—letters and memos now carried only the writers' names, not their positions. The idea was to stress the content of communications, not their sources, and to replace, at least in part, a hierarchical system among managers with a collegial system stressing not position but merit.

To carry the changes further, the bank began to measure all staff functions on their value to their users (internally in the bank). Suddenly being expert was not sufficient in a staff position— it became necessary to be useful as well. Surveys were taken of the users' opinions about the quality and utility of staff services and the results were published. Slowly, and far behind the New York bank, a change in personality began to metamorphose the West Coast bank.

In their own way many industrial companies are looking for personality changes as dramatic as those occurring in banking. Many American manufacturing companies have lost a commitment to quality in production—a weakness that foreign producers turned against them in the marketplace with devastating effect. In an attempt to rectify the situation, the American companies have begun to stress quality—but some have learned that much more is involved than they had suspected.

A commitment to quality turns out in many instances to be less a technical matter of controls, sampling, and inspection, than a behavioral matter in which the attitudes of people in all branches and functions of the organization are involved. People have to think about quality, have a commitment to it, and make sacrifices for it. Hence, quality requires a personality change in the corporation.

While the banks have had to undergo personality changes in order to get into new businesses, industrial companies like GM are changing their personalities in order to match competitors' quality in the marketplace. Perceiving this, General Motors Corporation has stressed quality not only as expertise in engineering but also as an ethic. The statement "New Quality Ethic at General Motors Corporation" was issued bearing six points and beginning with the sentence: "Quality is the Number One operating priority in General Motors." Materials accompanying the one-page ethic statement stress techniques of quality control (including a design quality index, statistical process control, and "just-in-time" inventory control) and also employee involvement, product development teams, and the role of suppliers.[6]

The existence of the personality changes under way in many of America's major business organizations, both service and industrial, is significant because many managers are reluctant to

[6] *1983 Public Interest Report* (Detroit: General Motors Corporation, 1984).

believe that the personality of a corporation, or even a division or a plant, can be effectively changed. Many managers believe it is easy to establish a constructive personality if you start at the beginning like Hewlett–Packard Company, IBM, or People Express Airlines, Inc. did, but it cannot be done after the organization has had years of a different kind of personality. They are certain that an organization cannot develop a new personality. Yet, examples such as GM show that personality changes can and are happening, even in large organizations with decades of experience and old, traditional personalities.

If a manager is working from top down and wants to see a personality change in a division or facility, how is it best accomplished? "The best way to get a change of personality installed," said the senior vice president of a large consumer products manufacturing company, "is to get the division or facility managers to ask for it." They may be persuaded to ask for help in changing their organization's personality if they have had the opportunity to see the success that has accompanied a different personality elsewhere in the company. Further, top managers can get people to change behavior (often the first step toward an attitude and personality change) by the questions they ask, by the purposes to which resources are allocated, and by what matters they are interested in when they visit a facility.

Whether for quality or to fit new businesses a personality change cannot be accomplished if structured as a project, competing for priority with other projects under way. Instead, a behavior change must be insisted on for itself, as the separate value it represents. The difficulty is that accomplishing changes in behavior requires time and persistence, neither of which is readily available to many American managers.

Finally, the care with which a constructive personality can be created in a new organization is usually very much misunderstood by many managers. They seem to think that if the company is new, its managers need only express their wishes about people's behavior, and all will do as directed. The experience of new companies indicates that much more hard work and persistence are required. As Don Burr at People Express says, attitudes brought by new employees from the outside are often in conflict with the personality of the airline, and it is a very difficult task for the company to open new employees' minds to a different set of attitudes and behavior. (See Chapter 11.)

Society has programmed people; a company must either accept the programming, or incur the costs and efforts of changing it. This is as true at a brand new company as a long-established firm. Costs can be minimized by selecting people who are inclined to fit the personality of the company, but there is still much that has to be done. This is why IBM, Hewlett–Packard, People Express, Smucker, and similar companies pay so much attention to training new employees in the company's values, and why frequent updating is provided. The influences of the general society are always bearing on people. If those influences promote quality consciousness, hard work and commitment, ambition and initiative, and cooperativeness, then a company which needs these employee values in order to be competitive can accept them and avoid the costs and efforts of training. If the general society does not endorse these values, then the company has no real recourse but to attempt to develop and nurture them itself.[7]

In some companies staff people are given a special role as custodians of the company's personality. At Hewlett–Packard the personnel staff audits the quality of communications, including business communications, between sales, production, research and development, and so forth. Where there is anger, pique, or misunderstanding, staff people try to clear the air. In this way the staff contributes to the better functioning of the business and tries to preserve the personality of the company.

In other companies people cannot be promoted to a high general manager's job without being signed off by the executive manpower staff. This staff is sometimes part of the personnel office, as at General Motors and sometimes separate as at General Electric

---

[7] Arthur P. Brief, "Undoing the Education Process of the Newly Hired Professional," *Personnel Administrator*, 27, no. 9 (September 1982): 55–58.

Company. The purpose is to be sure that people who will assume key executive jobs in an organization have an understanding of its desired personality and the ability to convey it to others. Both new companies and established companies need to train new people, to reinforce the initial training for those who have been there, and to be sure that persons in key executive positions are committed to the company's personality.

ASSESSING THE PERSONALITY OF A MANAGER'S OWN ORGANIZATION

Many companies are unconscious of their personalities, lack explicit statements of them, and do not consciously manage them. This leaves some aggressive and value driven managers who are members of the new generation very frustrated. They see the contribution to the organization's success that top management leadership could make if they would articulate and exemplify a corporate personality. New generation managers would also be more comfortable in such an environment.

Other than suggesting such a course of action to top management whenever possible, there is not much an individual can do to change the company as a whole. Individual managers, however, can do a great deal in their own parts of organizations. Even if the company lacks a clear personality, a subunit in the organization can acquire one.

The place to begin is by identifying the unit's current personality and the manager's own role in it. Managers can learn a lot about their own organizations and themselves by obtaining answers to such questions as, What do my subordinates think gets rewarded by me? Since the answers may not always be flattering, it is often useful to get someone else to talk to employees and peers about such matters and then relay the comments.

Once conscious of their organizations' personalities and their own managerial styles, managers can shape the desired personalities for their units. When a new team of General Electric managers took over a plant, they drew up a statement of philosophy. Fitting their own values, it emphasized shared decision making, commitment to both family and business, and commitment to quality. The philosophy was discussed with each employee, and he or she was asked to "buy in." The process shaped each person's expectations and also enhanced commitment. An additional key element of the philosophy was a commitment to change—to acquire the best technology of the factory of the future as it became available, and to change the organization as errors and other experience required.

The days of top performing managers simply accepting the attitudes and behavior which schools, the media, and other companies have developed in people seem to be ending. Today the manager who values competitiveness helps to create a personality in the organization that shapes people's expectations and enhances their commitment.

SUMMARY

Training is a largely unexploited opportunity to engage everyone in an organization in its mission. The effective manager has values which contribute to business success and conveys them to others through an enhanced concept of training, one devoted to values as well as skills.

The personality of a company is also an important influence on the level of performance of its people. Effective companies are conscious of the personality they wish to have, convey it explicitly to employees, and manage it with a variety of levers and devices.

This is not the only area in which top officials have a key contribution to make. Today's challenge to staff managers to increase their value to the company comes from the very top of the corporation.

15

Adding Value

Early on a Saturday morning Sol Robbins sat in his office, his thoughts twisted one way then another trying to avoid what seemed to be a trap. He thought of himself as an executive who combined hardheaded business sense with humane consideration for the people with whom he worked. Ordinarily, he believed the two attitudes went hand in hand, reinforcing each other. People who were treated well performed well in a business sense, and his own commitment to business success helped ensure job security and advancement opportunities for the people with whom he worked.

Unfortunately, his own advancement had suddenly brought him face-to-face with a situation in which he could not successfully combine business needs and support for his people. And, he reflected, it was neither his fault, nor the fault of the people reporting to him. His difficulty was the direct result of an external environment that had altered; now the company would undergo a drastic set of changes.

AN UNEXPECTED CHALLENGE

Recently Sol Robbins had received a major promotion, his first to the vice presidential level. To his surprise a staff job had been offered him. "What preparation have my years in operations given me to manage a group of professionals?" he had wondered. But apparently operating experience in the business was exactly what was being sought by the company's chairman, Lawrence Spencer. Few executives at Lancaster, Inc. had as broad experience in its various divisions as Robbins. Only after a lengthy conversation with Spencer did Robbins understand why operating experience had been a prerequisite for the staff job. Also, only after that conversation did Robbins begin to glimpse the difficulty of the assignment he had been given, and the nature of the dilemma in which it placed him. It was ironic.

As Sol Robbins opened the door to his office for his first day as a corporate vice president, he had felt excited and awed by the challenges ahead. He was no longer a division general manager, but rather an officer of Lancaster, Inc., a diversified manufacturing firm with $1.4 billion in sales, 20,000 employees, and 20 operating units.

When Larry Spencer first raised the question of his new assignment, Robbins had been told that Spencer saw him as the person to carry out a newly formulated corporate objective, "opportunity for people." This objective committed the company to provide, in the language of a letter Spencer subsequently sent to him, "both opportunity and security for our people in a corporate atmosphere of growth and change and to provide enlightened motivational programs and benefits."

This broad mandate and a series of one-to-one meetings with the company's CEO provided the context within which Robbins agreed to carve out an area for himself that would contribute to moving the new company forward and also enable him to make a larger contribution within its fast changing environment.

Robbins was aware that this was not an easy task. But he reassured himself that he had taken the job *because* of the changes the company was undergoing. Lancaster was successfully transforming itself from a rather staid company with a reliable but unexciting product line to an innovative high technology company.

Robbins liked that change. It would give him a chance to pitch in, contribute, and learn in a way that would be impossible in a company not responding as quickly to the new competitive environment. While he saw opportunities abounding here, Robbins also saw some big hurdles to get over; but only more slowly did he see that he would have to bring a lot of other people over those hurdles with him. Months later Robbins described his feelings that first day: "I had the expectation that my job would concentrate primarily on management planning and management development; the other areas would have people who were knowledgeable in them and maybe would be fairly routinized.

"I didn't really know exactly how to behave as a senior corporate officer . . . to me it was low risk in that I had a sense of my basic competence and felt that although there might be a less than perfect fit between me and the position there wouldn't be any disaster."

He knew his ability to succeed would be due in large part to his ability to garner and sustain the support he needed from top management, a task his five predecessors over the last three and a half years had been unable to accomplish. The rapid changes made by the CEO in Lancaster's product line and, indeed, his very insistence on change itself had caused turmoil in management. The rapid departure of Robbins's predecessors was just an outward sign of a company going through a metamorphosis. Robbins also knew that the changes were now the status quo at Lancaster. The company had transformed its business but the rapid product changes and Spencer's pressure on people were not going to ease up. Change and innovation were the means of doing business.

Robbins began his first day by scanning the kinds of problems which came his way. They were multitudinous and varied: The chairman requested that he straighten out a mailing to his polo partner that had been sent by surface mail to Paris, the slowest route possible, by the administrative service division that reported to Robbins. An employee's question about his pension had been unattended for two months; there was a seemingly unending stream of requests for interpretation of policies in a corporate policy manual which was difficult to understand and at many points virtually impossible to use. He also learned that Lancaster's people planning consisted of having a report about who was in line to succeed whom prepared by each division and sent to corporate manpower planning where it was promptly filed away.

With this brief introduction to his position, Robbins had gone to meet with Spencer to begin to lay out his plans. After having accepted the vice president's job, moving to corporate headquarters, and starting to deal with administrative tasks, Robbins's first glimpse of what Spencer must have known all along occurred at this meeting: In order to contribute to Spencer's vision of Lancaster, Inc., Robbins would not initially concentrate on service to the operating divisions in the traditional sense. Instead, he had to carry out a transformation in his staff function.

As Robbins's understanding grew, he recognized a kind of inevitability. Over the past several years the company had been transformed from its emphasis on electromechanical devices, particularly pumps, to electronics, particularly process control systems. Division after division of mechanical devices had been phased out or sold, and acquisition after acquisition made of smaller companies or divisions to fill out the new Electronics Age Lancaster.

Many managers, engineers, and production workers had left with the older product lines. Thousands of new people had entered the company. Robbins had presumed that he had been selected to continue to assist in this process of transformation, but now he recognized suddenly that Spencer considered it largely accomplished and that the continuing process was routinely manageable. The challenge Spencer had in mind for him was of a different nature. Spencer's new targets were the staff functions; he had asked Robbins to manage—and transform—a significant one. Spencer was never one to spend much time on preliminaries.

"Lancaster is changing and is going to continue to as long as I'm around. A big part of our ability to keep the momentum going will depend on forgetting the old idea of running a business by having people find a secure niche in a staff function, insulated from both the line and the market.

"It's just too expensive to run a business that way anymore. And we're not the only ones. At board meetings, I've heard how other companies have reduced and decentralized staff jobs. The old way has got to go, beginning now, with you. It's too expensive. There's not enough value added.

"Sol, I'm counting on you to change the way the personnel function has been practiced here at Lancaster. Maybe by your example you can lead some of the other staff functions into this way of thinking about their jobs, too. That would be a big contribution. I think they will have some things to teach you, too."

Robbins had been reading about the large and continuing middle management layoffs at American companies. At first he thought they were just a response to the deep recession of the early 1980s. But as the business cycle turned upward, the layoffs that began as a crisis response continued. They now appeared to be an ongoing characteristic of companies trying to renew their competitive vitality in a world where increased domestic and foreign competition had not vanished with the recession. Spencer continued, "What we've got to have is a leaner, crisper organization. Your job is to get value from the staff organization you run and as a whole from the function you're in charge of." Thus was Robbins launched on an entire reconceptualization of the human resource function just as all the other functions in the company had been rethought.

All of the services that reported to Robbins seemed to be in good working order. But he soon realized he was increasingly dependent on the entire business in order to take the first step in reformulating the mission of his department. Spencer's mandate to create "opportunity and security for people" depended not only on the staff that Robbins headed, but also on the resources available for the task, which in turn depended on the company's success at selling its present products and competing in the future. Robbins realized that he had to find a new orientation for his function and that this was exactly what Spencer wanted him to do. Robbins was going to have to reach beyond the bounds of the ordinary activities of personnel as he had found them and discover some way to contribute to the overall success of the firm.

He wondered how human resources would begin to make this kind of overall contribution. He concluded that the staff would have to become more active in a nontraditional sense. In this requirement lay the seeds of the dilemma in which Robbins found himself. He had inherited from his predecessors a group of personnel specialists. He knew many of these people from interactions with them while in his previous jobs. They were professionals in what they did, but they had been as frustrating as they had been helpful while he was an operating manager. Now he saw that it was precisely this perspective—that of the corporate staff as seen from field operations—that Spencer had wanted in a corporate staff executive. This perspective was why Sol Robbins had been promoted.

He put his mind to work recalling the merger of two divisions in which he had been involved. What had personnel done? They had checked off, as almost from a list, a set of activities to be accomplished: transfer or outplacement of surplus managers and professionals, lay off of surplus blue-collar and clerical employees, reevaluation of jobs and establishment of new pay scales, merger of benefit programs. These had been things that needed to be done, Sol recognized as the merged divisions' general manager, but they were not what he most needed. What I had to do, he reminded himself, was to keep people performing their jobs at top levels, despite the confusion, uncertainty, and rumors prevailing during the merger. I needed assistance in how to do that. Without offering any other ideas personnel thought that merging benefit plans and outplacing people would probably help to minimize disorder.

In a more active stance, Robbins reasoned, the personnel or human resources manager's first step upon learning of a merger would be to set broad objectives to support line managers who would perform the actual tasks associated with the integration of the two units. A successful merger of the units would minimize cost, enhance productivity, and improve morale. To achieve this Robbins decided the human resources manager would assess the function's resources—the budget, people, and levers (counseling, transfers, realigning)—and match them to the objectives. This would form the central theme of his new conception of the human resources manager's role. And if human resources managers are to grow past the service function image, they must be able to not only practice the new active human relations but also to work closely with the CEO in explaining the approach. If he as personnel vice president did not move quickly to create a more active staff, he would be overlooking an important opportunity to clarify and strengthen the personnel function within the firm and to make the firm's human resources a greater and more recognized element in the company's capacity to respond and compete.

Robbins knew the current opportunity to change and become part of the competitiveness of the firm would not be taken as an endorsement by managers of personnel as traditionally practiced. Nor should personnel people suddenly forego their professional responsibility to become new kinds of straw bosses to get productivity out of people. Spencer did not intend to give Robbins's staff more power by delegating greater authority. Instead Spencer wanted his line manager to take a larger role in the human resources area in consultation with both Robbins and his staff. The human resources function was being given a chance under Robbins's leadership to combine its two major tasks in support of business objectives. One task was to get the right numbers and skills of people; the other, to motivate them to high performance.

This would only be accomplished by a staff committed to close interaction with line managers. The general manager would continue to have major responsibility for the management of the firm's people, but he should have and use a staff capability to enhance effectiveness. A good general manager would begin to use this capability more broadly; to build commitment, encourage contributions, and build the competitiveness of the firm.

ALL IN THE SAME BOAT

Robbins's first weeks at his new job seemed to fly by, but he took occasion to talk with managers in other areas about his new vision for the human resources function. He found many of his peers thinking about the same kinds of issues. Ralph Jones, the vice president of finance, was himself going through a similar kind of process and he concurred with Robbins's assessment, "In the finance area staff and line are beginning to change. But each function will have its own unique way of organizing to enhance competitiveness. The finance function has carried with it a certain aura of certainty. Because the language of finance is numbers, people in other functional areas have tended to give to it a certain legitimacy and importance not given to other functions. After all, business is about the bottom line and the finance function is best able to locate it. Finance has had a comforting certainty attributed to it in an environment of rapid change.

"But to tell you the truth, more complex financial wizardry within the finance function won't necessarily clarify the choices Spencer must make in consultation with us. To the extent that the financial function becomes more accessible, not less, and more compatible with the other languages of the company, it will enhance my ability to add value to my job, the jobs of my staff, and to the company.

"Corporate finance in the future will be less and less a specialized staff function isolated from operations and concealed in certainty based on complex manipulation of precise numbers.[1] In general, the overall mission of my function will be the same—to ensure that I have access to a continuous flow of funds to direct to all strategically important programs. An important corollary is, of course, that funds be employed for the maximum benefit of the firm when not in use. But, the flow of funds will increasingly become analogous to the service function, your function, of human resource management, but with an increasing emphasis on processes and a decreasing importance attached to certainty as an end goal."

Robbins asked one further question. "Spencer pushed me on how much value personnel was adding to the company. Functions or people in them who weren't adding value were going to have

[1] Thomas Piper, "Notes on Financial Management," Harvard Business School, mimeo, pp. 1–3.

to go, he said. In finance, where do you see the value-added in the future? If it's not in refinements of your calculations, as you say, where is it?"

"I think," Jones replied, "that the financial function will have to have a better integration with the line to add value to the competitiveness of the firm. We will have to be tied in not only to the formal benchmarks of corporate plans for three, five, and ten years from now, but develop a greater capacity to move in response to changes in the company's marketplace and in other functions—in production or marketing—to help the company be flexible. It'll mean a tighter integration of the finance function into other areas of the business. We'll still be doing contingency planning and hedging in foreign currencies to minimize risk, but we'll be doing more. My problem is when to find finance professionals who can understand and relate to the business."

"And that's my problem also, in the personnel area," Robbins concluded.

Within the first month of Robbins's arrival he was asked by the vice president of marketing if he would like to sit in on a presentation for some newly hired salespeople. Robbins eagerly agreed, hoping to gain some insight into the VP's view of the marketing function.

The VP began his talk: "There was once a time when the products drove the people to a greater degree than now. That is to say, in many cases demand for a product could be created or enhanced by Lancaster's marketing efforts and the benefits recouped by us. But one of the major impacts of the new competitive world is that there will be fewer opportunities to be the only supplier of a product and a greater opportunity of choice by consumers. Many different firms will compete with us to fill created demand. In an increasingly competitive environment the company must become more consumer than product driven. It will be less and less possible to create and hold on to a market niche unchallenged by others either at home or abroad. This has already changed the approach here at Lancaster and at many other companies, too.

"Here are two examples I picked up in recent weeks. In the heavy equipment industry, John Deere Company and Caterpillar Tractor Company face heavy competition from the Japanese. In response, both have tried to turn their dealer networks into market research functions. In late 1983, American Telephone and Telegraph Company (AT&T) reorganized a subsidiary so that each division had its own product and its own marketing, sales, and research and development departments.[2] Once production driven American companies are becoming increasingly market driven. And this kind of sensitivity to the market is key here at Lancaster. You as salespeople, are one very important link to that market.

"Gone are the days when the engineers and technical people developed a product that was then sold to the American public through demand created by marketing efforts. The American car companies couldn't sell big cars, not because of any problem in marketing, but because of the gap between product development and the marketplace. This gap must be sharply narrowed if companies are to avoid getting out of touch with what the marketing function can accomplish—and reap only the ensuing financial disasters. So we have an obligation not only to sell products, but to keep the company in touch with what's really going on out there.

"Marketing must be increasingly tied to the production of the firm. If we as marketing people are to build value we will have to bring the environmental information gleaned from research and sales efforts to bear more directly on the development of new products and the cultivation of new markets. Line and staff functions are going to have to really cooperate. A greater adaptability to customers' product suggestions and modifications will give us the edge we need to extend the life of supposedly mature products; perhaps we can break out of the restraints on innovation and responsiveness imposed by the concept of an inevitable product life cycle.

"This means that, as salespeople, we can have a lot to do with not only selling Lancaster's products, but also letting our pro-

[2] "To Market to Market," *Business Week*, 9 January 1984, 70–71.

duction and R&D people know how to develop new products that will sell or improve the ones we have. We have a greater opportunity than ever before to contribute to what kind of company Lancaster is. I know that people here are ready to listen.''

Robbins's final exposure to the thinking of his peers came from a discussion with the vice president for manufacturing services at the corporate headquarters. Manufacturing services, the VP said, in cooperation with line managers, would have to view its mission more broadly. It would have to respond to a larger number of constituencies both inside and outside the company. With the proliferation of new product technologies, the acceleration of new process technologies, and the increasing importance of product quality, service, delivery, and reliability in the competitive market, manufacturing will have to enhance its ability to respond and innovate.[3] Flexibility will determine the degree to which Lancaster can respond to changes, said the manufacturing VP.

Lancaster's strategic planners, Robbins surmised, would continue their fall from grace as the soothsayers, the exclusive visionaries of the company. And he saw this as a healthy development. The acquisitions he had been involved in had brought him into contact with strategic planners in many different companies. Over the years many had seemed to become more isolated, estranged from the other functions within companies. It was not that they no longer had an important contribution to make, but that in a way too much was expected of the function and in a way, too little. This imbalance would have to be rectified if their contribution was to be understood and effectively coordinated with others. Instead, today's new staff planners would have to vault over the traditional assumptions of planning as an academic haven within the company, where they had time in which to reflect, analyze, and propose. If their contribution was to continue to be valued by the company, the new staff planners would have to do less reflecting and more broad analysis aimed at providing active assistance in positioning the company in the market.

[3] Wickham Skinner, "The Taming of Lions: How Manufacturing Leadership Evolved 1790–1984," Harvard Business School, Division of Research, March, 1984, pp. 64–65.

Robbins's mental tour of the staff functions at Lancaster confirmed that all functions including human resource management were potentially important to Lancaster. The management of the company's human resources was just as much a factor in whether the company could compete successfully as how well marketing, finance, or manufacturing did their jobs. For years, management of the people side of the business had been a staff activity with little explicit connection to the line. This, he knew, had been a costly error. Line people always had the actual responsibility on a day-to-day basis for supervision, direction, and morale. These responsibilities have frequently been difficult and uncomfortable ones because direct supervision and evaluation is often unpleasant. There are few instant successes and the results usually show up only in the long term: Are line people acknowledged and rewarded for success? Does good work lead to enhanced employment security and opportunities for advancement? Are maximum contributions effectively solicited? Are poor performers told they are not meeting the test and shown the path to improvement? An effective personnel function has to contribute to getting the right answers to these questions in practice.

Corporate staff is expensive. It is analogous to a major capital investment. Robbins decided to try to produce greater value from the human resources function through a three-part approach: First, he would involve his function to a greater degree in the corporation's long-term planning and by so doing better acquaint people on his staff with the company's direction. With their help, he would be able to guide his own function's future direction more securely on the company's chosen path.

The second part of his approach was to build a closer interface between the corporate staff and the personnel staff in the operating divisions. His responsibility was almost as great for the people in the field as for home office staff. Beyond a closer relationship between home and field, he would try to develop closer ties between operating managers and staff people in the manufacturing plants, distribution centers, research facilities, repair shops, and sales offices—in each sector of the line organization.

Finally, the third part of his approach was to work hard on how to implement the first, long-term planning. What had gone wrong with corporate planning generally, he believed, was that it focused too much on objectives and too little on how to realize them—too much on purposes and too little on means. To try to remedy this in his own planning he built in an implementation or action step as part of his basic objectives. An analytic planner would probably tell him that his grouping of objectives and means was illogical, but he was more concerned with what would work for him than with formal structure.

Robbins undertook a survey of people planning activities at corporations of a similar size. He found that where a company has moved to long-term planning for its human resources, 35 percent of the time top management had initiated the planning based on a vision of the strategic importance of planning for people. In another 20 percent of cases, the planning process simply evolved. It frequently began with one or two components related to human resource planning being incorporated into the company's long-term business plan. From these modest beginnings more fully developed human resource plans grew. But in a full 18 percent of companies surveyed, planning for human resources began as a reaction to a crisis. Left without potential successors to a departing key executive or facing shortages in scientific or technical personnel, many companies waited too long and assumed that the people with the talents they needed would always be available. This proved to be a very wrong assumption and costly mistake in many cases.

Human resources planning must be worked at continuously and be "home grown." A senior vice president of a major insurance company told him: "Human resource planning takes a lot of hard work and there is no company you can look at to see how to do it . . . . The danger is that when you try to go on to the next stage you find more pressing things to do . . . we must try to work at it every day."

Among those who do plan for their human resources the consensus was summarized by an aerospace industry vice president who said: "Planning for people certainly pays. It becomes a discipline for upper management to look at subordinates. It causes satisfaction on the part of the subordinates because of management's concern."

Robbins soon recognized from his conversations with his counterparts in Lancaster's other staff functions that what had become true of human resources planning in many major companies was also true of the other functions. Line managers were no longer relegating long-term planning and analysis of business opportunities to specialized staff. Corporate planners in any function now had to know the business, both its core and its frontiers, and be more tightly integrated into it. They were relying less on models and extensive reviews. In the effective company, line and staff were working with greater synchronicity or staff was not there to work at all.

Line managers no longer accepted excessive professionalism in whatever functional area. They demanded that staff processes be performed within the context of an overall understanding of the company's current competitive market stance as well as possible repositioning by the company to anticipate, or respond to, competition.

In order not to be sloughed off as a superfluous luxury too expensive for today's market, specialized staff was finding that it must add more value, becoming less remote and more accessible to the heart of the company. As a result, the traditional supportive, research, and planning activities performed by the staff of corporate functions were shifting from detailed, technically based, lengthy documents to activities that related plans to actions and scenarios to responses.

What General Electric's CEO has called "staff on staff" was becoming a thing of the past in many American companies. Because of value added questions about staff positions, managers beginning or in the midst of their careers would not automatically expect that their contributions in staff activity would continue to be valued by their company. Unless they were able to reconceptualize their roles and tie them more directly to the firm's competitiveness, their roles may continue to diminish and eventually disappear entirely.

Planning, or more informally looking ahead, continued to be important but its effectiveness increasingly lay in the involvement of line people and the degree to which it could be kept informal. The marketplace was changing so rapidly that line managers dared not delegate looking ahead to a professional bureaucracy. Companies could no longer afford to support high staff overhead when there was not enough value added.

PROBLEMS IN OPERATIONS ALSO

Robbins's background in the operations side of Lancaster gave him important insights into the role personnel staff could play in influencing line executives. The objective for his group was to contribute to the business's long-term success. No other element of a business was as significant in this regard, he reflected, as helping line managers understand their own jobs correctly.

Today, because of technological developments, a key problem is arising in exactly this area. The personal computer is at its source. The personal computer makes it possible for line managers to have up-to-date and comprehensive information on operations to a degree previously unknown. Several layers of managers whose jobs had been to gather and refine information on the state of the business are now unnecessary. In Lancaster several hundred middle managers had been released from line activities, saving the company millions of dollars. It was not only staff specialists whom Larry Spencer required to justify their value to the corporation.

Spencer believed that operations were as efficient with the superfluous layers of management gone. Robbins agreed, but was concerned about the longer term. If high level operations managers were now involved with the details of plant floor or sales office operations, Robbins asked himself, who was looking at the needs of the organization as a whole? Who was preparing for the next new product introduction, for the next generation of production equipment, for a needed reorganization?

Robbins feared that top managers were increasingly mired in the details of operations. How ironic, he thought. What we thought we were doing was eliminating lower level managers and preserving top level people. Instead, we've converted our top level people to lower management jobs, and have left key higher level positions undone by default.

Robbins also thought he saw a parallel danger in the attempt he was making to bring staff professionals much closer to operational needs. The danger was that the staff organization would not just reduce unnecessary bureaucracy, but would lose all its professionalism as well. The staff needed to complement, to supplement operational managers, not to mimic them.

All managerial jobs require carefully balancing between opposite extremes, Robbins thought. His old job as division general manager required him to cut unnecessary managerial levels without sacrificing a broader picture of the business and its needs. His new staff vice presidency required him to bring specialists' attention more closely to bear on the business's present problems without sacrificing too much the professionals' dispassionate views of what was required for the future.

A DILEMMA RESOLVED

Responding to these considerations Robbins began to implement his program. He thought that by looking ahead at business needs in an informal but comprehensive planning effort, he could help his people to visualize and prepare for the future. This would contribute to a generation of staff personnel people who could add value to the company.

He took the lead himself in demonstrating to the professionals at corporate level and in the field how to communicate with line managers and develop a working relationship. With a videotape camera and recorder he visited key divisional personnel, recording lengthy discussions of the business situation. By careful preparation, he knew what to ask. Encouraged by his advance preparation and interest the general managers were obligingly frank about their needs and objectives. With the videotapes Robbins was able to communicate up-to-date business knowledge to his own people and show them how to build trust with line managers.

He brought corporate and field personnel staff together for a series of two- and three-day conferences. They went over problem after problem in the various divisions, always searching for a way for personnel to more actively support business needs. When line managers had already started on a course of action with which the personnel staff did not agree, he challenged his staff to develop a better course and to sell it to line managers.

Looking to the future Robbins insisted that field personnel who had been preparing management succession plans do more than simply keep lists. "You've got to participate in the choice of who goes on those lists," Robbins told them. "One of the things Larry Spencer told me was to enlist motivation for our people generally," Robbins continued. "One of the most important ways to do that is to keep off the future management team managers who would be potential Neanderthals. But you can't do that unless you can affect who gets chosen for promotion, and you can't do that unless the general managers respect you."

At the termination of one such conference Robbins's assistant vice president came up to him. "I think we made a lot of progress in this conference," he said.

Robbins demurred. "We won't know a thing," he said, "until we see if these people do anything differently back at their plants and offices."

After the conferences Robbins required each field person to develop his or her own site specific plan of action. He and his staff at corporate spent days reviewing and commenting on the plan. They also identified in this process who in the field was progressing into the new vision of an active function and who was not.

Whatever his efforts, Robbins harbored few illusions. Despite all that he did, despite Spencer's clear warnings, some of his professionals would cling to the past—to a service rather than business orientation; to external professional contacts rather than to internal management counterparts; to elaborate planning and program exercises rather than to rough, quick, and timely solutions to business problems. Robbins knew he could not keep these people at Lancaster. Spencer would not permit it. The new competitors heading Lancaster's businesses would not be willing to carry the cost of people who contributed so little to the business. Even if Robbins liked and respected them as professionals, he could not keep them at Lancaster. His dilemma was resolved. I can't support a person who won't adapt, he admitted to himself. Today's intensely competitive business world has made obsolete insulated, outside-directed staff professionals. Probably their demise was to be regretted—but it could not be avoided.

SUMMARY

Increased competition is forcing companies to ask what value is added by their staff functions. Where there is not a satisfactory answer, staffs are being reduced. As a result, the staff career once seen as a professional haven within the business corporation is beginning to disappear. Tomorrow's successful staff executive is one who can provide clear evidence of his or her group's contribution to the business.

At the highest levels of business, people expect to make decisions. Yet no decision from the top is sometimes the best decision.

16

To Decide Or Not To Decide

This chapter is about the most basic elements of management: decision making, delegation, and responsibility. It is placed near the end of the book because it involves an advanced application of the preceding principles. Subtleties and nuances are critical in this chapter. Basic principles are applied in a manner so natural, yet so dependent on all the executives involved having a deep understanding of each other's role that to the eye of less experienced managers it is often not clear what is happening. Yet the chapter offers an example of American top management at its best—handling poorly structured, messy problems which nonetheless have a significant potential impact on the corporation. This is done with care, inbred through experience, for the personalities involved and for a careful balancing of long-term and short-term considerations. It is in the subtleties and nuances of the application of basic managerial principles that outstanding executives reveal themselves.

PROBLEM OF THE BENJAMIN PROJECT

In July the management committee of a large business products company was scheduled to review the status of an advanced technology project. Already, the company's two principal competitors had invested some $25 million to develop the technology and for pilot production. According to the company's best estimates, all potential competitors now had more than 500 engineers at work on the effort.

The problem for discussion was their own company's efforts. Already key executives were in sharp disagreement; that fact had brought the matter to the attention of top management. On one side of the issue were the group executive and the president of the company's computer division (CD). A seasoned manager with 28 years in the company, the group executive now headed CD, the company's largest group. He possessed a doctorate in physics; for the first decade of his career he had held positions in the company's research effort. The president of the division also held a doctorate in physics and had long service with the company.

The computer division was responsible for developing the technology in question. Until recently, development activities had been located in the company's research laboratories; but the effort had been determined to be sufficiently far advanced to be brought forward into the product application labs of the computer division. Early in the previous year, the division sent a business plan forward for corporate-level review which included three separate efforts on the technology: programs identified as Andrew, Benjamin, and Charlie respectively.

The technology involved an attempt to create a new and very rapid memory system for computers. The effort labeled Andrew was intended to bring the technology to the stage at which an initial mass data storage device was in operation.

The Benjamin effort was a follow-on to Andrew intended to enhance the performance and cost of the memory unit after its introduction. Charlie was a longer range program intended to develop a radically new approach to the basic memory design employed in Andrew.

Anxious to get a product to market, CD proposed in their business plan to take Andrew forward rapidly, but to devote little attention to Benjamin. Charlie, for its part was fully staffed since it involved a different memory technology and did not compete with Andrew for engineering talent. In the opinion of CD, however, a clear competition existed between Andrew and Benjamin.

To operate Benjamin at full staffing for 1980 required only 30 engineers, in a corporation that employed thousands. Yet these were highly skilled persons, conversant in a technology with which few persons in or outside the corporation were knowledgeable. Engineers who could work on Benjamin could also contribute to Andrew and the Andrew project was not yet completed. "We don't even have a product yet," the executive responsible for computer division complained. "How can I push its next generation ahead?" Needing the engineers to work on Andrew, CD gave low priority and few resources to Benjamin.

At corporate level, CD's plan came under review from various staff agencies, including the office of technology (OT). Headed by a physicist of long experience, both within the company and in major technical positions for the federal government, the office of technology was custodian of the corporation's technical future. The OT head was concerned about the low priority given Benjamin. He argued, "This technology is advancing rapidly, and our competitors are hard at work on it. Should they succeed in bringing it successfully to market and quickly follow with a second generation, we could be badly damaged. CD is placing far too much priority on initial product development. As a division which has both sales revenues and costs, and must also try to reach target levels of profitability, CD has an incentive to press the level of development closest to the marketplace. So it stresses Andrew and slights Benjamin, hoping to get sales from Andrew quickly, and to cut costs by doing little on Benjamin. The result may be greater short-run profit in CD, but it is likely to be at the cost of the long-term position of the company in the marketplace."

Meetings between executives in CD and OT were unable to resolve the disagreement, and on July 30, 1979, the key executives in CD and OT entered the room in which the top management committee of the corporation awaited them.

TOP MANAGEMENT DISCOMFORT

In reviewing the minutes of that meeting and the reflections of those who attended it, the conclusion is inescapable that the top corporate officials were uncomfortable with having to deal with this problem. Perhaps this discomfort derived in part from the issue itself: Was it important enough to be at their level? After all, only 30 engineers were involved and a tiny percentage of the operating budget of the CD. However, the question of the corporation's posture with respect to a very significant emerging technology was of great importance for the future.

Possibly the discomfort reflected the background of the company's top officers. Not a single one had a technical background of the depth which both CD's president and OT's head possessed. The corporation's chief executive officer had been trained as a political scientist before obtaining an MBA. He had spent more than 30 years with the company, rising through sales and general management. The company's chief operating officer, also an MBA, had similarly risen in the company through sales and marketing. The executive vice president on the committee was an accountant, later controller, and thereafter vice president of finance for the company. Yet here were these three executives, key players in determining the future of a major corporation, confronted with an issue which was largely technical: What, after all was the probability that the technology in question would be a major factor in the computer memory systems of the future? The company's top scientific talent disagreed on the matter, so it was now presented to a group of businesspeople for resolution.

WHAT WAS THE ISSUE?

What was the issue presented to the top management committee? At one level it was to determine the amount of resources, or the priority in the allocation of resources, which CD was to give to the technology development effort labeled Benjamin.

At a somewhat higher level, however, it was to review the corporation's previously established strategy that assigned an important role in its overall planning to this new technology. Was CD resisting devoting more resources to Benjamin because it had doubts—not yet expressed or perhaps fully recognized even by itself—of the feasibility of Benjamin or even of Andrew itself?

Or was the issue not real at all? Was it possible that there was no actual disagreement between the top technologist and CD; after all they insisted they were agreed that Benjamin was important, and that the only division between them lay in what resources to devote to it. Could it be that the apparent disagreement was merely a device by which CD could come to corporate executives for additional resources, using the office of technology as leverage to gain them?

Finally, was there an important status or even internal political issue involved? The technologist occupied a staff position, and his ability to influence the decisions of operating managers, such as those in CD, depended upon the degree of support by top management. Rarely did the technologist bring a disagreement with a line manager up to the top management committee. When he did so, it must be presumed that he thought it important, and knew the risk he was taking. For if the committee failed to support him, would CD or any other operating division, pay any heed to his positions in the future? Further, the technologist was specifically responsible for the long-run technical position of the company. Could his position on an issue such as the Benjamin project be disregarded by top management without effectively undercutting the technologist's role?

Probably in their own way these questions about what was really at issue before top management in this clash of staff and operating executives were more complex than the questions of physics involved with them. Once when Einstein was asked why the human mind could conjure up concepts such as quantum mechanics and the relativity theory, but could not reconcile divergent political theories, he replied, "But politics is so much more difficult than physics."[1] And the top executives might have added "Business seems so much more complicated as well."

AN ANSWER IS GIVEN

The top management committee listened to both sides of the issue. Then the board chairman commented, probably in reference to his lack of expertise about the technological issue involved, that he did not believe he could add any insight to the decision. Nonetheless, he seemed to say, his inclination would be to pour the coals to the effort.

As they were leaving the meeting, the CD executives turned to the technologist and asked what he thought the chairman had decided about Benjamin. "I believe you were told to do it," the technologist replied. "We were afraid that was what you thought," the CD managers responded. Thereafter, the top management committee informed CD that it would receive no further resources than it already possessed, so that additional staff, space, and funding for Benjamin must come from other programs.

WHAT DID THE ANSWER MEAN?

What had been done? The top management committee had met with the disputing executives, and something had occurred. But what was it?

Several years of discussing this incident with managers from a variety of companies have indicated that five different outcomes suggest themselves to managers; that is, five different interpretations of what had occurred, depending in part on how each manager would have viewed the character of the issue put to the top management committee.

[1] Quoted in Bernard O'Keefe, *Nuclear Hostages* (Boston: Houghton Mifflin, 1983), 240.

A Decision Was Made

Some managers insist that the committee made a decision, telling CD to go ahead with the Benjamin project at full steam. This, they argue, was the committee's responsibility, to decide the issue presented to it, and this it did.

But, if a decision was reached, on what basis was it made? The corporation's chairman prefaced his remarks at the meeting by saying he was not sure he could add any insight to the matter. Surely, the committee did not make a decision on technical terms.

Was there a decision on the significance of the technology to the company's competitive position? But CD had not disputed the technology's potential importance; only the high priority for 1980 which the technologist assigned to it. There had been no review of the marketing strategy issue. Would the top management committee have made a decision on business strategy without any review of the broader issues? Unlikely.

Perhaps a decision was made on the political issue? The technologist was upheld. But was his position thereby strengthened? How would CD's executives thereafter respond to suggestions from the OT? Most executives insist they would pay as little attention as possible. Why? To repay the injury given them by the technologist in overturning their position and thereby embarrassing the executives of CD before the top management committee. It would appear then that this decision by the top management committee would have been unwise.

There Was No Decision

Many managers reviewing this incident insist that the top management committee made no decision about the Benjamin project. The CEO simply expressed the opinion that he would be inclined to apply the coals to it, at best a possibly futile hope.

Some believe this failure to decide was a fundamental derogation of top management's responsibility to give the technologist and the CD executives a clear answer to their dispute. That, they argue, is the responsibility of management at all levels: to decide.

Others argue that there was no decision, and should not have been. The issue was thrown back to the managers who had brought it forward. But nothing had been accomplished by the top management committee's involvement in the matter. There was no value added. Things stood just as they had beforehand. The CD executive, they argue, finally took the initiative after the committee meeting by asking the technologist his view and apparently deciding to go ahead with Benjamin to placate him.

The Committee Punished the Disagreeing Executives

Many managers grow very angry in reviewing this incident, insisting that a matter of so little significance should never be brought to top management. In their view the executives who brought the matter of the Benjamin project forward should be penalized for their action. Evidence that the top management committee acted in this way may be inferred from its refusal to decide the issue, giving it back to the disputing executives, and in the refusal of any additional resources to CD.

In this view, any subordinate manager who takes an issue forward to his superiors initiates a process of review and evaluation by doing so. Rather than deciding the matter, or assisting in its resolution, the boss may decide he or she should not be bothered with it, adversely affecting the evaluation which the boss gives the subordinate.

This, it can often be agreed, is a dangerous pattern of behavior for the boss. If a subordinate manager is unsure of the importance of an issue—the most important issues of all may be only dimly perceived at first by a subordinate—and fears to take it forward, then the boss may have broken a crucial line of communication.

The Committee Worked Out a Resolution between the Managers Involved

When top management has no particular expertise in the issue given to it (as in this incident), then perhaps the best course is to try to bring the disputing managers to an agreement. Perhaps that is what happened here.

The chairman leaned in the direction of the technologist, who had little power in the situation, and left it up to the CD executives to work out a deal with him. But it is surprising that the top management committee would have left its work so much undone if it wished to mediate an agreement between the technologist and the president of CD. To mediate an agreement someone from the top management committee or from the chairman's staff would ordinarily have been assigned to work with both the technologist and CD's executives until an agreement was reached. To simply send the disputing executives away to work out something if they could, leaving their relationships and the destiny of the Benjamin project to fate, is a very unlikely course of action for the committee to take.

An Opportunity Was Seized to Coach the Executives Involved

The position in which the top management committee found itself in this incident was unpleasant. Key executives were in disagreement (the issue hardly mattered), and were so far estranged that they had brought their dispute into the open at the top level of the corporation. Because the conflict was now evident at so high a level both had an enormous amount at stake: the status of their respective organizations, the respect of their subordinates (who were watching closely to see how their bosses fared before the committee), and the top managers' evaluation of their own performance. A decision in favor of one would be potentially damaging to the other and destructive of their working relationship. Yet both had to work together for the future good of the company.

With so many pitfalls in how this matter was handled, it is easy to see why top management might have become impatient and/or frustrated at having to deal with it. It was tempting to wish it away by insisting that the technologist and the CD executives should never have brought the matter to top management. To refuse to deal with the issue would not resolve it, but leave the Benjamin project in limbo, and more importantly, leave the working relationship between CD line managers and the staff executives of the OT badly strained.

Where was the opportunity in this situation? What constructive advantage could be gained if the top management committee acted carefully?

The opportunity lay in assisting the executives involved in the dispute to resolve it, and any others in the future, by indicating to them top management's conception of how executives should do their jobs, including what relationship they should have to one another.

The key position was that of the group executive for the computer division, since his was the overall business responsibility, covering thousands of employees and many millions of dollars of costs and profits. His was the responsibility for the profitability of the divisions reporting to him, including CD. In some ways the greatest peril faced by the top management committee in handling this incident was the risk that its action might undermine the group executive's responsibility for his unit's performance, or his authority and status with the people who worked for him.

Hence, the message from top management to the business executives for CD had to be: "Yours is the responsibility for CD, including the Benjamin project. It is your responsibility to keep CD abreast of the technology, and to take those actions necessary to achieve this." In the words of one member of the top management committee, the message to the group executive was, "You make sure you're doing the right advanced technology work . . . and you get it done . . . the top management committee shouldn't have been asked to make the decision on Benjamin." The group executive was to use his judgment even to kill Benjamin, if necessary, and keep top management informed.

Though reinforcing the responsibility and authority of the key line manager was the first priority, it was not the end of the function of top management. The brilliance of this company's top executives was demonstrated in the succeeding step.

It was not enough to tell the executive that he had to make the decision on Benjamin; he also had to be subtly counseled in how to do it. It was at this point that the CEO's comment acquires meaning. He did not know how he could add any insight to the decision (*that is, you are the responsible executive with the necessary information and it is your responsibility to take the correct action*), but it was his inclination (*and therefore yours, if you wish to follow my lead*) to pour the coals to it (*that is, to take seriously the advice of the technologist*).

The CD executives gave every evidence that they had understood the lesson when, leaving the meeting, they raised the matter, ascertained that the technologist's view remained to push Benjamin ahead, and then reviewed again the advisability of diverting further resources to the effort.

The ambiguity in the action of the top management committee which permitted so many different interpretations of its action is explained by the need to avoid doing the group executive's job for him, instead counseling him on how best to do it. Proper handling of the matter requires subtlety and deliberate ambiguity plays a role.

Any doubt that the top management committee was aware of its role as a coach is resolved by learning that the company has a name for the process—"tone-setting." Tone-setting is different from a decision, but is accepted as a fundamental function of management.

A REAFFIRMATION OF RESPONSIBILITY AND DELEGATION

Does there still seem to have been a decision reached by top management in the incident described previously? Perhaps there does. The chairman did say to pour the coals to the effort, the technologist did echo that instruction, and the managers of CD did suggest that they could carry Benjamin forward.

So if one were to conclude that there was a decision, that Benjamin got done, would one be correct? No. Another member of the company's top management committee commented: "The fact that the CEO said let's go to it does not mean a subordinate manager does it even if it sinks the corporation. Whether or not the results of the 'decision' get implemented remains to be seen. We are not sure the CD people will work on the project. They may decide the effort isn't useful and instead devote the resources to another project.

"The operating executives have to have the option to make changes. There may be problems with the Andrew project. They have to have the opportunity to allocate the resources to their best use.

"So what did the top management committee really say? We said, 'Come on you fellows in CD, this is a fundamental technical problem. Figure out some way to push Benjamin forward to see if it will work. In spite of all the problems you've got, give Benjamin some management attention. If it looks like its going well, keep putting resources on it; if it stalls, divert them to other uses.'

Five months later, despite the top management's apparent decision to push Benjamin ahead, CD had only eight engineers working on Benjamin. And the corporation's top executives were satisfied with this performance. The Benjamin technology had not been successfully developed at this company or any other.

The top management's role had been to reaffirm where responsibility lay. The computer division's executives had been delegated the responsibility for technologies of the Benjamin type. Their responsibility was to keep the company abreast of technological changes. In doing so, top management counseled, they were to pay careful attention to the view of the technologist, but not to act slavishly at his direction.

Regarding the sources of failure of CD's executives, they were measured by CD's performance on many dimensions. With measurement went an assessment of performance—and from the quality of performance, a commensurate reward.

From delegation to responsibility to measurement to performance to reward—these are critical elements in the chain of management. Decisions about these matters are an important and continuing aspect of managerial responsibilities. Decisions about substantive matters, such as how rapidly to push ahead the Benjamin project, often are not appropriate for managers and best left to subordinates.

THE WISDOM NOT TO DECIDE

To have made a clear, incisive decision in this incident would not have been wise for top management. The two possible consequences of such a decision were both bad. First, a decision in favor of CD management against the technologist would have seriously undercut the latter's position. His choice to take this issue to top management was not lightly made. Like the Lone Ranger, a manager at this company had to use the silver bullet of an appeal to top management sparingly. To have been overruled would probably have caused the technologist to resign, in the opinion of his acquaintances outside the corporation. But a decision in favor of the technologist was only a little less perilous. For CD management might well have been angered and turned a cold shoulder to future cooperation with the OT. Recognizing this, the top management committee shied away from a clear decision about Benjamin.

This is a hard lesson for many managers to learn. When they start out in an organization, they feel themselves always carrying out someone else's orders. They long for the day they can make the decisions and tell subordinates what to do. In middle management positions, they may in fact behave this way, making operational decisions quickly, and expecting others to implement them. Further, subordinates who are used to clear directions may view any hesitation by managers in issuing a decision as weakness, or indecisiveness which they do not admire.

Aspiring to top management, middle managers see merely an enlargement of their role as decision makers. But as a manager advances in an organization, the value of crisp decisiveness is somewhat lessened. Not that a crisp decision is not important—it is, but only when it is appropriate to the situation. Too great a willingness to step in and decide an issue can undercut the responsibility of lower level managers; and it can damage the relationship between key subordinates who must respect each other and work together if the organization is to flourish.

As a manager advances, he or she must develop the ability to decide when crisp decisions are appropriate and when they are not. The manager must acquire the self-discipline to eschew decisions when they are not appropriate. The manager must learn to live with ever greater reliance on the capabilities of those who report to him or her. While still a decision-maker, the manager must possess the subtle quality of understanding when a decision is required and when it would be an error.

An aggressive manager might have seized the dispute over the Benjamin project as an opportunity to make a clear decision; and in doing so, that manager would have made a mistake. Some managers would have felt compelled to decide the issue. After all, the question had been brought for a decision. But that is exactly where restraint is required. Just because a subordinate asks for a decision does not mean that a manager should make it. Tone-setting may be more important.

A manager must have courage to let a subordinate make a key decision—one where the company stands to gain or lose a great deal. Often, as in this case, the subordinate is the best person to make the decision because of training and information possessed. Very good managers recognize their own limitations when they are significant. They recognize that just because an issue is important does not mean that the highest level manager should make a decision about it. The decision should be made at the level of the responsible and most knowledgeable manager—even though the corporation could stand or fall on it. This is the right answer—but it requires courage for managers to accept.

Some readers who are experienced managers may recognize that they have behaved in this way, often without knowing why. They have solved issues in their minds, choosing which ones to decide themselves, and which to coach subordinates into deciding. Yet, often, these managers may have been uncomfortable. Should I have decided that? they worry. Was I avoiding my responsibility to decide?

It should encourage them to know that top managers in very good companies also decide when to decide or not to decide an issue, and that they have a term (tone-setting) for coaching subordinates when a decision by the top is not well advised. Being able to recognize and label what one does by experience and to develop instinct is often as important as being comfortable with it.

The passive manager might have tried to bring the OT and CD managers to an agreement about Benjamin. That too would probably have been an error. For it may have implied that staff managers had a veto power on line managers; that CD could not move without the technologist's approval. Such a requirement would have imposed too great a limitation on the decision of the operating people. It would be too rigid a formula.

So the company's top management sought a middle course. They reinforced the responsibility of the operating managers to decide what to do about the Benjamin project and showed them the importance of paying real attention to the views of the technologist.

Even had the company's top executives been certain of what they wanted done with respect to the Benjamin project, and confident of their own judgment, they would still have been well-advised to proceed cautiously. It would have been wise to express the view tentatively and let lower management conviction develop in response to an understanding of both the situation and top management's inclination.

Ordering a subordinate to do something in which he or she has no confidence is not likely to result in a very good performance by the individual. Although it requires patience, persuasion is a better method of obtaining performance than direction. Managers who are too busy to persuade key subordinates, simply solve one problem, keeping to their own busy schedules by evading another— resentment which may affect performance in the person who has to accomplish a task.

If there was a flaw in the handling of this matter by the top management committee, it lay in failing to follow up on the technologist's side. Apparently the technologist left the committee meeting believing that the committee had made a decision, and not that the matter had been left to the group executive. Further, the technologist was not encouraged to assist the operating division on the Benjamin project, a failure which many operating managers consider significant. To make the technologist's recommendations more acceptable, they argue, he must be willing not to just pressure for more effort from operating people, but to be helpful in finding additional engineers to assist in the project.

The outcome? "We got a better understanding within the top management team of what we're trying to accomplish," said a member of the committee. The top managers had dealt with a touchy situation without loss, had helped key executives to better understand their responsibilities and their relationships to each other. They had gotten the Benjamin issue resolved at the level at which it should have been in the first place, between the group executive and the technologist, and had made less likely a recurrence of such an incident returning to the top management committee.

A top performance indeed.

SUMMARY

It is a myth that top performing managers are those whose key function is to make decisions. This approach does not and cannot work in the hierarchy of major companies because it elicits too little from people. This is not a new idea; it is an old one. This is a place where the old verities come into their own. Management must set the tone, delegate, assign responsibility, and manage. But management must not do the subordinate's job. There are many reasons for this, the most important being that the subordinate is probably better at it. This is a late chapter in this book, not because it is less important than what has come previously, but because it is subtle.

The manager's success will be determined to a large degree by the style of his or her leadership.

17

What The Boss Should Do

The members of the audience at Westover Company's annual management meeting turned to each other in absolute dismay; a murmur nearly drowned out the second paragraph of the CEO's speech. They couldn't believe what they were hearing. Their CEO of many years, Frank Steele, long noted not only for his ability to turn a profit and build the company, but more notorious for his aggressive, autocratic style was speaking like a different person. The words that rocked the crowd from its rather sleepy attention began: "There will be no more killing the messenger in this company. Henceforth, we all will solicit the ideas, suggestions, and comments of all employees. And I guarantee that there won't be retaliation for problems brought to my attention or for a try that fails."

The managers looked at each other in stunned disbelief, muttering, "Who has Steele been talking with? What's happening? Is this for real?" It was. They were witnessing a 360-degree turnaround in the way the CEO planned to deal with people in the future. For the managers assembled, it was a very welcome although not immediately believable development.

CEO AS VISION MAKER

A new day dawned at the Westover Company. Westover's corporate executive office was catching up with developments that had been under way in America for 20 years. Frank Steele was determined to be a leader, even if he had to run fast now to get back in front of those he wished to lead.

What had led to this dramatic change? The CEO was a war history buff. Frank Steele's change in style was fueled by a growing desire to not only manage the company but also to lead it. His reading of military history had taught him that the task of generals was not only to move troops and materials by command and plan strategy, but to keep the lines of communication open. More than that, the great military leaders he admired were able to build images and symbols that kept the troops moving in unison toward a goal.

He identified himself with military heros and drew analogies to his life as a corporate leader. But recently, a powerful statement from a military classic had begun to stick in his mind: "The psychological factor, loss or gain of morale by the soldier and loss or gain of prestige by the supreme command was, as it still remains, the determining factor in war."[1] What form, he asked himself, did the psychological factor take in today's business world?

Steele's profound change in style was not due to a reading of military history alone. The times had changed around him. He had come to the conclusion that he had to adapt. He read and talked with other CEOs at various professional meetings. He began to admire managers with a more relaxed style, one apparently rewarded by fewer adversarial encounters with the managers who reported to them. For a while he had passed off their success at more cooperative relationships by thinking they could afford to be cooperative. They were in a less competitive industry and

[1] Major General J.F.C. Fuller, *A Military History of the Western World* (New York: Funk and Wagnalls, 1954), 51.

his was a dog-eat-dog world. Over time, however, this seemed to have a less and less convincing ring to it. Other companies seemed to survive, adapt to new competitive challenges and thrive. Could it be *because* of the more cordial style of the CEOs rather than in spite of it, as he had always believed? He began to think it worth trying a style change.

Adding leadership abilities to a repertoire of management skills is a long reach for many managers. Today the search for leadership is being undertaken for a variety of reasons; it can be achieved through a range of methods. Leadership ultimately involves a mixture of inspiring the company, managing and communicating change, setting values, and serving as an ambassador of good will, all practiced while carrying out what is generally understood to be the unchanging core of the job—managing for a return on stockholders' investments. Sometimes current CEOs recognize that a change in leadership style is necessary but rather than change themselves, sponsor successors who are able to bring a new leadership style to the CEO's job.

AWAKENING A COMPANY

In a small Ohio town, George Smith owned a manufacturing company employing 100 people. Across the street from his plant stood another manufacturing facility belonging to a different company. Smith's company was making money, the plant across the street was not. So Smith had decided to acquire it.

His board of directors told him not to. "We have as much as we can handle now," his brother, a member of the board told him. "Don't take on more."

"It's a different business," said a successful local businessperson, also on Smith's board. Smith's company made large metal storage tanks, using a very simple and long established technology. The key to the company's ability to compete was high productivity, which kept costs low and discouraged new firms from entering into competition. His costs were so favorable that his customers, oil and chemical companies much larger than Smith, were unwilling to begin producing the units themselves, believing that Smith could always supply tanks more cheaply than they could do it themselves.

The firm that Smith was thinking of buying was different. It employed double the number of people and had a considerably larger complement of skilled workers and technicians. To a large degree, this different work force was required by the different nature of its product: a complex component provided to the automobile industry. The product was reengineered frequently to customer qualifications; quality was a key element in retaining customers and a lot could go wrong. It was a different business and a far more complex manufacturing task, Smith's directors reminded him.

Even Smith's banker, as a board member, advised him not to take on a company that was losing money. Smith's own pockets were none too deep, and if the other company were acquired and then experienced further substantial losses, the storage tank company could be taken down with it.

In the very losses that worried his banker Smith saw his opportunity; that same loss of money made the other company's owners willing to sell.

A key part of Smith's successful strategy in his own company was keeping in close touch with the people who worked for him. Smith knew all his employees personally. He was a familiar presence in the plant and in the community. Smith cared about the people who worked with him and expected them to care about him and his business. He paid moderate wages for the community, received good productivity, and kept his costs low. This formula, he thought, could turn around the company across the street.

Smith was also a good enough manager not to do everything himself. He had confidence that the managers in his own business no longer needed much of his attention. Because he had slowly delegated more and more of his own administrative functions, he now had the time to take advantage of the opportunity offered by his money losing neighbor. Because his board had pointed out legitimate matters of concern in making the acquisition, he was determined to spend his own time and effort to make it successful.

Alone he would not have dared to risk the acquisition. But his own company had enough good hands that Smith was prepared to take two or three key supervisors to the new acquisition. By letting his most capable supervisors take increasingly greater responsibility in the past, he had encouraged their initiative and developed their capability. It had not been unduly risky in Smith's relatively simple business. Now he was prepared to see what they and he could do in a new setting.

At sunup the morning after receiving the transfer of ownership, Smith stood at the front gate of the larger plant greeting employees as they arrived. He was there at dawn for several days thereafter, and intermittently in the weeks following. He became well known at the gate and on the plant floor. He also spent time getting to know his customers. The same style of personal leadership he had employed at his first company transferred successfully to the new one. Costs came down as people accepted more efficient design and production techniques. Smith had to borrow these techniques from the previous managers at the plant, but he found a storehouse of good ideas that the old management had been unable to implement. Smith's personal style melted away human barriers to these ideas, and as costs declined his business improved. In a few months the company was profitable.

Smith's success story is not unique. Several years ago a young man bought control of a profitless company in the sleepwear business. The company was located in a small southeastern town. On his first day as chief executive he called all the company's employees into a meeting. Dressed in a chicken suit to capture their attention, he told them that things were going to be different in the company. The word "problem" was no longer to be used. All problems were opportunities, he said.

At that time the company had just under three hundred employees. Today it has substantially the same number, and, in fact, the same individuals. Today the company is very profitable, and the young chief executive officer is now president of a major management association.

What these two managers had in common was an ability to deal directly with and inspire confidence in the people in their companies. Equally important, they were willing to do so. They did not limit themselves to decision-making duties.

Yet, in a sense, these situations had special advantages. Both were turnarounds—companies which had great potential, but which were currently performing poorly. Both were located in small towns. The people who worked at the companies were willing to help the company succeed, if only management asked their cooperation. The task facing the new owners was straightforward: to cut costs, concentrate on sales, and make the company do better at what it was already doing.

OPENING WINDOWS TO THE OUTSIDE

A much more complex task faces the manager of a previously successful company whose market is now beset by competitors, and whose products and technology of production are undergoing rapid change. For George Smith the task was to get the employees of his new acquisition to work more effectively at what they were already doing and knew how to do. For Joe Callahan, at a successful financial services firm, the task was to get his employees to work successfully at what they had *not* been doing before.

Fifteen years ago few would have believed that financial services, so long a bulwark of conservatism, so long tightly regulated by government and so resistant to any but the old ways of doing things, would today be a whirlwind of change. Joe Callahan had helped to make the transition.

He was not, however, a popular man. Aware of criticism from his top staff, he convened a meeting in late 1982. "You are driving us crazy," his managers said. "We agree on one set of plans on Monday, and by Friday you have changed them. We are confused; our people are confused, and we all are worried that you don't know what you are doing."

This direct challenge to Callahan's leadership had its roots, he knew, in an adverse reaction to his management style. It was not his personality that was at issue, but instead his deliberate choice of a management style.

He had built his organization from a small and fledgling enterprise to a large and rapidly growing major player in the financial services industry. This had been done by continual innovation; by new service after new service—always a step ahead of the competition. Changes in interest rate levels, in government regulations, in customers' saving and spending habits, each provided the occasion for a new product or service. The financial world had become a whirlwind of change, and Joe Callahan was at its center.

But how was he to sustain his organization's drive, its impetus, its momentum? All derived from creativity. Unlike George Smith, he lacked the luxury of driving his organization down a learning curve, pressing it to find ever less costly ways of producing a largely unchanging product. Costs were secondary to Callahan; what mattered was newness; to be first in the marketplace with the latest in financial service products. People who could accomplish this, he reasoned, were not people who concentrated long and hard on a single problem—like how to reorganize a production line to further reduce costs. Instead they were people in the maelstrom of a rapidly changing environment who formulated ideas quickly, and turned them into products for the marketplace, also very quickly.

Callahan's solution was to create a fluid organization—to mock the reports and forms of a bureaucracy. He ran meetings without published agendas, trying to force his managers to participate wholly, as people, rather than to rely on professional roles and professional detachment. Opinions, criticism, new ideas, complaints—all were aired without regard to rank or position in the organization.

Callahan rotated his executives among jobs frequently—no sooner did an individual learn one job than that person was off doing something else. He created project teams continually, not only for specific projects but also for routine management tasks. No organization chart was going to rigidify his people.

Callahan refused to read reports. Upon receiving a memorandum he called the executive into his office. Before the unbelieving manager's eyes, Callahan tore his memorandum to shreds, tossing it into the wastebasket. "I didn't read it," he said. "Now tell me what this is about."

"I think," began the executive.

"Is this about a business decision?" Callahan asked him.

"Yes," was the reply. Had it been no, Callahan would have ended the conversation.

"Then don't tell me what you think," Callahan responded. "I want to know what you feel. Is this something you want to do or not?"

Another executive faced with another discarded report protested to Callahan, "Why should I write reports if you're not going to read them?"

"That's a pretty good question," Callahan responded. "Quit writing to me. Just tell me what the report said."[2]

Callahan evaluated employees on their ability to react in an effective manner to the changing circumstances in which the company found itself. The bottom line could be up or down according to a changing situation—top performance was to be found in adverse as well as favorable conditions.

Perfection, the carrying out of a task to the final stages, was not something Callahan looked for. Things had to be done so quickly in the marketplace that he recognized that they could not be done in the organization exactly right. To get something exactly right too often meant to be late, and last, in the marketplace.

Callahan knew the marketplace; he felt its rapid shifts, its winds of change. He saw the great opportunities of being first, and the great disappointments of being late. Rewards were enormous for the initiators, often nonexistent for the imitators.

What is my job? Callahan thought, turning over the question for the hundredth time. Should he stand as a barrier between his

---

[2] J. Steward Dougherty, November 28, 1981, conversation at Boston.

organization and the turmoil of the marketplace, attempting to shield it from the confusion—hoping that in stability and security his employees would find productive opportunity? Or should he stand aside, as it were, letting the cold blow down the corridors of his organization, allowing his managers and their staffs to shiver in the cold, just as he did himself? Could he stand aside, then counsel, even challenge his managers when they came to him with their ideas for responses to the demands of the marketplace?

To simulate the external environment, Callahan consciously manipulated the climate in his own organization to create constant internal change. He wished to have his executives experience an environment as much like the shifting winds of the marketplace as possible. Few welcomed it; few cared for him. But the company prospered.

Joe Callahan sought no change agents in his organization—no managers who saw themselves as knights-errant battling the bureaucratic ways of the corporation. He was his own agent of change, employing the organization itself to challenge the creativity and adaptability of his people.

That they revolted from time to time did not surprise him. It was only human to wish for greater stability and security than they possessed. This would be a false security, Callahan was convinced, because it did not mirror the real world, but attempted to be an island removed from it.

MANAGING CHANGE

How are people able to tolerate this amount of ambiguity? How are they able to respond to change? What is in it for them?

Understandably there will be reactions from long-term employees to efforts to reshape the spirit of a company to make it more competitive. And perhaps the best employees, the ones who are most committed, may be the most questioning. For employees who have a long-term investment in the firm, or hope to, this questioning should not be interpreted as resistance to change. Rather than being discouraged by this reaction, some managers welcome it and hear that the employee may really be saying: "How can I continue to contribute? Can I make a place for myself in the new environment? Will the organization help me make the change if I need to?"

On January 4, Carl Berk, manager of Wells, Inc.'s midwestern sales division, arrived unannounced in Lester Wells's private office in the First National Bank Building. Wells had stayed on as a member of the board since his retirement as president of Wells, the preceding year. Berk apologized.

"I don't mean to just barge in on you like this, but I thought you'd want to know that our most promising young manager just quit. We've lost three division managers and a couple dozen middle and first-line managers in the last ten months. I need your help in talking to Eliot. Wells has become a corporate Vietnam."

Lee Eliot, a bright young executive, had been hired as the new president and CEO of Wells a year ago. He divided the company into semiautonomous profit units and measured sales and profits on a monthly basis. Bonuses and presumably future promotions were based on these monthly figures. To Berk, he seemed to be dividing up the company in other ways, too.

Berk explained to Wells: "Sure, the results are good; Wells has made a significant improvement in profits this year. But Lester, the costs, the costs! We are destroying the Wells spirit. Most of us have given our lives to build this company—for what?

"I don't want to be critical, but when you and your brother sold that last block of shares to the new control group, you didn't just sell shares, you sold lives, our heritage, our aspirations, our jobs—our way of life. Was that honoring the words of your grandfather—to take care of your corporate family?

"It's frightening to me to see how fast you can turn a cooperative group into a competitive jungle. The name of the game is win—by whatever means you can—as long as you don't get caught. Steal sales from other divisions, refuse to take back poor merchandise, and if a man can't produce can him no matter what his past record has been."

Berk remembered the annual management conference a year ago at which Eliot's selection as the new president was announced. At the meeting with the divisional vice presidents that followed Eliot had emphasized his goals of infusing Wells with "a fighting spirit" and "competitiveness."

Berk's feelings crescendoed: "What's the balance, Lester? What's the balance? Where is the protection for those of us who have given most of our lives to Wells? Is a $360,000 salary bonus payment to Eliot and a 10 percent increase in shareholder dividends worth the destruction of so many lives?"

Wells began, "In a way it's exciting to see someone like Eliot take over, with his youthful drive and ambition. On the other hand, the mix between people and profit is delicate. Sounds like our Eliot needs to pay more attention to what the old guard used to consider key to the company—people.

"I remember that I used to keep saying that we'd take care of people who worked for Wells. And we did. I used to require that no manager—first-line, middle, or senior level—would be dismissed without my reviewing the case personally. As a result, executive turnover has always been very low at Wells. Executives at all levels viewed their jobs as lifetime careers. We also led the industry in other areas that showed our concern for people.

"We had a private family trust that provided help to any employee—manager or production worker. We also were leaders in giving educational scholarships, in medical insurance for employees and managers. We encouraged everyone to give corporate and personal time to community problems and organizations."

Lee Eliot had changed all this, Lester Wells now recognized, possibly without even realizing it. Eliot certainly had failed to see that these various aspects of life at Wells, Inc., were important in giving its managers a well-rounded life, and indirectly, but importantly, contributed to their effectiveness for the company. When Eliot downgraded everything but return on equity, key managers began to leave—and the first to go were the hot shots of Eliot's own generation.

Could Lee Eliot have avoided this problem? Lester Wells asked himself. Could he have added vigor to the company without sacrificing its values? Puzzling over the question for several days, Wells decided that Eliot could have acted differently and been more effective.

Lester Wells recognized that Eliot knew what he wanted to do at Wells, Inc. when he was hired to be CEO. In fact, Eliot's plans for Wells, Inc., had been a key element in why he was selected. But Eliot had been far too direct in how he tried to change the company.

It was not smart of Eliot to take his key plans—establishing profit centers and paying managers on a bonus tied to return on investments—and simply impose them on the company in his first month in office. In retrospect, it was almost as if Eliot was trying to prove how smart he was—that he knew what needed to be done and did not need any assistance. This approach had been a mistake.

It would have been far smarter, Lester Wells concluded, for Lee Eliot to have talked to the key managers in the company first. To let them volunteer that they wanted a more profitable and bigger company—since Wells believed they did. Probably Eliot's ideas would have come out in these conversations, and possibly key executives would have accepted them as if they were their own. Then they would have "owned" the ideas.

Rather than saying, "I've decided," Lee Eliot could have said, "You've suggested," then he could have gone the next step, asking them what problems they foresaw in taking the company toward profit centers and bonuses, and ultimately to improve return on investment.

There was a further advantage to this approach, Wells realized. Had Eliot encountered pockets of opposition, he could have used other managers to persuade, or, if necessary, isolate objectors. Instead, Eliot tried to mow down all resistance, and the whole organization had begun to resent him.

"You haven't been very smart about this," Lester Wells told the younger man frankly in a private meeting two days later. "Lee, go straighten it out. Fast."

Eliot left Lester Wells's office in confusion. Yes, there were problems in the organization. He recognized that now. But where had he gone wrong? What should he have been smarter about? Wells had said it was the way he had implemented ideas.

Thinking the matter over, Eliot came to a different conclusion than Wells, and one more fundamental. It wasn't just how I did it, Eliot decided. It was also what I did. Not that the profit centers and bonuses were a bad idea; on the contrary, they were necessary and appropriate. But I think maybe I set the wrong objectives. I think I tried to get the division managers to think too much as one. They are not the CEO, I am. They do not have to do my job, and possibly do not want to. So they should not have to see the company as I see it. And I really ought to be able to see their jobs from their viewpoints and to help them do those jobs better.

The problems had stemmed from Eliot's failure to see other people in the company as different from himself. He had made a personal choice that he would subordinate every other thing in his life to business success until he obtained it. Because he was very capable as well as ambitious, Eliot was far advanced in his career at an early age. Only a few more years of all-out effort would provide financial security for him. At that point he visualized himself relaxing a little, taking up the hobbies and ancillary activities of an established business leader. His difficulties had arisen when he tried to transmit his single-mindedness to other managers in the company.

The first inkling of difficulty had come at the annual management conference some eight months earlier. Eliot had been in his job only a few months, but already he had announced a major reorganization of the company. The annual management meeting was to be his first opportunity to reveal his goals for the company. About three hundred managers were assembled from all over the country. Some he knew well, but many of them Eliot had met only briefly before—for a handshake at the reception held on the day he was formally made CEO. Others he had not even met.

He began his talk that evening somewhat self-consciously and self-disparagingly, admitting that he was the "new kid on the block." But following this unaccustomed touch of modesty, he moved quickly to his key point. "This is a company with a lot of potential," he told the assembled throng, "but it hasn't been realized. We are going to grow this company, and make it much more profitable."

So far so good, Eliot thought, as he watched the faces before him. He sensed a desire to have a bigger, better company. With his next words, he stumbled. He saw the lights go out in many eyes, but he did not understand why. It made him angry and he plunged ahead. "The purpose of this company," he insisted, "its only purpose is to make a top return on the capital invested in it. The key thing you must keep in mind is the return we make on investment," he said. "That's what makes the stock price go up. If we can get our return up, the market will reward us, with rising stock prices and bonuses.

"We're not around to build radios or the best fasteners; those are just what we do to get a return on equity. It's a ratio: profits over equity. So we can increase it by raising the top or lowering the bottom. That's what you should be thinking about. That's what the top corporate officers are thinking about—how we can get the ROE up."

Even to Eliot's ears, his speech now seemed strangely dated and one-dimensional. In a very competitive environment the products Wells made had better be the best or sales and profits would fall. Further, Eliot now had begun to realize, the production of the best products is contingent upon many factors and key among these is the commitment of managers to quality and to the customer. Substituting a commitment to profitability only threatened to undermine the whole system.

Eliot had failed to recognize that he had a responsibility to provide leadership in a variety of dimensions. Profitability and return on investment were very important, but so were such values as attention to the customer, concern for quality, and teamwork in the company. A single-minded pursuit of profit too often undermined other objectives which were the real keys to profitability.

A renewed commitment to leadership in several dimensions is frequently an important element when a business's management passes from the founder/owners to professional outside management as at Wells. This was the challenge given Eliot, but he had failed it. Along with goals of a financial nature, he should have been alert to implicit covenants that had been made by the founders to the consumers, employees, the community, and the stockholders. Had he looked around, Eliot would have seen that other companies are becoming more explicit in the expression of accountability to their various constituencies.

MANAGERS AS LEADERS

These glimpses of life at the top of a company have implications for today's middle managers who may aspire to be the CEO or may wish just to better understand the role of the CEO in order to support and facilitate it. A significant leadership role goes with the job, but not all managers cultivate leadership qualities.

A person who has become manager has already made an important decision about his or her type of work. That person has decided to move from making an individual contribution within the company to a position as a manager whose essential task is to get things done through other people. With this increased formal authority over others, the manager may acquire something equal or greater in importance. As a vice president of a large computer company states: "As you rise in the world, you come to understand that influence is often much more powerful than authority." Without influence, managers will founder and CEOs sink.

Leadership is not authority. Leadership must be accepted by others in order to be effective. As such, it is more akin to having influence with others than having authority over them.

In the past a top manager's ability to garner influence along with formal authority has resulted from the manager directing the flow of information within the organization. By letting a subordinate see more of the context in which he was acting, the top manager was able to persuade him to a certain course. The computer is making this source of influence much less central because it has allowed others within the company to have increased access to information. With the control of information abolished and the top manager's influence reduced, what role should the manager assume? Increasingly, it is coach, goal setter, and teacher in addition to decision-maker. Honeywell's vice chairman, Jim Renier, says that management's role is to set the goals and then manage the environment so people will achieve these goals. "People would manage (supervise) themselves."[3]

Today managers aiming for top positions have to add a facility with image building and leadership through goal setting and example to their collection of technical and other managerial skills. When a manager makes a successful transition to the top, it will be in part due to an ability to lead and to inspire others. Longevity at the top will depend on a continuing ability to do so.

Up-and-coming managers are often too impatient. It is not necessary to be in a rush to get to the top. In some ways the top job fits into a particular and concluding portion of a person's career. At an earlier time in life it may be surprisingly unsatisfying. The most important reason is that in well run companies there is less action at the top. Most important decisions and the efforts to implement them are made at lower levels in the company. There are rewards to be had at each level of a manager's career that can be missed in a hasty charge to "get ahead."

[3] R.J. Boyle, "Wrestling with Jellyfish," *Harvard Business Review*, 62, no. 1 (1984): 80.

Life at the top will involve less action and direct participation. More frequently it will involve dealing with problems at arm's length and through delegation. For those used to—and good at—hands-on problem solving, the change can frustrate and shock. This is especially true for those with ambition who are most likely to find themselves as CEOs.

As a group the new generation of managers is aware that today need not be all preparation for tomorrow's living. Many new competitors have made a commitment to greater participation in athletic challenges and family life than their predecessors did. Health experts have extolled the balanced life that encompasses commitments outside of work as important and sustaining to both energy and spirit. The one-dimension workaholic has come to command our sympathy more than respect. This dramatic change in values is now reflected in the rate of advancement up a corporate ladder that many of today's managers desire.

The new competitors see life as having many dimensions and envisage developing themselves as well-rounded people, not just as business managers. They recognize that there is a sequence of times in a person's life into which the various stages of a business career fit. People who understand this are particularly well suited for the latter stages of an executive's life, when he or she is called upon not so much to do, as to lead; not so much to push, as to persuade. Well-rounded executives have the more profound understanding of other people which enriches their leadership ability.

It follows that the headlong rush to the top which characterized so many younger managers in the past is one aspect of traditional management today's new competitors need not emulate. In the past too often the workaholic who got to the top was discovered to have few of the leadership attributes needed. The decline in competitiveness of American companies in the international marketplace has some of its roots in the inability of many American top managers to fulfill the broad human and social requirements of their jobs. There is no need for today's rising managers to make the mistake of being single-dimension persons.

A NEW STYLE FOR THE OLDER GENERATION

Earlier chapters gave examples of managers' efforts to improve work life for blue-collar and clerical people by accommodating to the attitudes and ambitions of today's work force. Many companies have discovered that such efforts have had a favorable impact on cost, quality, and production by building commitment and enhancing morale. Have such efforts reached to the inner offices of managers themselves and changed their way of working? Has there been an equal commitment to fit the quality of work life among managers to the values and aspirations of today's generation of managers? The answer is mixed.

For one thing, middle managers have been suspicious that the process of winning rank and file commitment has been at their expense. Middle managers recognize that when the work force does more, there may be a need for fewer middle managers. In addition, the nature and style of middle manager jobs are much affected by these innovations in the organization of work. Managerial style has to change. Managers feel a loss of control without a reduction in responsibility.

Top management at companies pledged to enhance the commitment of the rank and file supports these programs through speeches, budget increases, and the recognition and promotion of those who advance innovative efforts. So far, however, in most cases the top level has not been prepared to practice what it preaches as best for the bottom. For the most part, top executives have not given their support through a change in their own personal styles.

Often today's American company is in actuality two different companies. Increasingly it is imaginative, innovative, participative, and competitive at the plant, sales office, and distribution center level. In contrast, it is sluggish, tradition-bound, autocratic, and insular in the corporate headquarters. The operating level general manager who has learned to delegate, to listen to subordinates, and to patiently watch and develop top performers is ordered about, brow-beaten, and verbally abused at corporate headquarters.

Perhaps surprisingly, this major difference in management style—the lower levels of an organization becoming increasingly participative, while the higher levels remain autocratic—does not necessarily imply hypocrisy on the part of top management. Entire companies used to follow the more autocratic style. Changing generations have brought the emergence of the participative style. Only if change is seen as a top down process are top managers hypocritical to encourage participative management for others while remaining autocratic themselves. In fact, participative elements have always drawn their long-run strength and energy from the shop floor; from here their effects have begun to filter upward in the organization. This is not usually the way that we think of change taking place within American companies, but it is now the reality.

This chapter began with an account of how one top executive acknowledged to his managers that the time of change had come for himself and for the corporate office. Frank Steele's slowly dawning perception that a nonautocratic management style was effective at lower levels in Westover caused him to suddenly do an about-face. In his last act as an autocrat, Steele decreed a new and open style of management for Westover's corporate officers. Just as the waves slowly eat away at the base of a cliff until it suddenly tumbles with a great crash, the foundations of the older management style had been critically weakened long before Steele had recognized it. When he finally saw that the crash was imminent, he took the occasion of the annual management meeting to make it happen. To his listeners Steele's comments were as deafening as the crash of a tall cliff into the sea.

There was no hypocrisy in Frank Steele's having for years allowed his managers to develop a new style in dealing with their subordinates while he retained the old. Instead, he was slowly learning from them. Steele understood all along his need to lead the company, but he was slow to recognize that the style of leadership acceptable in our country had been changing. To his credit, however, he did recognize the change, and embraced it, even if a bit belatedly.

COMMUNICATING CHANGE

Joe Callahan's fluid organization described earlier is an extreme response to the challenges of today's marketplace; a response not readily available to many managers in older, larger organizations where new competitive winds that might blow gales in the executive suite are dissipated and lost in the caverns below. Until problems confront operations-level managers, how are people to be challenged? How is the pace of change to be communicated to them?

At General Electric Company Jack Welch became CEO in the midst of a substantial recession. Responsible for an enormous organization with several hundred thousand employees, he did not have available to him the options of Joe Callahan in a far, far smaller company. But like Callahan, he saw the necessity of challenging the organization to meet the requirements of a rapidly changing external environment.

Welch's answer was both brilliant and simple. He insisted that General Electric, a diversified company in hundreds of businesses, was to be *first or second* in each business that it undertook and that it would get out of those areas where it was not. General Electric was not just to have a business plan, it was to have a vision to inspire and direct its activities.

An ability to challenge or inspire an organization is found in all great managers; they are leaders as well as administrators. This quality is found not only in leaders of business firms, but also in other organizations ranging from military units to evangelical churches.

General George Custer once addressed the Seventh Cavalry as follows: "Men die. A regiment is more than men—it has an immortal soul. Our task is to discover the soul of the Seventh Cavalry—the spirit that makes men die for it. The rest is merely hard work, hard fighting, hard riding." With this insight, it is not surprising that Custer believed, even if erroneously, that his regiment could defeat ten times their number of Sioux warriors.

The problem with too many managers is that they believe hard work from themselves and their organizations is enough. They have no concept of spirit, and their people cannot identify the spirit of the organization. A business, like a regiment, has an immortal soul. Its managers must be able to help others find it.

Managers should live in the future. Most people live at best in the present. Some people, sad to say, live primarily in the past. As a matter of course businesspeople must forecast and plan for the future. And the best ones do.

In many businesses today's events are already ancient history to its management. The objectives, plans, and mechanisms which created today's production and sales were established many months ago. The actual playing out of the script is anticlimactic. This is true both in stable industries, where products and processes are little changing, and in Joe Callahan's financial service business where everything is in a state of flux.

This characteristic of living in the future gives good managers' behavior a paradoxical quality to other people in our society. For example, today business is excellent, profits are booming; but management is preparing to lay people off—foreseeing a recession months ahead. Alternatively, stuck in the depths of a business downturn, with many people on layoff, with red ink flowing like water, management is investing in new equipment, building new facilities, or even considering acquisitions.

A vision of the future is itself an element of leadership, a means of inspiring the organization. This fundamental tool of leadership lies readily at hand to virtually all managers. Like the person in the bow of a sailboat, the manager is first to see what is ahead.

How then is it that so few managers communicate their vision of the future to others, especially to the rank and file of their organization? In step with the future themselves, too often managers allow others in their organizations to plod along in the present. This is a major failure, because people generally can respond to a goal, if they are permitted to see it.

Does it matter that the manager's vision of the future may be limited, or even flawed? Yes, to a degree. But people who live in the future quickly acquire a certain flexibility, knowing that nothing is certain in forecasting.

At a large plumbing supply company, a manager commented, "Like any long-run plan, our vision of the future is hazy. Nonetheless, it helps to prepare. When we do it well, and keep on top of it, it eliminates surprises." And, he might have added, it gives direction and purpose to what we are doing today.

LEGACY OF LEADERSHIP

Constructive relationships are always two-way: The manager provides vision, challenge, and direction for subordinates; he or she also works for them. Jack Welch is the chief executive officer who challenges the GE organization. He is the boss to whom its sector, group, and division executives report. At the same time he is also a servant of the organization and its people. He is, par excellence, an ambassador for the company to the outside world.

In 1982–1983 as General Electric's capital goods business stagnated, Welch became a spokesman for what he termed a quality economic recovery. This recovery would pay off by contributing to America's economic potential and international competitiveness in the years ahead. His was often a minority view, when political leaders and Wall Street analysts were satisfied with a brief boom in consumer spending. By 1984 Welch's views had an impact. Investment spending recovered as General Electric and other firms introduced new technology to help keep American facilities competitive.

Many managers are, in part, promoters for their organizations; selling new products and obtaining new customer relationships. It is a hard job, requiring salesmanship and diplomacy, and is a long way from the popular misapprehension of the manager as an autocrat issuing directives to the staff.

At the Continental Group, CEO Bruce Smart traveled to the upper Midwest, then down to Texas in a single day, stopping to see key customers. He was assessing the customer–supplier relationship his company had built up and, where it was weak, taking steps to strengthen the relationship.

The top performing manager is also a helper. In frequent meetings with subordinates the manager listens to their reports of progress or difficulty and offers assistance. "I met with Johnson today to build a fire under her," the subordinate reports.

"Do you need help?" the boss replies. "Can I do anything?"

Managers also can be catalysts of change and interpreters of events both internal and external to the company. They can signal which events are important to react to and which are not. Their radar screens can become the company's.

Today's middle managers are anxious for the opportunity to show what they can do. Does the top manager take over, asserting control and direction? What subordinates want is advice and assistance.

Big things depend ultimately upon small things. Small contributions build trust, tolerance, and satisfaction in a group of people who work together. Top performing managers recognize this. They look for high performance and high commitment from the people who report to them. They view themselves not primarily as decision-makers, but partially as leaders and partially as helpers; they are prepared to operate in these ambiguous roles. When the best corporate leaders conduct a meeting, it is imaginative and brings out more from people than the people thought they had brought in.

The best CEOs understand their organizations, and ultimately factor into all long-term decisions the question: What can my organization do well? The strategy is fitted to the people's capability and the organization's structure is fitted to the strategy.

Top managers' most lasting impact on the companies which they head will not be through the policies, strategies, and programs designed under their tutelage or the structures set up to carry them out, although these will consume most of their time. The manager–leaders will carve out from the demands on their time the opportunity to develop the human side of the organization. This is difficult within an environment with many demands on managers' time. But ultimately the most important contribution managers can leave behind is not the policies but the people—the way they look at things. This will be the manager's footprint.

Central to this legacy will be the manager's talent in picking good people to hire and to develop. For managers who came to their positions through formal graduate programs the importance of hiring good people may be a lesson lost in the formal structure of some business programs. But as Jack Welch of GE insists: "If you pick good people and give them the opportunity to spread their wings and put the compensation carrot at the back, then you don't even have to be a very good manager to succeed. It's that important."

SUMMARY

The boss sets values, provides tone, and makes certain key decisions he or she is best suited to make. The boss takes a long-range view, for the organization's day-to-day operations keep others from doing so. It is fun to be the boss, but it is also fun getting there. It is a mistake to rush it.

The most lasting contribution a manager can make is not policies and strategies but through the management of people. And attention to people will pay off in the competitive marketplace.

18

It All Pays Off In The Competitive Marketplace

Today's intensely competitive environment helps to shape the new executives, to make them different from the previous generation. Examples of the differences can be found in many places, but none is more dramatic than those in family-run companies.

UNCONVENTIONAL MANAGEMENT

In the early 1980s at a small regional airline two brothers succeeded their father, who had founded the company thirty years before. One brother commented to a business magazine reporter, "Dad's philosophy was to entrench himself and avoid competition. When someone would threaten to come in on top of Dad, he would run to the state public service commissions, the Civil Aeronautics Board, and the Federal Aviation Administration to complain. That's the way things were done back then.

"But we were younger. We were willing to take risks. And we're not afraid of competition—in fact, we're pretty awesome competition ourselves."[1]

[1] Curtis Hartman, "PBA: A Tale of Two Airlines," *Inc.* (February 1983).

When airlines were deregulated the brothers saw that competition would require their small company to expand, or it would be slowly choked to death. To survive they embarked on a program of rapid expansion financed by debt and a public equity offering.[2] To the company's base in the northeastern United States they added a Florida operation. Not only did the new operation add business in winter, when northeastern traffic was slow, to help even out the flow of revenues year-round, but it also provided an opportunity for a summer life-style all year round for busy company executives.

With these initiatives the company has prospered and continues to grow, but the older generation resisted strongly. As the company took on its first rate war with a competitor, the company's founder told his sons to stop the expansion or buy his stock out entirely and immediately. "He felt that we were squanderers, too flashy, too eager to try new stuff," one of the brothers said. So they bought him out.[3] Certain aspects of the company did not change, including commitments to passenger service and reasonable fares. These were old ideas in the company, as indeed commitments to customers and quality are old ideas in many other business.

Similarly, many of the management ideas stressed in this book have been around and applied successfully for a number of years. The circumstances, however, have changed; so much so that to hold to the old ideas without modifications would doom a company to a lingering death. The greatest change of all has been the new competition's erosion of protected positions in the marketplace. Because of this change old ideas of all sorts have to be tested for applicability in the current context. The founder was right about some things but he was not 100 percent right. His demand to be bought out showed that he was not able to adapt his business strategy sufficiently to the new age. His company was fortunate that his sons were there to take it forward by making

---

[2] The pressure of competition can also lead a company astray, as it did at PBA when FAA regulations, sometimes ignored, led to a brief closing of the airline's operations.
[3] Ibid.

the necessary changes. This unconventional management led into the future.

The free market offers an opportunity for great success. Victories over the competition can bring enormous rewards. But it also means some rough going. The general manager of a major construction company is another example of the new generation of managers and its impact on competition. His father had built a very successful mechanical construction company. Like virtually all successful companies in that industry in the 1950s and 1960s, it was fully unionized. In the mid-1970s, the company began to encounter significant nonunion competition, which had by then moved into all major markets. This new source of competition has made the job of management much tougher. The younger generation of managers is holding its own, but lives in a faster, riskier world than did its predecessor. To remind himself of the realities of the bumps and thumps of the competitive marketplace the company's young general manager keeps two signs on his desk: "MAKE A DECISION," says one, and the other adds, "NOW PICK YOURSELF UP AND START RUNNING AGAIN."

While the stories of small companies, such as the airline and construction firms, make the transition between generations evident, they unfortunately make it seem easier than it often is, especially in larger companies. The airline and construction companies are each in only one industry, so each company's financial situation is relatively directly and clearly tied to its operations.[4] The complexity of meeting competition in large and diversified companies is much greater, but has to be done nonetheless.

IBM is very large and operates in many markets, producing thousands of different products for the office. Competitors come and go, some persisting indefinitely, others emerging in a single limited area, then disappearing. How does IBM attempt to judge whether a small company will constitute a long-run threat in some particular segment of the marketplace? "Any start-up can have one hot product," an IBM vice president responded. "The

[4] PBA, Annual Report, 1983, published in 1984, p. 10.

key thing in new firms is whether they're putting dollars into engineering. That's where future products must come from."

For established companies already putting money into engineering new products, the key thing is the quality of their strategy and execution. Behind these lie the ultimate resource, the imagination, resourcefulness, and tenacity of their key people. Recognizing the long-term competitive threat in competitors' people, IBM and similar established companies look to their people for their competitive viability.

IBM and Hewlett–Packard Company are commonly listed among our country's most successful business enterprises. They are also widely recognized as companies which make an unusually serious commitment to the recognition and development of their employees. Many American managers watch these two companies attentively, admiring aspects of their management which keep them performing successfully. Especially admired are each company's clear understanding of its mission, the attention devoted to its core businesses, the willingness to change both products and technologies as required, and the response when challenged.

Both business equipment and instruments are highly competitive businesses, and have been for decades. Both industries are populated with far less successful companies. Both IBM and Hewlett–Packard are credited by other companies in their core businesses with being very tough competitors indeed.

Clearly, these two companies are not successful simply because of the industries they have chosen to be in. Those industries are cluttered with too many less-than-successful firms for this to be true. It is far too simple to conclude that IBM and Hewlett–Packard are successful simply because of the businesses they chose to enter. Both are successful because of what they do. And from early in their histories many of the policies described earlier have been part of what they do.

Though it is probably too much to conclude that IBM and Hewlett–Packard owe their business success to certain of their employee policies, it is also a mistake to conclude that success and policies are unrelated. These companies draw long-term competitive strength from their employee policies because of the high performance these policies bring forth, and competitive success helps allow them to continue those people policies. This cycle in which management policies contribute to business success and permit continuation of the policies is not a vicious cycle, but a benevolent and profitable one.

Managers in other companies often say of IBM and Hewlett–Packard, "We cannot afford financially to provide the benefits those companies provide to employees." Failing to use the same policies, they fail to get similar performance. Can the other companies afford not to make a bigger investment in the human factor in their businesses?

A top executive at White-Westinghouse once told a group of managers that all managerial problems are either money or people—there are only two piles. Starting with the money side, if a manager does not get a project approved, then it was not good enough. There is a priority in business for everything. A manager's job is to be on top of the priorities.

In a more fundamental sense, all money problems come down to people in the end. When carefully looked into, the financial disasters turned out to be people problems. There were two types of problems—the employee who could not do the job and led the company into a financial loss, and the boss who did not see the problem coming.

Because the performance of people is so fundamental to business success, managers who cannot afford to try to improve performance by improving their own and their companies' people policies are revealing that they do not know business very well. Unfortunately, competitive pressures do not ensure that a company will discover the path into the benevolent circle. Quite the contrary, competitive pressures can make it seem that there is no time to do the things necessary to improve the performance of people in the organization. This is especially true today as the competitive environment heats up.

Eight years ago a major American manufacturer embarked on a series of experiments to improve the performance of people in its manufacturing facilities. Nonconventional plants of the type described in Chapter 11 were established. Despite problems, the plants prospered, and by the early 1980s had given the company 15 to 20 percent cost-effectiveness above its own conventional plants and its competitors' conventional plants. But in 1984 the company was less than bullish on its nonconventional plants.

The reason was that East Asian manufacturers had entered the American marketplace with products of reasonable quality selling at up to 40 percent below current American prices. The 15 percent advantage of the nonconventional plants was not sufficient to meet the new competitors. Today the company searches for some response to its new competition, and has begun to move its new manufacturing investment to Asia. The promising experience of the nonconventional plants is in danger of being lost because of pressures from foreign competition.

Perhaps it is too late for the company just described, but its experience shows that there is an urgency for improving performance in organizations not yet hit by the forces of competition. Urgency exists because when competitive pressures suddenly emerge, it is often too late, or seems too costly to respond. Far from always forcing a company to become more effective, competitive pressures may remove the opportunity to do so—forcing the company to retrench and retrench until little of its former size or opportunities remain.

The vice president for manufacturing of a textile company described his company's efforts this way: "Before the force of foreign competition hit us we had seen that the people-performance equation was not right in several of our plants. We acted by really increasing communication; performance increased and the bottom line numbers improved. We developed more corporate pride, and it turned out we needed it, with the customer as well. We're viewed as a company that cares, and that helps us hold our customers despite the increasing pressure of foreign competition."

DECLINING SHELF SPACE IN THE MANAGER'S MIND

Making the right business choices in the current environment is a central element of management. It becomes more difficult as the number of choices rise. Recent years have added to the complexity of choice by increasing the number of things being managed.

Managers have long paid attention to production, finance, investments, budgets, and sales. But today a group of new items has been added to the list of things that executives must manage. In the last eight years, companies have developed careful programs for the management of cash. With high interest rates, unused cash can constitute a major lost opportunity to the firm. In consequence, procedures for cash utilization are being established and general managers are becoming conscious of cash as a resource of the corporation to be carefully tended. For companies active abroad, foreign exchange fluctuations add another significant dimension to financial management.

Many companies have become active in the management of energy use. These companies have established corporate and divisional level capabilities in energy conservation and have encouraged managers to become more conservation conscious.

The management of technology has entered a more sophisticated phase. In some industries there are now too many opportunities for firms to exploit all of them simultaneously. Many opportunities require large capital investments and long lead times. Companies considering technological advances face problems of possible adverse reactions from consumers and government regulators, and potentially stiff competition from other firms. As but one example, consider the problems of managers pondering whether to begin producing home appliances which conserve on energy and water usage. Will customers accept appliances which use little water? Will the consumer believe that clothes or dishes can be cleaned in an almost dry washer? When a housewife looks in the front of a washing machine, and does not see splashing water, will she try to exchange the machine?

The fast pace of technical change is causing many employees to become less effective in their work. In the modern world many companies do not simply abandon these people. Instead, management of the careers of employees is being developed through an adroit mixture of retraining, transfer into other jobs in the organization, early retirement, and outplacement. Managers plan in the present for potential future obsolescence for people just as for products.

Government and the public generally are demanding to know more about the practices of business. Product safety, environmental impacts, community impacts, and the personal ethics of executives are subject to outside scrutiny as never before. To avoid embarrassing and possibly costly exposures, corporations are having to manage the external impacts and internal ethics of the firm more completely than before. Some writers on auditing are proposing that corporations develop a group of auditors to evaluate the effectiveness, efficiency, and propriety of managerial actions. They suggest that such broadened internal auditing may reduce the pressure of public review on firms.

How does today's manager cope with the increased complexity of today's business environment? Think of a manager's mind as if it contained the shelves of a retail store. In the same way the consumer goods companies compete for shelf space ("You can't sell the product if the customer can't see it and reach for it.") more and more items compete for the manager's attention. But like a retail store with limited shelf space, the manager can address only a restricted number of topics.

The volume of material which a manager must review continues to expand; the number of persons inside and outside the firm with whom communications are necessary continues to rise; and the number of activities which must be managed continues to grow. This increasing complexity requires managers who are able to scan the environment at a very rapid pace. Some things are not important; some things are significant but can be left to assistants; and other things are significant and should be handled personally. The modern executive scans material quickly; gives directions and receives reports at a fast clip; and allocates his or her own time carefully.

As complexity grows, managers are faced with a threshold choice: to attempt to master the new subjects, or to keep the number of variables down by simplifying. There is much to be said for the latter course, but it cannot be done successfully merely by ignoring what may be key elements in the business equation. Simplifying can be done by an individual manager only by delegating the responsibility for dealing with excluded issues to others; and this can be done safely only if the others are competent. Hence the importance firms are placing on management development as described in Chapter 5.

While top performing managers are attempting to free themselves by delegation from numerous complex issues competing for their attention, surprisingly they have not been content to isolate themselves further from the day-to-day realities of their businesses. They have not retreated behind enlarged staffs, trying to preserve simplicity by being further divorced from their companies. Instead, they have sought both to delegate more and to be more knowledgeable about the performance of the people to whom responsibility has been given.

Hence, there has been a shift in recent years in many of our most successful large firms to a much more hands-on style of management, even at top levels. The effective manager now keeps on the go. He or she visits the company's locations. Decisions are made in the field with people directly involved. An insistence on doing something is replacing lengthy study and analysis. Detached, arm's length control by management is too risky when the economy shifts suddenly and when competitors can emerge with lightning speed.

Jack Welch has told his people to avoid what he calls the anchor-man syndrome: the plant manager who calls his boss on a Friday night and says: "Jack, the plant just burned down. Everything's a total loss—I'm going to a dinner party now, but I'll be in to give you a full report on Monday morning."

"This is terrible," says Jack Welch. "I don't want a news report.

The question is: What can we do now? How fast? With whom? It's war out there—do something!"

LONG-TERM COMPETITIVE ADVANTAGE

Management is about building value. Broadly speaking, value is built through financial and human leverage. Such leverage entails risk. Since risk is involved, there are elements of choice about the nature of the risk and its degree.

Choice, which receives so much attention from management theorists, is an important part of building value. The issue of business strategy, for example, gains theoretical power when thought of as the choice among a portfolio of the firm's real options, that is, those investment options which are not merely financial but also involve plant and equipment, organization, or even questions of acquisition or merger. In recent years the rules for portfolio-type choices which maximize corporate returns from various investment options have been elaborately developed and publicized.

Of equal interest, however, are those activities which add to the set of real options from which managers can choose. Investments in the people in an organization, get little attention from management scholars who are interested in investment choices, but nevertheless play a critical role in widening a firm's potential range of choice. Managers in many top companies plan ahead for the people side of their business because it gives them the option to do profitable things.

Faced with what appear to be potentially lucrative investment opportunities, many companies shy away, recognizing that they have no one to whom they could successfully entrust the opportunity. Even in companies with a substantial reputation for developing managers, good opportunities sometimes go begging for lack of the right persons to manage them. "Our biggest limitation is not capital for new ventures," says the top executive of one such company, "but is always the managers to whom to entrust it."

In recent years CEOs at many firms have been favoring financial investments rather than new business opportunities that require plans, equipment, and organization. This is because the CEOs are not confident in the ability of their managers to run a new effort successfully. Although the choice to avoid new business is usually described as a result of a poor expected financial return, underneath the numbers lies a shortage of managers who could be expected to overcome operating and cost obstacles to make the enterprise sufficiently profitable. The problem is not that profit hurdles are set too high, but in many instances that managers are not available who could do a really good job.

A company is correctly positioned when it has the managerial talent to seize important business opportunities. In the late 1970s officers of a large electrical manufacturing company headquartered outside the United States saw that semiconductor technology would be crucial to its business in the future. They reviewed a list of possible ways to enter the semiconductor business, and finally decided to go in directly. At that time American companies dominated the market.

At a press conference called to announce the company's decision to enter semiconductor manufacturing, business reporters challenged the company's chairman. "Why are you doing this?" the reporters asked. "The Americans have the most advanced technology; your materials costs will be as high as theirs and you are farther from the large markets."

Because his company's need to have a secure source of semiconductors for its future product line was well known to the reporters and needed no elaboration, the company's chairman pointed to a different aspect of his decision. "We have very good people," he responded, "and they are doing very well in our current markets. They need a new challenge. This is the one they believe is most important."

The company had both the business need to enter semiconductors, and the people resources to do so. With good people, the company could anticipate profitability; despite vigorous competition in semiconductors, it has achieved it.

As important as people are in establishing a wider range of business possibilities for a company in the short run, they are also important to the continuing success of a business in the long term.

Value building has always been a search for the protected niche in the marketplace, the position of quasimonopoly from which substantial financial rewards could be generated. Today is different only in kind. It is far more difficult to keep a protected niche than it used to be. Competitors are faster to copy new products, to make patents obsolete by developing alternative technologies, to match services in order to lure away new customers, and to prevail on government to remove protection by deregulation. Where there is free and active competition, in the long term all profits tend to disappear—this is a fundamental conclusion of economic analysis. It follows that long-term profits are the result either of a series of short-term monopolized niches, or of some permanent competitive advantage.

Let us consider an example of how the two strategies interplay with each other. The large electrical power plant equipment division of a major American company has for years seen its market eroding due to the lower costs of competitors who are largely copying its technology. Then in the recent recession the American market for new power plant equipment all but disappeared. Desperate for orders, the division looked abroad. Because of continued spending on research and development, the division could offer the most advanced technology available in the world.

The largest electric utility in a foreign country offered a large order for the division's product. The government of the foreign country attached a provision to the import licenses. The American company could have five-sevenths of the order; two-sevenths of the order went to two companies in the foreign country. Furthermore, as a condition of the import license, the American company had to provide all technical plans and the assistance necessary for its two foreign competitors to build and supply the electric utility with the American company's most up-to-date technology. In essence, to get the order the American company had to give its technological know-how to two competitors. It would still license the technology and derive royalties, but it would lose the more lucrative role of supplier since its foreign competitors had lower labor costs.

The American company accepted the utility order on those conditions, and proceeded to transfer its technology to its competitors. Why? The Americans needed the business. Would they ever sell another such order, when their competitors would have the technology, they were asked. Probably not, they admitted; at least not that same technology. They were banking on research and development to provide yet another technological advance which would open sales opportunities in the future.

For many companies this story gets to the reality of today's marketplace. Competition is intense with foreign competitors in league with their governments against the Americans. The protected market niche, so important to value creation, disappears very quickly.

Where then does a company's permanent competitive advantage, the other source of value building, come from? It comes from the creative potential of the company; from its ability to stay a step ahead of the competition—in technology, in service, in sales, in finance—in whatever is necessary to get and retain customers. At the root of this creative capability lie the people who make up the organization—who have to create continually, providing a long sequence of short-lived profitable niches for the company.

As managers come to see their long-term business strategy in this light, they focus less exclusively on particular products and deals, and more on depth, quality, and internal renewal of their organizations. The focus on creating and changing directs attention to the management efforts illustrated in previous chapters.

Decision making becomes less important than developing the capacities of subordinates. Situations that seem to be difficult call forth the question, "Where is the opportunity?" Whatever is good in the situation is salvaged; the rest is recognized and then forgotten.

The conditions in an organization which encourage people to perform at a high level are recognized as crucial to the company's success. Compensation has to be flexible enough to reward top performers. Managers who are placed in charge of a business have to be effective enough to recognize when it is entering a dematurity stage—leaving a business to a caretaker is too risky to the company as a whole. The values of an organization which promote performance are identified, made explicit, and are communicated to managers and employees.

Managers who stress competitiveness are necessarily outer directed. They compare themselves not with others in their own organization, but with the companies on the outside with which they compete. Striving for an advantage in the marketplace, they stress quality, cost control, and innovation. Recognizing that virtually everyone in a company can contribute in some significant way to these objectives, they encourage people to participate, to give a higher level of commitment to their jobs. Compensation systems with a large performance component make it possible to reward those who make important contributions.

Managers frequently see other managers and top technical people as important potential contributors to the enterprise, and encourage them to participate. Less frequently managers recognize the less glamorous but still significant contribution which the rank and file can make. Managers in the top companies are quite aware of this. They recognize employee loyalty and commitment as major assets of the corporation, and so they manage with employees in mind. They recognize that they must often compromise their own interests and not push other people to extremes, in order that on their own initiative the rank and file will play the game which is business enterprise; and play to win, which is competitiveness.

Risking a little oversimplification, it may be said that there are three kinds of managers as measured by their dealings with subordinates: First, there are those who do not wish to hear subordinates' views. These managers structure meetings as a series of presentations and lectures; subordinates are to listen and be silent, to be seen but not heard. The manager is comfortable only when explaining, instructing, and giving direction—only, that is, when he or she is talking.

In today's competitive world a manager like this is not of much value to a company. If the manager is a top-notch scientist, engineer, salesperson, or financial deal maker—that is, a significant individual contributor—then that is where the person should be, in a professional or staff role, not trying to function as a manager. This is true even where this person is a founder of the company.

Such persons are disasters as managers because they get too little leverage from the human resources entrusted to them. They use others to leverage their own ideas, but gain nothing from the ideas of others. They do not listen, so they cannot learn. They solve the problem of deciding how far to delegate by not delegating at all. They resolve the issue of how much participation to encourage from subordinates by encouraging none at all. Both of these extreme solutions are wrong.

The second type of manager encourages subordinates to speak up, but only to have cause to reprimand or correct them. This manager's meetings require subordinates to report, but each slight failing is met with criticism. Short on praise for contributions or performance, this manager will sometimes offer private congratulations.

Ordinarily this manager is driven by insecurity, by the need to continually demonstrate who is boss, who is the expert. Managers like this have potential, because they know how to listen, if only their supervisors can counsel them to overcome their insecurity. This type is very common in up-from-the-ranks managers or among young managers who have significant responsibilities.

The third type of manager encourages subordinates to speak up, to report on performance or difficulties, and to offer ideas. These managers listen, learn, and offer advice or praise. When necessary, this type may remonstrate or counsel. These managers are valuable because of the knowledge they acquire about their organizations and their people, and because they are building capability in their people. Their leverage is great, extending not only to their own ideas but to those of the people for whom they are responsible.

The group vice president of a major clothing chain described his efforts to develop managers of the third type in his company. "We've doubled in size in the last three years after being stagnant for many years. To do this we established a flat management structure. We provided training to managers in sensitivity to people. Today's employees are more 'me-oriented,' so we're trying to help our managers be aware of this and its implications. We instituted an internal promotions policy and so reduced employee turnover. We've also noticed reduced absenteeism and better training at our locations. We've made all levels of management accessible to employees, and we're stressing their involvement."

Although building value is measured by the accumulation of capital in an enterprise, it involves more than financial and bricks-and-mortar investments. What defines a business, as opposed to a profession, is that the work involved can be organized and replicated in such a way that it can be done by rank and file people. If a task cannot ever be delegated out of managerial or professional ranks, then it probably cannot be perpetuated after key individuals have gone. And if the organization has to have that task performed, and it cannot be delegated, then the organization probably cannot be perpetuated. The indispensable person is an enemy of value creation in a business sense, just as a person who does not perform is an enemy of value creation. The indispensable person and the nonperformer are opposite extremes — the creation of value in a business proceeds between the extremes.

Good managers recognize that if they are not refining processes into tasks that can be delegated, they are not building the company. They also recognize that if they are not building the capacity of people to perform higher level tasks, they are not preparing the company for the long-term. The manager's task is to take the expertise of the professional and transfer it to work for others and to develop the rank and file's ability to perform that work. Efforts to let the work force do more are described in Chapter

11. These are the most recent and promising attempts to move forward the process of transferring work to rank and file. For a long period in our country many managers and entire corporations lost sight of the importance of this process in building value.

There has not been a period in American history when building value in this fundamental way was more important to the long-term survival of companies. It is a fundamental principle of our free enterprise system that a company which pays more for money than it is able to earn with the investment is going to lose a bundle for its shareholders. Bill Fruhan has documented important examples of this in the *Harvard Business Review*.[5] Today American companies face the highest real interest rates (i.e., adjusted for inflation) in our nation's history. In consequence, for an investment to pay off, it has to make returns at an unprecedented rate. To be successful in this treacherous economic environment, a manager must know the costs and have them under control, must know what the customer wants and be able to provide it, and finally must assume tough competition can be met in the marketplace.

The balance of risk and potential reward, of change and continuity, of old verities and new approaches, of delegation and oversight—these are central to successful management. What keeps management from being a science—with its emphasis on optimizing behavior and wringing the final dollar from the margin of the firm's revenues and costs—is this need for balance. The manager has to respond to many conflicting pressures—to satisfy many conflicting requirements. It can be done in a rapidly changing business environment only by a continuing feel for whether the right balances have been struck.

Among the most important balances are those directly involving the human factor in a business. Generally firms and divisions of firms with excellent performance achieve it by finding an appropriate balance between two apparently opposite elements of human nature: the need for individual recognition and reward,

[5] William E. Fruhan, Jr., "How Fast Should Your Company Grow?" *Harvard Business Review* 62, no. 1 (1984): 84–95.

and the necessity to act as a member of a group or team in order to get things done.

What distinguishes top performing organizations is their ability to make a well-functioning unit of a group of people, while still identifying and recognizing individual merit. To be world class, a company has to work at this balancing of opposites continually and for large numbers of people.

What makes it possible for world class companies to successfully attain this difficult balance is a combination of elements developed in the last 30 years or so which have been described in this book. At the core of these policies is a sustained and self-conscious effort supported by top management and accepted by functional and operations managers to attract and retain committed people and to motivate high performance at all levels of the organization. Key methods to implement these policies include hiring selectivity, value imprinting, assessment of the individual's contribution, pay for performance, career education and development, and reinforcement and reiteration of the company's principles and ways of doing business.

A LAST WORD

The opportunities in American companies for applying these policies and techniques remain enormous. Because of publicity in recent years, most managers have a sketchy view of various components of this new style in management. Most managers, however, are unaware of how the components fit together into an overall system of management which is far more effective than any of its individual parts. And most managers have failed to make the connection between the new systems and competi- tiveness. Instead, managers outside these systems by and large view them as frills—when to those actually in the systems their purpose and result is to enhance the survivability and success of the business. Instruments of profitability alone they may not be, because they reflect values independent of profitability as well, but without a doubt these systems contribute to the long-term competitive advantage of the company.

As one bank official put it in our interview, "There is a crisis in our industry. We've always responded short-term in the past, and our long-run plans were neither objective nor realistic. But we got a new president recently, and great changes have been made under his direction.

"We're a financial services organization. When our people are made aware of what their own accomplishments are, somehow they have more appreciation for our customers. When customers are treated fairly, it has a favorable impact.

"To broaden our managers' expertise we are moving them around, training them across the business units. We try to expose managers to the corporation as a whole and give them a multi-dimensional view of the company. This increases their appreciation for the trade-offs that have to be made in order to maximize profits."

Our interviewees also included the vice president for operations of a very large brokerage house, one of the strongest companies in America's current financial services industry. Does the company plan ahead for management development and recruitment of key staff? "No." Does the company try to manage or improve morale? "No." Does the company integrate its personnel functions into long-term business planning? "No." Does the company have a personality of which it is conscious and which it tries to foster among employees? "No, what are you talking about?"

The two companies just mentioned are competitors and became so in the past three years. Each is attempting to build a secure future in the financial services industry, where the integrated financial service concept is still primarily an idea whose full ramifications are not yet evident. The concept is to provide all financial services for a client, so that a competitor's agents cannot gain a foothold by providing a particular service and later adding other services.

The full service concept can only work in a financial services company if people in the different services see the opportunity for interconnection among the services offered. This will not be easily done in the financial services companies of today, because by and large they employ not broad-gauged people, but specialists. If the interconnections are not made, both financial services institutions and the customer will lose. The customer will fail to get the convenience and efficiency of a single relationship, and the financial services companies will end up as conglomerates deriving no synergy from their many separate activities.

The competitive struggle to create the interconnections to provide a full range of financial services to the consumer is very hot. Of the two companies just described, the one which is attempting to apply the modern systems of delegation, morale building, management development, and up and down communications is surely ahead in the race to make the necessary interconnections in its organization. In the end, these practices and the competitive fervor which motivates and inspires that company will surely pay off in the marketplace.

SUMMARY

Today's new managers are strongly driven by values, yet live in a time of intense foreign and domestic competition. They are profoundly changing American companies as they move through the ranks of management. A new system of management is being created. It is the special interaction of this generation of managers with their environment that holds the potential for American companies to recapture the ability to compete more successfully in our own and foreign markets.

Index